The Constitution
Between Friends

The Constitution
Between Friends
*Congress, the President,
and the Law*

LOUIS FISHER

New York   St. Martin's Press

To Ellen and Joanna:
Too young to understand constitutionalism,
but learning what is fair and just

Cover design: Mies Hora

Library of Congress Catalog Card Number: 77–89993
Copyright © 1978 by St. Martin's Press, Inc.
All Rights Reserved.
Manufactured in the United States of America.
098
fedcba
For information, write: St. Martin's Press, Inc.,
175 Fifth Avenue, New York, N. Y. 10010

cloth ISBN: 0–312–16530–7
paper ISBN: 0–312–16531–5

Preface

This book borrows its title from an anecdote about President Grover Cleveland, who once refused to endorse a bill sponsored by a Tammany politician. Asked for a reason, Cleveland explained that the legislation was unconstitutional. His statement brought forth this bewildered rejoinder: "What's the Constitution between friends?"[1] Here we have in capsule form the perennial conflict between constitutional principles and short-run political objectives, as well as the struggle between the two political branches of government, the executive and the legislative.

A more contemporary example comes from the administration of Lyndon Johnson. In August 1964 Johnson enlisted the support of almost every member of Congress for his Gulf of Tonkin Resolution, granting him extraordinary powers over the military. Passage of the resolution put Congress in the back seat, legally, in determining the scope and direction of the Vietnam War. Johnson's use of the resolution, particularly as a "functional equivalent" to a declaration of war, seemed to many dismayed legislators a violation of congressional intent. But Johnson did not misread the statutory language, which represented a blanket and careless abdication of authority to the president. A few years later the Senate Foreign Relations Committee publicly apologized for its part in this episode. It admitted that Congress, in adopting the resolution, committed the error of making a *personal* judgment as to how a particular president would implement the resolution when it had a responsibility to make an *institutional* judgment, to ask whether it

[1]Whereas this anecdote usually is attributed to Cleveland, Teddy Roosevelt is reported to have had the same experience with a Tammany politician, who replied: "What the divil is the Constitution between frinds?" (William Howard Taft, *Our Chief Magistrate and His Powers*, 22–23 [1916]. A slightly different version appears in *The Works of Theodore Roosevelt*, XX, 92 [1926].)

was appropriate under the Constitution to grant such authority to any president.[2]

These two examples illustrate a tension that runs throughout the American system of government. Statutory and constitutional restrictions are erected to keep the actions of the executive and legislative branches within certain legal boundaries. The drive for political power continually tests those boundaries, often stretches them to satisfy momentary needs, and sometimes succeeds in doing what the law forbids. Because the demarcations between the branches are imprecise and subject to varying interpretations, periodic protests about "encroachments" and "usurpations" are to be expected. At any given time one branch may appear to be dominant, the other subordinate. Fortunes wax and wane; struggles for spheres of influence are inevitable.

A certain amount of friction is, of course, invited by the American Constitution. Conflict between the branches serves the useful purpose of preventing an accumulation of power and the abuses that flow from unchecked power. Equally important, it develops public policies that have a broad base of support and understanding. However, as Attorney General Edward H. Levi has noted, the framers

> did not envision a government in which each branch seeks out confrontation; they hoped the system of checks and balances would achieve a harmony of purposes differently fulfilled. The branches of government were not designed to be at war with one another. The relationship was not to be an adversary one, though to think of it that way has become fashionable.[3]

Unfortunately, in recent years the conflict between the president and Congress has bordered on stalemate. Each branch has sensed that its vital powers and prerogatives were endangered. Cooperation and good-faith efforts have been little in evidence. Reaction has led to overreaction, the pendulum of political balance has swung unpredictably, constitutional roles have been confused. In-

[2]S. Rept. No. 129, 91st Cong., 1st Sess. 23 (1969).

[3]Edward H. Levi, "Some Aspects of Separation of Powers," 76 *Colum. L. Rev.* 371, 391 (1976).

stead of moving ahead with urgent public problems—energy, the environment, foreign policy, the economy—political leaders have filled the air with mutual recriminations and countercharges. These paralyzing conflicts obviously resulted from something more basic than partisan bickering. What the country lacked was an agreement on the appropriate roles for the two branches, particularly on large policy questions such as national defense and budget.

Although the nature of government and our constitutional system call for some overlapping of functions, and to good effect, it should be possible to clarify the authorities and responsibilities of each branch. Clarification could reduce the frequency of head-on confrontations, contribute to accountability, and produce a more constructive relationship between political leaders. This book contributes to such a clarification by examining the central legal and constitutional conflicts between the president and Congress today.

Too often law and politics are viewed as if they were isolated sectors of public policy. The Supreme Court reinforces such a view by announcing, on various occasions, its unwillingness to decide "political questions." This doctrine survives on circular reasoning. Declared one federal judge in refusing to decide a war-powers case in 1968: "Though it is not always a simple matter to define the meaning of the term 'political question,' it is generally used to encompass all questions outside the sphere of judicial power."[4] That definition does not push the frontiers of human knowledge very far. As John Roche has noted, it is like the dictionary that explained: "violins are small cellos, and cellos are large violins."[5]

The fact is that today, as in Tocqueville's time more than a century ago, what begins as a political question often ripens into an issue appropriate for the courts. Regrettably, a large element of the citizenry—including many political scientists—cringes from serious debate on constitutional issues. The mere mention of a "legal" dimension seems to stifle further discussion. Why this is so I have never fully understood. Perhaps the technical presentation of court

[4]Velvel v. Johnson, 287 F.Supp. 846, 850 (D. Kans. 1968).

[5]John P. Roche, "Judicial Self-Restraint," 49 *Am. Pol. Sci. Rev.* 762, 768 (1955).

decisions presents a barrier, and yet federal judges often write with a flair, lucidity, and intelligibility rarely matched by offerings in the scholarly journals.

Part of the resistance, I believe, comes from a habit of thought that associates political events with the real world while consigning legal matters to the realm of the remote and ethereal. This is a puzzling attitude, for constitutional and legal questions have their roots in tangible and concrete injuries. Someone suffers and seeks relief. Strong beliefs and deeply held feelings cause plaintiffs to take their grievances to the courts, often after being rebuffed by Congress and the executive branch. Great questions of constitutional law, Henry Steele Commager has remarked, are great "not because they are complicated legal or technical questions, but because they embody issues of high policy, of public good, or morality."[6]

The American Constitution is designed in part to protect individual liberties. That objective requires the consent, and the understanding, of the governed. But many of us shy away from constitutional issues as technical and abstract, preferring to leave those matters to legislators, executive officials, the courts, and a few academic specialists. That attitude is an unhealthy sign for democratic society. A dependence on the people, Madison counseled in Federalist 51, is the primary control on the government. This book is written to encourage a broader public understanding of some central constitutional issues that face us today.

[6]*War Powers Legislation,* hearings before the Senate Committee on Foreign Relations, 92d Cong., 1st Sess. 13 (1971).

Acknowledgments

Not until I taught a course in constitutional law at Georgetown University did I realize how far removed—in the literature—politics and law had become. The opportunity to teach the course, combined with the exceptional interest and talents of the students, gave me the stimulus I needed to prepare this book.

The manuscript was carefully read by three experts who have done much to keep law and politics from going off in separate directions: Harold G. Maier of the Vanderbilt School of Law, Walter F. Murphy of Princeton University, and C. Herman Pritchett of the University of California at Santa Barbara. Never have I received such detailed, penetrating, and constructive critiques. Those who read parts of the manuscript, alerting me to a number of deficiencies, include Arthur S. Miller of the George Washington University National Law Center; William M. Nichols, General Counsel of the Office of Management and Budget; and three colleagues from the Congressional Research Service—Marjorie Ann Browne, Kenneth D. Merin, and Harold C. Relyea.

Progress on the manuscript was helped by my teaching duties at the American University and Georgetown University; lectures I gave at the Federal Executive Institute in Charlottesville, Virginia, the Civil Service Commission, the National War College, the Department of Agriculture Graduate School, and the National Academy of Public Administration; a paper on "Presidential Budget-Making: Laws, Customs, Trends," which I presented at the 1975 annual meeting of the American Political Science Association held in San Francisco, California; and another paper entitled "The Constitution Between Friends," which I delivered at the Center for the Study of Democratic Institutions, Santa Barbara, California, in 1977.

A Note on Citations

All court citations refer to published volumes whenever available: *United States Reports* (U.S.) for Supreme Court decisions, *Federal Reporter* (F.2d) for appellate decisions, and *Federal Supplement* (F.Supp.) for district court decisions. For cases not yet reported, citations are to either the *United States Law Week* (U.S.L.W.) or to the civil action number and date.

Several standard reference works are abbreviated in the footnotes by using the following system:

Elliot, *Debates*
Jonathan Elliot, ed., *The Debates in the Several State Conventions, on the Adoption of the Federal Constitution* (5 vols., Washington, D.C., 1836–1845).

Farrand, *Records*
Max Farrand, ed., *The Records of the Federal Convention of 1787* (4 vols., New Haven: Yale University Press, 1937).

Richardson, *Messages and Papers*
James D. Richardson, ed., *A Compilation of the Messages and Papers of the Presidents* (20 vols., New York: Bureau of National Literature, 1897–1925).

Wkly Comp. Pres. Doc.
Weekly Compilation of Presidential Documents, published each week by the Government Printing Office since 1965.

Contents

The Constitution
Between Friends

1

The Constitutional Setting

Constitutional law texts have a disconcerting habit of evading discussions about the meaning of "constitutionalism." With little introduction, they plunge into an examination of individual court rulings. They provide few signposts to guide the reader in recognizing the characteristics that distinguish a constitutional system from other forms of government.

Constitutionalism is more than a shorthand expression for a constitution and the case law that accompanies it. To be worthy of the name, a constitution embodies a philosophy of government, an understanding between public officials and the people. The purpose of government is to promote the commonweal and protect individual rights, and toward that end a constitution simultaneously grants and limits power.

THE ELEMENTS OF CONSTITUTIONALISM

The main elements of constitutionalism are found in Bolingbroke's definition, written in 1733: "By constitution we mean, whenever we speak with propriety and exactness, that assemblage of laws, institutions and customs, derived from certain fixed principles of reason, directed to certain fixed objects of public good, that compose the general system, according to which the community hath agreed to be governed."[1] Governmental behavior is guided not

[1]Charles Howard McIlwain, *Constitutionalism: Ancient and Modern* 3 (1947).

only by laws, but also by institutions and customs, and legal principles must be set forth in a written document. Even the "unwritten" constitution of England—an amalgam of major enactments, minor statutes, judicial decisions, custom and convention, and parliamentary debates—is secured by publishing the fundamental principles for all to see: Magna Carta, the Habeas Corpus Act, the Petition of Right, and the Act of Settlement.

"Fixed principles of reason," Bolingbroke's second criterion, cannot be defined with any exact meaning and application. At the very least the concept eliminates political regimes that act in an arbitrary, irrational, and capricious manner. Constitutionalism cannot exist, even in the presence of a constitution, if the principles and standards of behavior are matters of whim for those in authority.

The American concept of "due process of law" depends on reasonableness. Courts strike down statutes when they exhibit the "vice of vagueness" (as in loyalty oaths). Citizens should not have to guess at the meaning of a law. Similarly, courts insist that legislative investigations relate to a legislative purpose. Questions during committee interrogations must be pertinent and relevant. When the judiciary finds that legislators have chosen a "rational basis" for carrying out, for example, the commerce power, the court's examination is at an end.[2]

Fixed principles of reason, as a constitutional standard, invokes the idea of natural law, "higher law," or *jus gentium*, which the Roman jurist Gaius called "that law which natural reason established among all mankind."[3] Natural law is given concrete meaning in a scene from Sophocles's *Antigone*. One of Antigone's brothers, Polyneices, joined in a military attack on the city of Thebes. Among the defenders was his brother. Both men, meeting face to face in battle, were killed. The regent of Thebes, Creon, issued an edict ordering Polyneices's body to rot on the battlefield. Antigone defied the proclamation and buried her brother. When asked by Creon if she chose flagrantly to disobey his law, Antigone responds:

[2]Katzenbach v. McClung, 379 U.S. 294, 303-304 (1964).

[3]Edward S. Corwin, *The "Higher Law" Background of American Constitutional Law* 17 (1955).

Naturally! Since Zeus never promulgated
Such a Law. Nor will you find
That Justice publishes such laws to man below.
I never thought your edicts had such force
They nullified the laws of heaven, which,
Unwritten, not proclaimed, can boast
A currency that everlastingly is valid;
An origin beyond the birth of man.

Even Haemon, son of Creon, tells his father that he is "at logger-heads with open justice!" The chorus uses just eight words to express the issue of constitutionalism: "Where might is right there is no right."

In one of the first examples of judicial review, in Dr. Bonham's Case of 1610, Justice Coke announced that when an act of Parliament was "against common right and reason, or repugnant, or impossible to be performed, the common law will controul [sic] it and adjudge such act to be void."[4] Common right and reason, Edward S. Corwin concluded, meant something fundamental and permanent: "it is higher law."[5]

The natural law doctrine enters American constitutionalism by way of John Locke's *Second Treatise on Civil Government* (1690). Locke believed that people living in the state of nature were governed by a law of nature, which obliged everyone to behave in a certain manner. Reason, "which is that law, teaches all mankind who will but consult it, that being all equal and independent, no one ought to harm another in his life, health, liberty or possessions." But humanity, biased and ignorant, failed to study the law of nature. When called upon to judge in their own cases, people punished others too harshly and excused their own transgressions. The result was that "inconveniences" (Locke's mild term) developed in the state of nature, creating the need for a common, unbiased judge to handle disputes.[6]

Although Locke regarded the legislative power as supreme, it could not be arbitrary. The purpose of the legislature was to pre-

[4]*Id.* at 44.
[5]*Id.* at 47.
[6]John Locke, *Second Treatise on Civil Government,* §§ 4–6, 13, 124–125.

serve life, liberty, and fortune. If it became destructive of this end, people would find themselves in a condition worse than the state of nature. Under such circumstances the people were at liberty to dissolve the government and establish a new legislature.[7]

The Lockean influence carries over directly into the Declaration of Independence. The opening sentence explains that the rupture with England was necessary so that Americans might "assume among the Powers of the earth, the separate and equal station to which the Laws of Nature and of Nature's God entitle them." The idea of constitutionalism, emphasizing individual liberties and Locke's philosphy of government, appears in the very next paragraph:

> We hold these truths to be self-evident, that all men are created equal, that they are endowed by their Creator with certain unalienable Rights, that among these are Life, Liberty, and the pursuit of Happiness. That to secure these rights, Governments are instituted among Men, deriving their just powers from the consent of the governed; That whenever any Form of Government becomes destructive of these ends, it is the Right of the People to alter or to abolish it, and to institute new Government.

These sentiments lead to Bolingbroke's last two elements of constitutionalism: (1) government is directed to certain fixed objects of public good; and (2) the community gives its consent to be governed. Both points are consistent with Locke, who held that the legislature's power, "in the utmost bounds of it," was limited to the public good of the society. The executive's emergency power (the prerogative) was "nothing but the power of doing public good without a rule."[8]

The principle of public consent and popular control is implicit in Locke's belief that human rights existed prior to government. If government fails to protect those rights the people can change the governnment. In this sense the *public's* interpretation of natural law—as developed over a period of time—becomes the ultimate

[7]*Id.* at §§135–137, 220–222.
[8]*Id.* at §§ 135, 166.

test of the legitimacy of civil law. The community can never agree to be governed by tyrannical or arbitrary regimes. It never loses control over the government it creates. While regimes of that nature may exist, even supported by a written constitution, they are not constitutional forms of government.

The conviction that individuals retain certain rights, never to be surrendered to government, was basic to other political philosophers. Spinoza believed that no man's mind can possibly lie wholly at the disposition of another, for "no one can willingly transfer his natural right of free reason and judgment, or be compelled so to do." Any government attempting to control minds was, by definition, tyrannical. It was an abuse of sovereignty to seek to prescribe what was true or false, or what opinions should be held by men in their worship of God. "All these questions," to Spinoza, "fall within a man's natural right, which he cannot abdicate even with his own consent."[9]

Sutherland and Friedrich: Modern Views on the Elements of Constitutionalism

These elements of constitutionalism, discussed centuries ago, parallel the principles we follow (or should follow) today. Arthur E. Sutherland, in a major study published in 1965, emphasized the "freedom of men, acting through an organized majority, to control their own political and economic fate." This principle rejects hereditary rule, divine right of kings, and rule by elites. Sutherland also holds that government, to remain righteous and just, must create institutions to correct its own injustices. Or, as Madison cautioned in Federalist 51: "In framing a government which is to be administered by men over men, the great difficulty lies in this: you must first enable the government to control the governed; and in the next place oblige it to control itself."

Sutherland recognizes that his second principle jars with the first. Governmental action may be unjust even if willed by a majority of the people. Judicial officers, less vulnerable to majoritarian pressures, may declare invalid any governmental action that is incon-

[9]*The Philosophy of Spinoza* 333 (Modern Library ed., 1954)

sistent with standards of constitutional justice.[10] This proposition is not the same as "government by judiciary." Charles Evans Hughes reached too far with his injunction: "We are under a Constitution, but the Constitution is what the judges say it is . . . "[11] The Supreme Court is a coequal, not superior, branch. In his inaugural address in 1861, President Lincoln denied that constitutional questions could be settled solely by Supreme Court rulings. If governmental policy upon "vital questions affecting the whole people is to be irrevocably fixed by decisions of the Supreme Court . . . the people will have ceased to be their own rulers . . ."[12] Constitutionalism is not entirely what the judges say it is.

In many instances justices conclude that Congress is a more appropriate forum for the determination of conflicts between individual rights and governmental action. Moreover, Congress frequently passes legislation that has the effect of modifying a previous decision of a court. Because of the "political question" doctrine, many important constitutional issues are left to Congress and the president. Even when the courts intervene they often regard as authoritative a set of practices already established by legislators and executive officials. Still other questions never reach the courts because of problems of jurisdiction, mootness, standing, ripeness, and other conditions for adjudication.

Sutherland points to three other criteria of constitutionalism. First, there must be fundamental equality before government. While human beings are not identical, the standard of equality serves to eliminate artificial and arbitrary inequalities, such as discriminatory treatment on the basis of race, sex, or religion. Second, the fundamentals of the constitutional system must be reduced to a written statement, either a concise constitution, as in America, or the fragmented, cumulative written record of England. As a final element, Sutherland depends on structure to restrain government: dividing power between the nation and the states, and then again within the central government (creating separate executive, legislative, and judicial bodies).[13]

[10]Arthur E. Sutherland, *Constitutionalism in America* 2–3 (1965).
[11]Charles Evans Hughes, *Addresses and Papers* 139 (1908).
[12]Richardson, *Messages and Papers*, VII, 3210.
[13]Arthur E. Sutherland, *Constitutionalism in America* 4–7 (1965).

To Carl Friedrich this division of power cuts across two planes: functionally (separation of powers) and spatially (federalism). The doctrine of separated powers has been heavily attacked in the twentieth century, first for impeding the flow of power to public administrators (who supposedly possessed expertise not found among legislators), and secondly for interfering with the demand for centralized authority during World War II. Friedrich warned that "Many who today belittle the separation of powers seem unaware of the fact that their clamor for efficiency and expediency easily leads to dictatorship . . ."[14]

THE DOCTRINE OF SEPARATED POWERS

The abuse of power by recent presidents, particularly Lyndon Johnson and Richard Nixon, generated some conventional and convenient arguments about the separation doctrine. Opponents of presidential power claimed that the framers distrusted government (especially the executive) and attempted to fashion an instrument of checks and balances to prevent tyranny. While the framers did indeed construct a system designed to restrain power, that was only part of their intention. It would be inaccurate and a disservice to their labors at the Philadelphia convention to believe that they created a document primarily for the purpose of obstructing and hampering the operation of government.

It is important to understand the practical forces that led to the creation of separated branches. Our structure of government owes its existence to the experiences of the framers, not the theory of Montesquieu or precedents borrowed from England. The framers

[14]Carl Friedrich, *Constitutional Government and Democracy* 175 (1946). See his "Constitutions and Constitutionalism," *Int'l Encyc. Soc. Sci.* (1968) and "Separation of Powers," *Encyc. Soc. Sci.*, XIII, 664 (1935), as well as Charles H. Wilson, "The Separation of Powers under Democracy and Fascism," 52 *Pol. Sci. Q.* 481 (1937). Arthur T. Vanderbilt, in the introduction to his *Doctrine of the Separation of Powers and Its Present-Day Significance* (1953), has written that individual freedom and the progress of civilization were attainable only by adhering to the principles of the separation of powers.

used Montesquieu selectively, adopting what they knew from their own experience to be useful and rejecting what they knew to be inapplicable. The product was more theirs than his. Having served in public life for many years, both in the colonies and in the fledgling republic, they knew firsthand the practical duties and problems of running a government. They were continuously and intimately involved in the mundane, down-to-earth matters of conducting a war and laying the foundation for a more perfect union. Their close familiarity with the classics in history and government, combined with the daily experience of public office, marked their special genius. It gave them vision without becoming visionaries.

British history, while valuable for the study of private and individual rights, is of marginal interest for the study of executive-legislative relationships in America. Questions of executive privilege, impoundment, and the war power cannot be resolved by harkening back to British practices. The Supreme Court made this valid observation in 1850:

> [I]n the distribution of political power between the great departments of government, there is such a wide difference between the power conferred on the President of the United States, and the authority and sovereignty which belongs to the English crown, that it would be altogether unsafe to reason from any supposed resemblance between them, either as regards conquest in war, or any other subject where the right and powers of the executive arm of the government are brought into question.[15]

It is said that powers are separated to preserve liberties. But separation can also destroy liberties. The French constitutions of 1791 and 1848 represented ambitious efforts to erect a rigid and dogmatic separation of powers. The first document produced the reign of Napoleon Bonaparte; the next effort led to the Second Empire.[16]

Instead of indiscriminately championing the virtues of the sepa-

---

[15]Fleming v. Page, 50 U.S. (9 How.) 602, 618 (1850).

[16]M. J. C. Vile, *Constitutionalism and the Separation of Powers* 176–211 (1967).

ration doctrine, we should remember that it can satisfy a number of objectives, not all of them worth seeking. The framers of the American Constitution did not want a political system so fragmented in structure, so divided in authority, that government could not function. Justice Story pointed out in his *Commentaries* that the framers adopted a separation of power but "endeavored to prove that a rigid adherence to it in all cases would be subversive of the efficiency of the government, and result in the destruction of the public liberties."[17] His observation has been underscored by others. Justice Jackson correctly identified the multiple goals that motivated the framers: "While the Constitution diffuses power the better to secure liberty, it also contemplates that the practice will integrate the dispersed powers into a workable government. It enjoins upon its branches separateness but interdependence, autonomy but reciprocity."[18]

Had this understanding prevailed in the 1960s and 1970s, we might have been spared some of the stark, corrosive confrontations between president and Congress. More recently, in *Buckley* v. *Valeo* (1976), the Supreme Court noted that the framers recognized that a "hermetic sealing off of the three branches of Government from one another would preclude the establishment of a Nation capable of governing itself effectively."[19]

This conclusion is driven home by studying the political climate in which the framers produced their document. If they wanted weak government, if they wanted it shackled and ineffective, they could have retained the Articles of Confederation. They decided against this, for very good reason. The framers had labored under a weak government from 1774 to 1787, and deliberately rejected that model in favor of stronger central powers. Consciously, at the national level, they vested greater powers in an executive.

The distrust of executive power in 1776—against the king of England and the royal governors—was tempered by two developments in the following decade. Americans discovered that state legislative

---

[17]Joseph Story, *Commentaries on the Constitution of the United States,* 5th ed. (1905), I, 396.

[18]Youngstown Co. v. Sawyer, 343 U.S. 579, 635 (1952).

[19]Buckley v. Valeo, 424 U.S. 1, 121 (1976).

bodies could be as oppressive and capricious toward individual rights as executive bodies. Also, many delegates to the Continental Congress watched with growing apprehension as the Congress found itself incapable of discharging its duties and responsibilities. Support began to grow for an independent executive, in large part for the purpose of assuring efficiency.

This interpretation challenges a famous dissent by Justice Brandeis, who claimed that the separation of powers doctrine was adopted *not* for efficiency but to preclude the exercise of arbitrary power.[20] Brandeis's dictum, invoked regularly by those who urged legislative reassertion in the 1960s, is a half-truth. The historical record is clear and persuasive that the inefficiency of the Continental Congress convinced the framers of the need for a separate and independent executive.[21]

The practical source of the separation doctrine is generally overlooked or ignored. Much more satisfying, emotionally if not intellectually, is the belief that the Constitution was pounded into shape from abstract principles, with the name of Montesquieu leading the list of theorists. Gladstone reinforced this impression by describing the American Constitution as the most wonderful document ever "struck off at a given time" by the mind of man.[22] But the framers did not create out of whole cloth the document that guides us today. They were alert to the excesses and injustices committed by state legislators. They were sensitive, very sensitive, to the demonstrated ineptitude of the Continental Congress, which had to administer and adjudicate while trying to legislate. One branch of government performed all the tasks.

Because of the repeated failings of the Congress, it soon began to delegate power—first to committees, then to boards staffed by people from outside the legislature, and finally, in 1781, to single executive officers.[23] These events occurred prior to the Philadelphia convention. The Constitution marked a continuity with political

[20]Myers v. United States, 272 U.S. 52, 293 (1926).

[21]See Louis Fisher, *President and Congress* 1–27, 241–270 (1972).

[22]"Kin Beyond the Sea," *North Am. Rev.*, Vol. 127, No. 264 (Sept.–Oct. 1878), at 185.

[23]I trace this process in *President and Congress.*

developments already underway. John Jay, after serving as secretary of foreign affairs under the Continental Congress, remained in office in the Washington administration until Thomas Jefferson could take his place. Henry Knox was secretary of war under the Continental Congress and under President Washington. Because of this orderly transition it has been said that the Constitution did not create a system of separated powers; rather, a system of separated powers created the Constitution.[24]

Several delegates to the ratifying conventions objected to the fact that the branches of government—legislative, executive, and judicial—had been intermingled instead of being kept separate. "How is the executive?" demanded one irate delegate at Virginia's ratifying convention. "Contrary to the opinion of all the best writers, blended with the legislature. We have asked for bread, and they have given us a stone."[25] This outcry enlisted some support, but not much. By the time of the Philadelphia convention the doctrine of separated powers had been modified to allow for checks and balances. One contemporary pamphleteer called the separation doctrine, in its pure form, a "hackneyed principle" and a "trite maxim."[26] Madison devoted several of his *Federalist* essays to the need for overlapping powers, claiming that the concept was superior to the impracticable partitioning of powers demanded by some of the Antifederalists.[27]

The system of checks and balances is not a contradiction to the separation doctrine. The two are complementary. Without the power to withstand encroachments by another branch, a department might find its powers drained to the point of extinction. The Constitution allocated separate functions to separate branches, but "parchment barriers" were not dependable. It was necessary, Madison concluded in Federalist 51, that "ambition must be made to counteract ambition," while in Federalist 48 he warned: "unless

[24]Francis Wharton, *The Revolutionary Diplomatic Correspondence of the United States*, I, 663 (1889).

[25]Quoted in Elliot, *Debates*, III, 280.

[26]Quoted in Vile at 153.

[27]Federalist 37 and 47 attempted to rebut some of the Antifederalist objections regarding blended powers. For the latter see Morton Borden, ed., *The Antifederalist Papers* (1965), papers 47, 48, 64, 67, 73, and 75.

these departments be so far connected and blended as to give to each a constitutional control over the others, the degree of separation which the maxim requires, as essential to a free government, can never in practice be duly maintained."

The case for a strict separation of powers was tested in the form of an amendment to the Constitution. Three states—Virginia, North Carolina, and Pennsylvania—wanted to add a separation clause to the national bill of rights.[28] The proposed language read as follows: "The powers delegated by this constitution are appropriated to the departments to which they are respectively distributed: so that the legislative department shall never exercise the powers vested in the executive or judicial [,] nor the executive exercise the powers vested in the legislative or judicial, nor the judicial exercise the powers vested in the legislative or executive departments."[29] Congress rejected this proposal, as well as a substitute amendment to make the three departments "separate and distinct."[30]

Although powers are not separated in a pure sense, it does not help to characterize the federal government as a "blend of powers." The branches have distinctly different responsibilities, practices, and traditions. A certain distance between the branches is preserved by Article I, Section 6 of the Constitution, which prohibits members of either house from holding appointive office. Congress is prohibited from reducing the compensation of the president and members of the judiciary. The Speech or Debate Clause was designed to protect legislators from executive or judicial harassment.[31]

Any occupant of the White House, after a short time in office, appreciates the degree to which an institutional separation exists,

[28]Elliot, *Debates*, III, 280, and IV, 116, 121; John Bach McMaster and Frederick D. Stone, eds., *Pennsylvania and the Federal Constitution* 475–477 (1888).

[29]Edward Dumbauld, *The Bill of Rights and What it Means Today* 174–175, 183, 199 (1957).

[30]For the congressional debates, see *Annals of Congress*, I, 453–454 (June 8, 1789) and 789–790 (Aug. 18, 1789). For action by the Senate, see U.S. Senate, *Journals, 1789–1794*, I, 64, 73–74 (1820).

[31]United States v. Johnson, 383 U.S. 169, 179 (1966).

whether Congress is in the hands of the president's party or the opposition party. That is as it should be. The president does not share with Congress his pardoning power, nor does Congress share with the courts its taxing and appropriations powers (although the judiciary is participating in the outer fringes). In 1974 the Supreme Court highlighted the separation that exists in the federal government by stating that the judicial power vested in the federal courts by Article III of the Constitution "can no more be shared with the Executive Branch than the Chief Executive, for example, can share with the Judiciary the veto power, or the Congress share with the Judiciary the power to override a Presidential veto."[32] Even in administrative agencies that discharge executive, legislative, and judicial duties, those tasks are kept separate. Someone who prosecutes a case, for example, would not be called upon to render a decision on the dispute.[33]

The Durability of the Separation Doctrine

Has the balance among political institutions, as fashioned by the framers, failed to meet the test of time? Have events overtaken theory? Tocqueville, quoting with approval a passage from Jefferson, believed that the "tyranny of the legislature" in America would continue for a number of years before being replaced by a tyranny of the executive.[34] Yet presidential power, after cresting with Abraham Lincoln, subsided in the face of a determined and resurgent Congress. Writing in 1885, Woodrow Wilson believed that Congress had become the dominant branch. He said that the Constitution of 1787 was a form of government in name rather than in reality, "the form of the Constitution being one of nicely adjusted, ideal balances, whilst the actual form of our present government is simply a scheme of congressional supremacy."[35]

Two decades later, glancing with covetous eyes at the White House, Wilson predicted that the president "must always, hence-

[32]United States v. Nixon, 418 U.S. 683, 704 (1974).

[33]Kenneth Culp Davis, *Administrative Law and Government* 174–191 (1975).

[34]Tocqueville, *Democracy in America*, I, 280 (1945 ed.).

[35]Woodrow Wilson, *Congressional Government* 6 (1885).

forth, be one of the great powers of the world . . . We have but begun to see the presidential office in this light; but it is the light which will more and more beat upon it . . ."[36] The new wellspring of presidential power, according to his analysis, was the burden of international responsibilities thrust upon the United States. The Great Depression of the 1930s, joined with the personal qualities of Franklin D. Roosevelt, gave further impetus to executive power. The reputation of Congress plummeted with such swiftness that Samuel P. Huntington, in an influential study published in 1965, suggested that unless Congress drastically altered its mode of operation it should abandon its legislative role and concentrate on serving constituents and overseeing the agencies.[37]   The condition of Congress appeared to deteriorate even further, for in 1968 Philip B. Kurland charged that it did not have the "guts to stand up to its responsibilities." Congress was prostrate, the president transcendent. Kurland invited us to visit the "sickbed of another constitutional concept—the notion of separation of powers." Not only was the patient diseased, the affliction seemed terminal. Theoretically a cure was possible, but Kurland saw no grounds for optimism. To him the patient had lost the will to live.[38]

These dire predictions suggest that the imbalance between president and Congress is chronic and permanent. At no time, however, has either branch been as all-powerful or as defective as critics maintained. Congress, though its particular life style may offend our tastes, is alive and well. The political system has shown a capacity for self-correction. Two presidents, testing the limits of their

[36]Woodrow Wilson, *Constitutional Government in the United States* 78 (1908).

[37]Samuel P. Huntington, "Congressional Responses to the Twentieth Century," in David B. Truman, ed., *The Congress and America's Future* 5–31 (1965). Writing a year later, however, Ralph K. Huitt argued that Congress played a more important part in legislation than its critics realized. See his "Congress, the Durable Partner," originally published in 1966 and reprinted in Ralph K. Huitt and Robert L. Peabody, *Congress: Two Decades of Analysis* 209–229 (1969).

[38]Philip B. Kurland, "The Impotence of Reticence," 1968 *Duke L. J.* 619, 621 (1968).

power during the 1960s and 1970s, were driven from office. Congress, flexing its muscles during this time of reassertion, ran into barriers erected by the courts. In 1976 the Supreme Court ruled against the Federal Election Commission because Congress had staked out a role for itself in the appointment of four of the commission's six members. The court held this procedure contrary to the separation doctrine. Congress could not both legislate and enforce.[39]

The separation doctrine, subjected to ridicule for much of the twentieth century, still retains vitality. A longer view of American history provides room for confidence. Senator George Wharton Pepper offered this sound perspective: "[I]f the geometers of 1787 hoped for perfect peace and if the psychologists of that day feared disastrous conflicts, history, as so often happens, has proved that hopes were dupes and fears were liars. There has not been perfect peace; but the conflicts have not proved disastrous."[40]

IMPLIED POWERS

In civics courses we are taught that the American Constitution is one of limited and enumerated powers. This is satisfactory only if we stay inside the classroom. Once we venture out and observe the actual workings of government, we must confront and resolve a perplexing array of powers that are not expressly stated. They parade under assorted names: implied and inherent, incidental and inferred, aggregate, powers created by custom and acquiescence, and delicate "penumbras," "interstices," and "glosses" that add strange and new qualities to the Constitution. Whatever the name the result is identical: the conferral of a power that is neither expressly stated in the Constitution nor specifically granted by Congress.

The "genius and spirit of our institutions are hostile to the exer-

---

[39]Buckley v. Valeo, 424 U.S. 1 (1976).

[40]George Wharton Pepper, *Family Quarrels: the President, the Senate, the House* viii (1931).

cise of implied powers." Thus spake the Supreme Court in 1821. After making the appropriate gesture it proceeded to deal amicably with these hostile forces. It was utopian, said the court, to believe that government could exist without leaving the exercise of discretion somewhere. In this particular case the court recognized that Congress possessed powers not expressly granted by the Constitution: the power to issue warrants to compel a party's appearance and the power to punish for contempt.[41]

If a constitution is intended to limit power, and if we admit powers that are not expressly stated, can government be kept within bounds? Let the imagination run to far corners and the answer is No. But let "experience be our guide" (the framers' preference), and the prospect is more reassuring. The American Constitution cannot survive purely on the basis of express powers or "strict constructionism," a phrase made popular by the Nixon administration.

The debate in 1789 on the Bill of Rights settled the need to grant implied powers to government. Members of the First Congress proposed that the Tenth Amendment be so worded that all powers not "expressly delegated" to the federal government would be reserved to the states. Madison immediately objected, insisting that it was impossible to limit a government to the exercise of express powers. There "must necessarily be admitted powers by implication, unless the Constitution descended to recount every minutiae [*sic*]." After elimination of "expressly" the Tenth Amendment was adopted with this language: "The powers not delegated to the United States by the Constitution, nor prohibited by it to the States, are reserved to the States respectively, or to the people."[42]

Chief Justice Marshall cited this debate when he ruled on the implied power of Congress to establish a United States Bank, even though not expressly permitted by the Constitution. Marshall observed that there was no phrase in the document which (like the Articles of Confederation) "excludes incidental or implied powers; and which requires that everything granted shall be expressly and

[41]Anderson v. Dunn, 19 U.S. (6 Wheat.) 204, 225 (1821).
[42]*Annals of Congress*, I, 761 (Aug. 18, 1789).

minutely described,"[43] A constitution represented a general structure, not a detailed instruction manual:

> A constitution, to contain an accurate detail of all the subdivisions of which its great powers will admit, and of all the means by which they may be carried into execution, would partake of the prolixity of a legal code, and could scarcely be embraced by the human mind. It would, probably, never be understood by the public. Its nature, therefore, requires, that only its great outlines should be marked, its important objects designated, and the minor ingredients which compose those objects, be deduced from the nature of the objects themselves.[44]

In interpreting the Constitution it is important to remember that government is created to carry out certain functions required for the people. A number of essential activities find no ready reference in the Constitution. As Marshall remarked: "All admit, that the government may, legitimately, punish any violation of its laws; and yet, this is not among the enumerated powers of Congress."[45]

The theory of implied powers was treated to an extended debate in 1793 after President Washington issued what is now known as the Neutrality Proclamation. His administration was subjected to bitter attacks, particularly from those who sympathized with France. Alexander Hamilton, writing under the pseudonym "Pacificus," denied that the proclamation had been issued without authority. Hamilton derived the power to issue proclamations from the general clause of Article II of the Constitution: "the executive Power shall be vested in a President of the United States of America." He believed that it was unsound to limit the executive power to the particular items enumerated in subsequent sections. They should not derogate from the "comprehensive grant" of power in the general clause, "further than as it may be coupled with express restrictions or limitations." With the exception of the Senate's participation in the appointment of officers and in the making of

[43]McCulloch v. Maryland, 17 U.S. (4 Wheat.) 315, 404 (1819).
[44]*Id.* at 406.
[45]*Id.* at 415.

treaties, and Congress's power to declare war and to grant letters of marque and reprisal, all other executive powers were lodged solely in the President.[46]

Jefferson, outraged by this doctrine, wrote to Madison: "For God's sake, my dear Sir, take up your pen, select the most striking heresies and cut him to pieces in the face of the public."[47] Madison produced five articles under the name "Helvidius," charging that Hamilton's reading of the Constitution must be condemned "as no less vicious in theory than it would be dangerous in practice." The expansive interpretation of executive power would mean that "no citizen could any longer guess at the character of the government under which he lives; the most penetrating jurist would be unable to scan the extent of constructive prerogative."[48]

Madison indulged in hyperbole, as did Hamilton. We could scarcely expect much else in the supercharged political atmosphere of 1793, heightened as it was by the intense rivalry between Hamilton and Jefferson in the cabinet. But the issue they raised was to remain active. By the end of the nineteenth century the issue of implied powers for the president reached the Supreme Court in the case of *In re Neagle* (1890). Justice Stephen Johnson Field, serving as circuit justice in California, had his life threatened by two malcontents. David Neagle, a United States deputy marshal, was assigned to ride circuit to offer protection. One morning during breakfast, Field was assaulted by David Terry, one of the malcontents. Neagle, after identifying himself, shot and killed Terry. No statute authorized the president to appoint a deputy marshal for the purpose of protecting a Supreme Court justice traveling in his circuit.

The court, split six to two, upheld the assignment of Neagle and his immunity from state law. His attorney acknowledged that there was no single specific statute making it a duty to furnish protection to a Supreme Court justice. To the attorney, however, whatever was "necessarily implied is as much a part of the Constitution and

[46]Alexander Hamilton, *Works* (Lodge ed.), IV, 437–439.

[47]Thomas Jefferson, *Writings* (Ford ed.), VI, 338.

[48]James Madison, *Writings* (Hunt ed.), VI, 152.

statutes as if it were actually expressed therein."[49] Justice Miller, announcing the opinion for the court, agreed:

> In the view we take of the Constitution of the United States,
> any obligation fairly and properly inferrible from that instrument, or any duty of the marshal to be derived from the general scope of his duties under the laws of the United States, is
> "a law" within the meaning of this phrase.[50]

The two dissenting justices did not dispute the proposition that "whatever is necessarily implied in the Constitution and laws of the United States is as much a part of them as if it were actually expressed." Nor did they question the propriety of Neagle's action. But they related implied powers to this clause in Article I which augments the powers of Congress: "Congress shall have power . . . to make all laws which shall be necessary and proper for carrying into execution the foregoing powers, and all other powers vested by this Constitution in the government of the United States, or in any department or officer thereof." Finding no such law, and believing that the United States government was powerless to try and punish a man charged with murder in this offense, they would have had Neagle placed in the custody of the sheriff of San Joaquin, California, to be tried by the courts of that state.[51]

Theodore Roosevelt and William Howard Taft, debating the boundaries of presidential authority, appear to have held diametrically opposed positions on implied power. Roosevelt asserted that it was the president's right and duty to do "anything that the needs of the Nation demanded, unless such action was forbidden by the Constitution or by the laws."[52] His argument follows the one presented in Hamilton's "Pacificus" writings. Taft maintained that the president

> can exercise no power which cannot be fairly and reasonably
> traced to some specific grant of power or justly implied and

[49]In re Neagle, 135 U.S. 1, 27 (1890).

[50]*Id.* at 59.

[51]*Id.* at 77–78, 83.

[52]*The Works of Theodore Roosevelt*, XX, 347 (1926).

included within such express grant as proper and necessary to its exercise. Such specific grant must be either in the Federal Constitution or in an act of Congress passed in pursuance thereof.[53]

Use of the words "express" and "specific" appears to put Taft in the camp of those who believe in enumerated powers. But it is clear that he recognized the need for implied powers—powers that can be "fairly and reasonably traced" or "justly implied." He even adds to the Constitution a necessary-and-proper clause for the president. When Taft's study is read in full, it is evident that he adhered to a generous interpretation of executive power: incidental powers to remove officers, inferable powers to protect the lives and property of American citizens living abroad, powers created by custom, and emergency powers (such as Lincoln's suspension of the writ of habeas corpus during the Civil War). Summing up, Taft said that executive power was limited "so far as it is possible to limit such a power consistent with that discretion and promptness of action that are essential to preserve the interests of the public in times of emergency, or legislative neglect or inaction."[54]

The general principles discussed in this chapter will be followed by more specific powers. But first it is helpful to understand other basic ingredients of a constitutional system: the delegation of legislative power to agents outside of Congress, the use of nonstatutory controls by Congress to monitor the delegated power, the impact of custom and of legislative acquiescence, the distinction between executive and ministerial duties, and the notion of an emergency power for the executive (the prerogative). These subjects form the basis of the next chapter.

[53]William Howard Taft, *Our Chief Magistrate and His Powers* 139–140 (1916), now available in paperback under the title *The President and His Powers* (1967).

[54]For specific references in Taft's 1916 edition, see the following: pp. 56 and 76 on removal powers; p. 95 on inferable powers, p. 135 for powers created by custom; p. 147 for suspension of habeas corpus, and p. 156 for the need for executive discretion and promptness of action. A comparison between Roosevelt and Taft appears in Fisher, *President and Congress* 33–37.

2

Boundaries of Power

The theory of constitutional limits—of powers enumerated and clearly defined—has lost ground to a number of stubborn forces. Even at the outset, two hundred years ago, the lines between the three branches of the federal government were not crisp demarcations. Madison confided to Jefferson that the boundaries between the executive, legislative, and judicial powers, "though in general so strongly marked in themselves, consist in many instances of mere shades of difference."[1] In Federalist 37 Madison paused to acknowledge the inherent limitations of our language. Just as naturalists had difficulty in defining the exact line between vegetable life and the animal world, so was it an even greater task to draw the boundary between the departments of government, or "even the privileges and powers of the different legislative branches. Questions daily occur in the course of practice, which prove the obscurity which reigns in these subjects, and which puzzle the greatest adepts in political science."

Madison, while supporting the need for implied powers, feared that transgressions would benefit the legislature at the expense of the executive. In 1789 he opposed the Senate's participation in the removal power on the ground that it would reduce presidential powers to a "mere vapor." On such specific issues he indulged in abstract and impracticable formulations about the separation doctrine, saying that "if there is a principle in our Constitution, indeed in any free Constitution, more sacred than another, it is that which separates the Legislature, Executive, and Judicial powers."[2] What

---

[1] James Madison, *Writings* (Hunt ed.), V, 26.
[2] *Annals of Congress*, I, 582 (June 22, 1789).

alarmed him, however, was not the blending of powers inherent in the checks and balances system but encroachments that might fundamentally alter the balance. Madison could not foresee the vast quantity of legislative power soon to be delegated to the president and his assistants. The extent of this delegation has sometimes reached the point of jeopardizing the system of separated powers. To retain control, Congress has evolved a highly sophisticated set of tools, many of them of a nonstatutory nature. Custom and legislative acquiescence also reshape the boundaries of power. We distinguish between administrative actions that are mandatory ("ministerial") and those that call for discretion and judgment ("executive"). Finally, there exists an executive prerogative that temporarily frees the president from statutory and constitutional inhibitions.

DELEGATION

Not since 1935 has the Supreme Court struck down a delegation of power to the executive branch because of inadequate legislative guidelines. In that year delegations of power were twice struck down. Both decisions involved the National Industrial Recovery Act (NIRA), which placed upon industrial and trade associations the responsibility for drawing up codes that would minimize competition, raise prices, and restrict production. If the president regarded the codes as unacceptable he could prescribe his own and enforce them by law. The court concluded that NIRA failed to provide adequate standards and guidelines for administrative action. In one of the cases, *Schechter*, Justice Cardozo exclaimed that "This is delegation running riot."[3]

The court did not object to delegation; it opposed delegation unaccompanied by statutory guidelines. In other situations, both before and after 1935, the court has recognized that the nature of government requires Congress to pass general legislation and leave to other branches the responsibility for, as the court put it, "filling

---

[3]Panama Refining Co. v. Ryan, 293 U.S. 388 (1935); Schechter Corp. v. United States, 295 U.S. 495, 553 (1935).

in the details."⁴ While Congress cannot surrender the legislative power entrusted to it by the Constitution, neither is it possible to avoid delegating major chunks of discretionary authority to the executive branch. The tension between these two competing values is relieved by some judicial tightrope walking.

One author suggested this humorous but accurate syllogism: (1) *Major Premise*: Legislative power cannot be constitutionally delegated by Congress; (2) *Minor Premise*: It is essential that certain powers be delegated to administrative officers and regulatory commissions; (3) *Conclusion*: Therefore the powers thus delegated are not legislative powers.⁵

This kind of self-serving logic reappears in many decisions on delegation. Typically the court declares that it would be a breach of the Constitution for Congress to transfer its legislative power to the president. After genuflecting to the theory of separated powers, the justices regularly uphold the delegation in question.⁶ Statutory language is sanctioned even when it is vague and ill-defined, such as general guidelines of "excessive profits," "reasonable rates," "unjust discrimination," and "in the public interest." The courts tolerate this kind of legislation not because the language is specific, which is far from the case, but because Congress supplies standards of due process to guide officials in administering the statute. Agencies are required by law to give notice and a hearing prior to issuing a rule or regulation. Also, findings of fact are supplied for the record and procedures exist for appeal. The Administrative Procedure Act of 1946 established various standards for agency rulemaking in order to guarantee fairness and equitable treatment. Through such procedural standards Congress tries to eliminate or minimize the opportunity for executive caprice and arbitrariness (see pp. 132–136).⁷

Still, there is an uneasy feeling that Congress has handed over to

⁴Wayman v. Southard, 10 Wheat. 1, 46 (1825).

⁵Robert E. Cushman, *The Independent Regulatory Commissions* 429 (1941).

⁶For example, Field v. Clark, 143 U.S. 649, 692 (1891) and Hampton & Co. v. United States, 276 U.S. 394, 406 (1928).

⁷In 1958 the Supreme Court upheld the Assimilative Crimes Act of 1948, which provided that, in a federal enclave, acts not punishable by any enactment of Congress were punishable by the then effective laws of

executive officials too much of its legislative power. A glaring example of contemporary delegation is the Economic Stabilization Act of 1970, which authorized the president "to issue such orders and regulations as he may deem appropriate to stabilize prices, rents, wages, and salaries at levels not less than those prevailing on May 25, 1970." The remaining sections of the act failed to provide for procedural safeguards—for example, giving notice prior to issuing orders, providing a hearing for affected parties, and establishing machinery for judicial review.[8]

In view of President Nixon's public opposition to wage-price controls, it is evident that Democratic members of Congress tried to embarrass him and create an election-year issue. Each time the expiration date of the act drew near, Congress extended it. Nixon's refusal to use the authority permitted legislators to chastise him for inaction. Then, on August 15, 1971 Nixon stunned Congress by placing a ninety-day freeze on all prices, rents, wages, and salaries. In part he based his action on the authority given him in the Economic Stabilization Act of 1970.[9] Congress had passed a domestic equivalent to the Gulf of Tonkin Resolution.

Private parties appealed to the courts to have the act struck down as an invalid delegation of legislative power. In one of the principal cases, Circuit Judge Leventhal upheld the legislation by noting that some of the legislative guidelines had been included in committee reports and the legislative history of the act: "Whether legislative purposes are to be obtained from committee reports, or are set forth in a separate section of the text of the law, is largely a matter of drafting style."[10] Yet it is more than that. Agencies are

---

the state in which the enclave was located. In a dissent, Justice Douglas objected that "federal laws grow like mushrooms without Congress passing a bill"; United States v. Sharpnack, 355 U.S. 286, 299 (1958).

[8]84 Stat. 799.

[9]Executive order 11615, 36 Fed. Reg. 15727 (1971).

[10]Amalgamated Meat Cutters & Butcher Work. v. Connally, 337 F.Supp. 737, 750 (D.D.C. 1971). See also California Teach. Ass'n v. Newport Mesa Unified Sch. Dist., 333 F.Supp. 436, 446 (C.D. Cal. 1971) and DeRieux v. Five Smiths, Inc., 499 F.2d 1321, 1329–30 (Temp. Emerg. Ct. of Appeals, 1974), as well as cases cited in footnote 11 of latter decision.

bound by law; they are not necessarily bound by nonstatutory controls (a point pursued in the next section). As for the 1970 act, Congress subsequently amended it to provide for more explicit standards and guidelines.[11]

In 1974 two members of the Supreme Court objected to excessive delegation of legislative power to the president.[12] This issue was lifted to more conspicuous heights when President Ford responded to the Arab oil embargo by placing a fee on imported oil. The purpose was to promote energy conservation, encourage domestic production, and reduce United States dependence on foreign sources. The chief purpose, however, was to pressure Congress into passing Ford's energy bill. After an initial fee of a dollar per barrel, imposed on January 23, 1975, the plan called for additional dollar increases on March 1 and April 1. The Ford administration took the position that while taxes and tariffs were legislative prerogatives, requiring specific authorization by statute, a "fee" on imported material "may be set for non-revenue purposes and need not be legislated."[13]

Congressman Robert Drinan, joined by other parties in litigation, regarded the fee as a circumvention of the duty system established by the Constitution. However, a district court decided that the fee program was one of several actions covered by the Trade Expansion Act, which permitted the president to "adjust imports."

[11]The 1970 act was extended by 84 Stat. 1468, 85 Stat. 13, and 85 Stat. 38, before being fundamentally rewritten by legislation in 1971 (85 Stat. 743) which provided for more specific standards, procedural safeguards, and judicial review. For critiques of 1970 act see Stanley H. Friedelbaum, "The 1971 Wage-Price Freeze: Unchallenged Presidential Power," *The Supreme Court Review, 1974* at 33–80, and Richard P. Carr and Robert P. Dutcher, "Phase V: The Cost-of-Living Council Reconsidered," 62 *Geo. L. J.* 1663 (1974).

[12]California Bankers Assn. v. Shultz, 416 U.S. 21, 90–93 (1974) (Justices Douglas and Brennan dissenting). Dissenting in another case, Justice Harlan expressed concern about the lack of standards in defining the limits of the interior secretary's power to apportion the waters of the Colorado River; Arizona v. California, 373 U.S. 546, 624–627 (1963). In a 1965 dissent, Justice Douglas objected to unrestricted delegation to the secretary of state: Zemel v. Rusk, 381 U.S. 1, 21–22 (1965).

[13]Algonquin Sng., Inc. v. Federal Energy Admin., 518 F.2d 1051, 1060 (D.C. Cir. 1975).

For those who criticized the statute as an undue delegation of legislative authority, the court observed that the "non-delegation doctrine is almost a complete failure."[14]

An appellate court reversed this decision, holding that the Trade Expansion Act did not constitute authority for the fees imposed by President Ford. A review of previous trade legislation convinced the court that congressional delegations had been "narrow and explicit in order to effectuate well-defined goals." Also rejected was the administration's interpretation of a fee on imported materials. The Tariff Commission had called the license fee mechanism "substantially a duty system." Furthermore, the fee imposed by President Ford would have generated an estimated $4.8 billion a year, which exceeded the total amount of revenue derived from customs in 1974.[15]

The Supreme Court did not analyze the fee-duty distinction in 1976, when it upheld the license fees. Writing for a unanimous court, Justice Thurgood Marshall stated that the fees were within the scope of the Trade Expansion Act. The court was not disturbed by the fact that the act delegated broadly, authorizing the president to "take such action, and for such time, as he deems necessary to adjust the imports of [the] article and its derivatives so that . . . imports [of the article] will not threaten to impair the national security." To Justice Marshall the president's action was authorized by the language of the Trade Expansion Act and its legislative history. He maintained that the legislative standards "are clearly sufficient to meet any delegation doctrine attack."[16]

It is evident from these examples that more explicit standards for administrative action must come from Congress, not the courts. But a number of technical and political factors discourage specificity.

[14]Commonwealth of Massachusetts v. Simon, Civil Action No. 74-0129 (D.D.C. Feb. 21, 1975), and Algonquin Sng., Inc. v. Simon, Civil Action No. 75-0130 (D.D.C. 1975), reprinted at 518 F.2d 1064 (D.C. Cir. 1975).

[15]Algonquin Sng., Inc. v. Federal Energy Admin., 518 F.2d 1051, 1056, 1061 (D.C. Cir. 1975).

[16]FEA v. Algonquin Sng. Inc., 426 U.S. 548, 559 (1976). See Thomas P. Preston, "National Security and Oil Import Regulation: The License Fee Approach," 15 *Va. J. Int'l L.* 400 (1975).

The Impulse for Broad Delegation

Vague and general grants of legislative power are criticized from various perspectives. Some critics insist that political accountability and democratic values depend on the establishment of clear guidelines for administrators.[17] Others point out that vague statutes make it difficult to conduct program evaluation, stressed in such recent statutes as the Legislative Reorganization Act of 1970 and the Congressional Budget and Impoundment Control Act of 1974.[18] How can Congress, assisted by the General Accounting Office and other staff support, determine whether programs are being carried out effectively unless the original legislative goals are clearly stated?

Part of Congress's hesitancy in writing explicit statutory language is rooted in a genuine dilemma: how successfully can Congress legislate for future events? William Blackstone, the eighteenth-century English jurist, observed that the "manner, time, and circumstances of putting laws in execution must frequently be left to the discretion of the executive magistrates."[19] Contingent (or conditional) legislation has had a long tradition in America. An early legal test involved a nonintercourse act against Britain. After the legislation lapsed in 1810, Congress left it to the president to renew the trade restrictions at his discretion. When President Madison revived the act, a merchant complained in court that the president's proclamation had the force of law and was thus legislative in nature, violating the separation doctrine. The Supreme Court rejected this contention in *Brig Aurora*, affirming that Congress could legislate conditionally and leave to others the task of ascertaining the facts that bring its declared policy into operation.[20]

For more than a century courts have recognized that it is essential to phrase statutes in general terms when events are "future and impossible to be fully known." Many subjects of government depend upon legislation which cannot be known to the lawmaking power

[17]Theodore J. Lowi, *The End of Liberalism* 298 (1969).
[18]84 Stat. 1168, sec. 204 (1970); 88 Stat. 325, Title VII (1974).
[19]William Blackstone, *Commentaries*, Book 1, *270.
[20]Brig Aurora v. United States, 11 U.S. (7 Cr.) 382 (1813).

"and must, therefore, be a subject of inquiry and determination outside of the halls of legislation."[21] Toward the end of the nineteenth century and during the first part of the twentieth, administrative discretion became ever more familiar and widespread. Conditions in the economy requiring regulations were increasingly complex, interrelated, and in process of rapid change. Administrators could not be expected to solve new problems when operating in a legislative strait jacket. They needed an opportunity to experiment and learn. Courts accepted broadness and generality in statutes as unavoidable qualities of legislation. Because of unique circumstances prevailing in different regions and localities, Congress need only declare a general policy and leave to administrative officers the duty of applying the statute to particular circumstances.[22]

Political motives sometimes lurk behind delegation. Congress may find a responsibility so irritating, so utterly lacking in political rewards, that it shifts the chore elsewhere. General tariff making exposed Congress to such ridicule that in time it delegated the bulk of that responsibility to the executive branch and the Tariff Commission. As one study concluded, "every favor which can be conferred is also a danger, because it must sometimes be refused. Responsibility involves blame. And, if the demands exceed what the congressman can effectively handle, then he may happily yield up a significant portion of his power. This is what happened with the tariff."[23]

As much as Congress tries to rid itself of unwanted tasks, it has difficulty breaking free entirely. In the case of international trade, industries and labor unions appealed to Congress for protection from foreign competition. Legislation soon appeared, providing federal assistance payments for dislocated industries and a variety

[21]Locke's Appeal, 72 Pa. St. 491, 498-499 (1873).

[22]For example, Buttfield v. Stranahan, 192 U.S. 470, 496 (1904); Union Bridge Co. v. United States, 194 U.S. 364, 386 (1907); Monongahela Bridge Co. v. United States, 216 U.S. 177 (1910); and United States v. Grimaud, 220 U.S. 506, 516 (1911).

[23]Raymond P. Bauer et al., *American Business and Public Policy* 37 (1963). For delegation of tariff power see Louis Fisher, *President and Congress* 133–155 (1972).

of nontariff barriers. The Trade Act of 1974 marked a reassertion of Congress in this area.

A similar pattern is emerging with postal reform. In 1970 Congress established the Postal Service to make it "independent" of political pressures. The purpose was to convert the former Post Office into a modern, "businesslike" operation. Yet Congress would not surrender some sensitive political decisions, such as assuring rural delivery and providing subsidies for certain classes of mail. Additional legislation, in 1974, extended the subsidies for several years.

Congress found other postal issues back in its lap. Each year the new Postal Service ran larger and larger deficits. Irate constituents complained about deteriorating mail service and higher postage. Congress passed another law in 1976 to supplement the federal subsidy and prohibit the Postal Service from increasing rates or decreasing service until a Commission on Postal Service could report on recommended changes. When the report appeared the next year, members of Congress immediately attacked the commission's recommendations to eliminate Saturday mail delivery, increase the annual federal subsidy, and push postal rates still higher. The promise of innovative and imaginative techniques, borrowed from the private sector, now seemed the product of fancy. There were even some within postal management who believed that governmental service should not compete with the technology (such as electronic communication) used by private industry.[24]

The recent history of federal pay adjustments illustrates the sticky quality of delegation. Congress adopted the principle of "pay comparability" in 1962 as a means of keeping the levels of federal salaries comparable to those in the private sector. On the basis of surveys conducted by the Bureau of Labor Statistics (BLS), as well as advice from the Civil Service Commission, the president recommended pay adjustments to Congress. But because of legislative inaction and delay, especially during election years, pay raises took effect long after the BLS surveys.[25]

---

[24]P.L. 93-328, 88 Stat. 287 (1974) and P.L. 94–421, 90 Stat. 1303 (1976). See statement by Congressman Hanley, 123 Cong. Rec. H4970–4981 (daily ed. May 24, 1977).

[25]See remarks of Senator McGee, 116 Cong. Rec. 44099 (1970).

Prior to 1967 Congress determined the rate of compensation for senators and representatives by a separate statute, setting forth the specific dollar amounts paid to legislators. In that year, as part of the Postal Revenue and Salary Act, Congress established a commission to recommend every four years the rates of compensation that should be paid to members of Congress, justices of the Supreme Court, federal judges, and certain high-ranking government officials. The president, after receiving these recommendations, would submit to Congress his own proposals for salaries. They would take effect within thirty days unless disapproved by either house or replaced by a different salary schedule enacted into law.

The issue is further complicated by another delegation included in the Federal Pay Comparability Act of 1970, which directed the president to have a report prepared each year to compare federal and private rates of pay. After considering this report, along with recommendations from the Advisory Committee on Federal Pay, the president proposes an adjustment in pay to satisfy the principle of comparability. He may also submit an alternative plan, taking into account national emergency or economic conditions. Unless either house vetoes his plan within thirty days, it takes effect.[26]

Through such mechanisms Congress hoped to remove "politics" from pay adjustments, but the issue continued to bounce around as a political football. Presidents Nixon and Ford, appealing to the country for spending restraints, repeatedly tried to delay salary increases or keep them below the line of comparability. In 1972 President Nixon, relying on an interpretation of the Economic Stabilization Act, refused to submit an alternative plan. An appellate court held that his action violated the law.[27] Members of Congress, responding to constituency pressures (particularly in election years), also helped frustrate the policy of pay comparability.

The first report of the Quadrennial Commission, responsible for rates of compensation to members of Congress, the judiciary, and top-level executive officials, resulted in a pay increase in 1969. The

[26]84 Stat. 1946 (1970).

[27]National Treasury Employees Union v. Nixon, 492 F.2d 587 (D.C. Cir. 1974). Earlier, in National Ass'n of Internal Revenue Employees v. Nixon, 349 F.Supp. 18 (D.D.C. 1972), a district court declined to decide the dispute.

second quadrennial report, submitted a year late, was defeated by Congress in 1974. As a consequence, by 1977, top executive officials had received only one raise. Since other federal employees continued to receive annual increases, middle-level and upper-level administrators—with vastly different responsibilities—became compressed in the same bracket. The lack of pay relief caused many officials to retire early. Subordinates often declined to move up and assume greater responsibilities without salary incentives, while replacements were difficult to recruit. The inequity was widely acknowledged but the political situation remained deadlocked.

Congressman Larry Pressler asked the courts to declare unconstitutional the statutory procedure for setting legislative compensation. He claimed that the system, allowing salary adjustments without affirmative action by both houses of Congress, violated the Ascertainment Clause: "The Senators and Representatives shall receive a Compensation for their Services to be ascertained by law" (Article I, Section 6). A district court in 1976 decided that the meaning of "ascertains" is satisfied by the statutory procedure.[28]

The lid on salaries for top officials was finally lifted in 1977, with a large catch-up pay raise, but only after Congress had deftly arranged its schedule so that a vote on the plan was practically impossible. The Senate did vote twice in tabling motions to disapprove the increase. Critics bewailed the irresponsibility of Congress, but Speaker Thomas O'Neill maintained that the increases would have been defeated "overwhelmingly" had they been brought to the floor for a vote.[29] Congressional inaction (that is, looking in another direction) seemed the only way to permit justified pay increases to take effect. Afterwards, Congress passed legislation to require an affirmative roll-call vote for all pay increases for members of Congress, federal judges, and high-level federal officials. This new procedure applies only to the increases recommended every four years by the Quadrennial Commission, not to annual cost-of-living adjustments.[30]

Broad delegations result from a number of conditions. Leg-

---

[28]Pressler v. Simon, 428 F.Supp. 302 (D.D.C. 1976), docketed as No. 76-1005 before the Supreme Court, *sub. nom.* Pressler v. Blumenthal.

[29]*Washington Post*, Feb. 21, 1977, at A6.

[30]P.L. 95-19, 91 Stat. 45, sec. 401 (1977).

islators and their staffs frequently lack the expertise needed to draft specific language for highly specialized subjects. Even experts in the agencies and the private sector find it difficult to develop strict standards that would be workable. An assistant general counsel in the Department of Health, Education, and Welfare (HEW) expressed misgivings about the lack of clarity in legislation being drafted for social services. But his boss, HEW Secretary Wilbur Cohen, had little patience with the demand for legal precision. For those who worried about details and specificity he offered this advice: "Put it in regulations . . . do it later. I can't think of an answer."[31]

These circumstances, faced by legislators and administrators alike, invite vague formulations of objectives. Furthermore, specificity of language may undermine the consensus needed to pass the legislation. A ban on "sex discrimination" can attract a majority of votes in Congess. Working out precisely what the phrase means in terms, say, of father-son banquets or boy choirs might fracture the coalition required for passage.

Instead of relying on more stringent legislative standards, Kenneth Culp Davis would prefer to have the guides furnished by the administrators who implement the program. If Congress fails to provide adequate standards, agency officials would have to use their rulemaking authority to establish criteria for further action.[32] Congress may also control administrative action by changing authorization language or by placing limitations in an appropriation bill.[33] In the event that the president issues executive orders, pursuant to delegated authority, and Congress wants to revoke the orders, such action is well within its power.[34]

Congress may also include in a statute a requirement for review at stipulated periods and may provide a termination date for delegated authority (so-called "sunset" or self-destruct provisions). The

---

[31]Martha Derthick, *Uncontrollable Spending for Social Services Grants* 8–9 (1975).

[32]Kenneth Culp Davis, *Discretionary Justice* (1969), and "A New Approach to Delegation," 36 *U. Chi. L. Rev.* 713 (1969).

[33]Eisenberg v. Corning, 179 F.2d 275 (D.C. Cir. 1949).

[34]Feliciano v. United States, 297 F.Supp. 1356, 1358 (D. Puerto Rico 1969), *aff'd*, 422 F.2d 943, *cert. denied*, 400 U.S. 823 (1970).

Senate Foreign Relations Committee has identified a number of legislative failings in the areas of foreign policy and war, such as the practice of passing general area resolutions that transfer power to the president. The committee recommended that each resolution should use the words "authorize" or "empower," to make clear that Congress had delegated power that the president would not have otherwise possessed. Also, the committee advocated a time limit in each resolution, "thereby assuring Congress the opportunity to review its decision and extend or terminate the President's authority to use military force."[35]

NONSTATUTORY CONTROLS

Vagueness in legislation is partially remedied by details that appear in the legislative history, such as committee reports, committee hearings, floor debates, and correspondence from review committees. This material considerably narrows the range of agency discretion. For example, the public works appropriation act for fiscal 1977 contained what seemed to be an extraordinary grant of power: a lump sum of $1.4 billion for construction by the Corps of Engineers. But the two houses of Congress had quite specific projects in mind in arriving at that sum. The projects appeared in the conference report, organized state by state so that each member knew what projects were to be carried out.[36]

Nonstatutory controls serve the purposes of both branches. Neither Congress nor the agencies are always certain of the specifics to be included in a statute. When judgments and predictions are wrong, the statute has to be rewritten. Putting guidelines and details in nonstatutory sources adds valuable flexibility to the legislative process. If an adjustment is necessary after a law is passed, committees and agencies can depart from the nonstatutory scheme without having to pass new legislation.

The system of nonstatutory controls is fragile. Much depends on

[35]S. Rept. No. 129, 91st Cong., 1st Sess. 33 (1969).

[36]P.L. 94-355, 90 Stat. 891; H. Rept. No. 1297, 94th Cong., 2d Sess. 18–29 (1976). For a general treatment of nonstatutory controls, see Michael W. Kirst, *Government Without Making Laws* (1969).

a "keep the faith" attitude among agency officials. They must want to maintain the integrity of their budget presentations and preserve a relationship of trust and confidence with congressional committees. Violation of that trust may result in budget cutbacks, restrictive language in statutes, and line-item appropriations. The House Appropriations Committee has reminded the Defense Department that, regardless of the lump-sum nature of defense appropriations, the department is expected to spend funds in accordance with its detailed budget justifications:

> In a strictly legal sense, the Department of Defense could utilize the funds appropriated for whatever programs were included under the individual appropriation accounts, but the relationship with the Congress demands that the detailed justifications which are presented in support of budget requests be followed. To do otherwise would cause Congress to lose confidence in the requests made and probably result in reduced appropriations or line item appropriation bills.[37]

The evolution of nonstatutory controls is reflected in the history of "reprograming" of funds by the Defense Department. Reprograming consists of the shift of funds within an appropriation account (for example, "Aircraft Procurement, Navy"), compared to shifts from one account to another (for example, from "Aircraft Procurement, Navy" to "Weapons Procurement, Navy"). The latter type of transaction, called a "transfer," requires statutory authority. Reprograming is essentially a nonstatutory development. Control is exercised for the most part through committee reports, agency directives, and a complicated set of understandings between the two branches.

Several decades ago the extent of legislative control consisted basically of review by two members from each of the appropriations committees: the chairman of the defense appropriations subcommittee and the ranking minority member. Gradually the subcommittee began to place restrictions in the committee reports. The Defense Department incorporated these restrictions in its directives and instructions to agency officials. Congressional review included

[37]H. Rept. No. 662, 93d Cong., 1st Sess. 16 (1973).

a greater number of committee members (extending to the full sub-committee and sometimes the full committee) and eventually the authorization committees (Armed Services). On occasion the com-mittees agreed that the decision was of such fundamental im-portance that it should be made on the floor of Congress rather than worked out as an agency-subcommittee agreement.[38]

Although the procedure has worked well, members of Congress have uncovered attempts to circumvent the understandings. Par-ticularly serious to Congress was a practice followed by some de-fense agencies: when funds for a program were not granted, other funds would be reprogramed to it. This practice made a mockery of congressional action on the budget. After warnings were issued by the committees having jurisdiction (both Appropriations and Armed Services), a restriction was placed in the defense appropria-tions bill. For a number of years it has been the practice of Congress to insert this language:

> No part of the funds in this Act shall be available to prepare
> or present a request to the Committees on Appropriations for
> the reprogramming of funds, unless for higher priority items,
> based on unforeseen military requirements, than those for
> which originally appropriated and in no case where the item
> for which reprogramming is requested has been denied by the
> Congress.[39]

Congress included the clause concerning "higher priority items" to discourage agencies from applying surplus funds to marginal and low-priority programs.

The tenuous nature of nonstatutory controls is underscored by an incident that took place in 1975. The conference report on the defense appropriations bill had directed the navy to produce, as its air combat fighter, a derivative of the plane selected by the air force.[40] The purpose was to increase commonality between the two services. Instead, the navy picked an aircraft that was not a deriva-

---

[38]For the development of defense reprograming see Louis Fisher, *Presidential Spending Power* 80–98 (1975).

[39]P.L. 94-419, 90 Stat. 1298 (1976).

[40]H. Rept. No. 1363, 93d Cong., 2d Sess. 27 (1974).

tive. A contractor, who had bid on the expectation that the navy would follow the understanding in the conference report, lodged a formal protest with the General Accounting Office (GAO), claiming that the contract was null and void. The contractor insisted that directives placed in a conference report were binding on an agency.

The GAO disagreed. The comptroller general ruled that such directives had legal force only when some ambiguity in the language of a public law requires recourse to the legislative history. Otherwise, agencies follow nonstatutory controls for practical, not legal, reasons. Agencies may ignore nonstatutory controls, said the comptroller general, but only "at the peril of strained relations with the Congress." To be legally binding, the directive on the navy aircraft had to appear in the public law.[41]

In case of litigation, an interpretation of a statute's legislative history can be decisive. But Congress and the public cannot enter the courts to resolve every grievance. Nonstatutory controls depend on good-faith efforts and a spirit of cooperation by agency officials. During the Nixon years, agencies demonstrated a studied contempt for nonstatutory controls, partly because of politicization in the top ranks of agencies and less influence by careerists. This record is largely an aberration, and yet similar breakdowns in executive-legislative understandings have marred the history of other administrations. If some type of shift is under way, producing an attitude of agency independence and White House autonomy, Congress will have to depend more heavily on statutory provisions and sharper legislative guidelines.

CUSTOM AND ACQUIESCENCE

Previous examples illustrate how Congress consciously shifts power and responsibility to the executive branch. Sometimes the shift is not so deliberate—some practices may have unintended consequences. The Supreme Court tries to discourage the idea that a precedent, even when repeated, represents an adequate basis for

[41]General Accounting Office, "LTV Aerospace Corporation," B-183851 (Oct. 1, 1975), at 21–22.

authority. In *Powell* v. *McCormick* (1969), the court stated that because "an unconstitutional action has been taken before surely does not render that same action any less unconstitutional at a later date . . ."[42] In more colorful prose Senator Sam Ervin used to remind his listeners that "murder and rape have been with us since the dawn of human history, but that fact does not make rape legal or murder meritorious."[43]

Still, an action based on usage may acquire legitimacy. To the extent that the action is favorably exposed to popular judgment, custom does expand power. The Supreme Court, upholding the president's removal power in a 1903 decision, based its ruling largely on the "universal practice of the government for over a century."[44] Here is an example where constitutional law is made not by the courts but by the conduct of the executive and legislative branches.

William Howard Taft, often associated with a strict reading of the Constitution and presidential power, recognized that executive authority is based partly on custom: "so strong is the influence of custom that it seems almost to amend the Constitution."[45] A specific example dates from his own administration. After Congress had opened public lands in the West to encourage oil exploration, settlers began to extract oil rapidly, fearing that entrepreneurs on adjacent lots might be tapping from the same source. Because of the limited supply of coal on the Pacific coast for the navy, it appeared that the federal government might have to purchase from the private sector the very oil it had given away.

Taft acted by issuing a proclamation that withdrew the affected lands from private exploration. A violation brought the case before the Supreme Court, where it was argued that the president could not suspend a statute or withdraw land that Congress had thrown

[42]Powell v. McCormick, 395 U.S. 486, 546–547 (1969).

[43]*Congressional Oversight of Executive Agreements*, hearing before the Senate Committee on the Judiciary, 92d Cong., 2d Sess. 4 (1972).

[44]Shurtleff v. United States, 189 U.S. 311, 316 (1903). Additional commentary on custom and acquiescence appears in *American Jurisprudence*, XVI, 264–270 (1964).

[45]William Howard Taft, *Our Chief Executive and His Powers* 135 (1916).

open to acquisition. The court declined to approach the controversy from the standpoint of abstract constitutional theory. The president's action, it said, was based upon and supported by years of precedents. Before 1910 there had been 99 executive orders establishing or enlarging Indian reservations, 109 executive orders establishing or enlarging military reservations, and 44 executive orders establishing bird reserves. While it was true that the president had acted without statutory authority (and in fact had acted against it), the court held that "nothing was more natural than to retain what the Government already owned. And in making such orders, which were thus useful to the public, no private interest was injured. . . . The President was in a position to know when the public interest required particular portions of the people's lands to be withdrawn from entry or location."[46]

Justice Frankfurter wrote about the cumulative impact of uncontested executive actions in these words:

> A systematic, unbroken executive practice, long pursued to the knowledge of the Congress and never before questioned, engaged in by Presidents who have also sworn to uphold the Constitution, making as it were such exercise of power part of the structure of our government, may be treated as a gloss on "executive Power" vested in the President by §1 of Art. II.[47]

Some scholars resist the gloss-on-life proposition, believing that it invites usurpation of power. They fear that, instead of following the provisions of the Constitution, or attempting to amend it, people with political ambitions and an impatience with legal niceties might "adapt" the Constitution to their own narrow ends. This is indeed a risk, but to prohibit adaptation based on custom would require several hundred amendments to the Constitution and a willingness to keep it in a perpetual state of agitation and flux.[48]

[46]United States v. Midwest Oil Co., 236 U.S. 459, 469–471 (1915). For a statement by the court on public lands held as trust for all the people, see United States v. Trinidad Coal Co., 137 U.S. 160, 170 (1890).

[47]Youngstown Co. v. Sawyer, 343 U.S. 579, 610–611 (1952).

[48]See Robert G. Dixon, Jr., "Article V: The Comatose Article of Our Living Constitution?," 66 *Mich. L. Rev.* 931 (1968). For a critique of "adaptation by usage," see the testimony of Raoul Berger, *War Powers*

Justice Frankfurter emphasized that custom is a source of executive power particularly when Congress fails to challenge and check. Acquiescence has been part of Congress's record in permitting the war power to drift to the executive branch. In 1969 the Senate Foreign Relations Committee tried to explain this tendency by saying that Congress was unprepared for America's new role as a world power and the extraordinary demands placed upon the Constitution. An atmosphere of real or contrived urgency encouraged this legislative passivity. Congress was also overawed by the "cult of executive expertise." In addition, a legacy of guilt remained in the Senate after its rejection of the Covenant of the League of Nations in 1919. Senators practiced a form of penance that has "sometimes taken the form of overly hasty acquiescence in proposals for the acceptance of one form or another of international responsibility."[49]

Legislators are said to acquiesce because of the superior information and technical knowledge available to the executive branch. One member of Congress exclaimed: "How the hell do we know what should be considered anyway? We mostly reflect what the military men tell us."[50] This comment conceals another motivation: an unwillingness to be held responsible for issues of national security and military preparedness. Delegation and acquiescence are natural by-products of the better-safe-than-sorry attitude.

EXECUTIVE-MINISTERIAL FUNCTIONS

The president may exercise a number of constitutional powers in accordance with his own judgment and discretion and without interference from any other agency of government. It is left to him alone to grant reprieves and pardons for offenses against the United States, "except in Cases of Impeachment." The act of submitting a

---

Legislation, 1973, hearings before the Senate Committee on Foreign Relations, 93d Cong., 1st Sess. 10 (1973).

[49]S. Rept. No. 129, 91st Cong., 1st Sess. 15–16 (1969).

[50]Lewis Anthony Dexter, "Congressmen and the Making of Military Policy," reprinted in *New Perspectives on the House of Representatives*, 2d ed., Robert L. Peabody and Nelson W. Polsby, eds. (1969), at 185.

name to the Senate for nomination to a public office is purely a presidential act (though greatly modified in practice). Recognition of foreign governments is a decision, on the basis of custom, reserved solely for the president.

Decisions that require judgment and discretion are called "executive." A responsibility performed without discretion is known as "ministerial." This distinction appears at least as early as 1803, in the famous case of *Marbury* v. *Madison*. John Adams, in his last few days in office as president, nominated a number of men to serve as members of the judiciary. The Senate gave its advice and consent; Adams signed commissions for the offices. The seal of the United States had been affixed to the commissions by the secretary of state to attest their validity. But after a change in administrations, the new secretary of state, James Madison, refused to deliver some of the commissions. The question was, could the Supreme Court compel him to act?

Charles Lee, attorney for several men who sought their commissions, advised the court that the secretary of state exercised his functions in two distinct capacities: "as a public ministerial officer of the United States, and as agent of the president." The secretary owed one duty to the United States and its citizens, the other to the president. A public officer, Lee reasoned, could be compelled by court order (mandamus) to perform a ministerial duty. Lee regarded delivery of the commissions as a ministerial act, particularly since they had been signed by the president and given a seal.[51]

Chief Justice Marshall accepted this distinction between executive and ministerial acts. The choice of nominating a person to office represented the "sole act of the president, and is completely voluntary." Appointment is shared with the Senate. But to grant a commission to a person appointed "might, perhaps, be deemed a duty enjoined by the Constitution."[52] Tentative here, Marshall then supplied firmer language:

> The last act to be done by the president is the signature of the commission. He has then acted on the advice and consent of

[51]Marbury v. Madison, 5 U.S. (1 Cr.) 137, 138, 149 (1803).
[52]*Id.* at 155.

the senate to his own nomination. The time for deliberation has then passed. He has decided. His judgment, on the advice and consent of the senate concurring with his nomination, has been made, and the officer is appointed. This appointment is evidenced by an open, unequivocal act; and being the last act required from the person making it, necessarily excludes the idea of its being, so far as repects the appointment, an inchoate and incomplete transaction.[53]

Turning to the statute of 1789 that created the Department of State and defined the duties of the secretary of state, Marshall concluded that the secretary's action in this matter had been prescribed by law. The secretary of state, as an officer of the United States, must obey the laws: "He acts, in this respect, as has been very properly stated at the bar, under the authority of law, and not by the instructions of the president. It is a ministerial act which the law enjoins on a particular officer for a particular purpose." Although Marshall decided that the withholding of the commission from Marbury was "not warranted by law, but violative of a vested legal right," he decided, for other reasons, that the court could not issue a writ of mandamus to compel Madison to deliver the commissions.[54]

The concept of ministerial acts reappears in the case of *Kendall* v. *United States* (1838). Amos Kendall, postmaster general under President Jackson, refused to pay the claim of an individual who had contracted to carry the mails and sought compensation for his services. Congress directed the postmaster to pay the amount, as did the circuit court of the District of Columbia. The Supreme Court affirmed that the postmaster general could not refuse this payment authorized by law. Payment of the claim constituted a "purely ministerial" act, in the same sense that "an entry in the minutes of a court, pursuant to an order of the court, is an official act."[55] For such duties there could be no discretion.

The court carefully distinguished its ruling from the question of judicial intervention in an *executive* act requiring discretion and

[53]*Id.* at 156.
[54]*Id.* at 157, 162.
[55]Kendall v. United States, 37 U.S. (12 Pet.) 524, 613 (1838).

judgment. The mandamus to pay the amount did not seek "to direct or control the postmaster-general in the discharge of any official duty, partaking in any respect of an executive character; but to enforce the performance of a mere ministerial act, which neither he nor the President had any authority to deny or control."[56]

When the issue concerns an executive action and the exercise of judgment, the court defers to the administration. As noted by the Supreme Court in *Decatur* v. *Paulding* (1840), "interference of the courts with the performance of the ordinary duties of the executive departments of the government, would be productive of nothing but mischief . . ."[57] And in *Reeside* v. *Walker* (1850) the court again distinguished between ministerial and executive actions. A mandamus is "only to compel the performance of some ministerial, as well as legal duty. . . When the duty is not strictly ministerial, but involves discretion and judgment, like the general doings of a head of a department . . . no mandamus lies."[58]

This approach can easily degenerate into an exercise of self-definition. If the matter is ministerial, the courts enter. If it is executive, they stay out. Some students of public law have abandoned the ministerial-executive distinction, regarding it as artificial and inapplicable to modern circumstances. But it still has use and was applied frequently during the impoundment disputes of the Nixon administration. One case involved agriculture funds. After heavy rainfall in parts of Minnesota had caused extensive crop damage, Secretary of Agriculture Earl Butz declared in 1972 that fifteen counties were eligible for emergency loans. Farmers in these areas were told that applications would be received through June 30, 1973. They were further advised to file after the harvest (late November and early December) to ensure that all eligible losses would be included in their applications. A heavy work schedule in the local offices delayed appointments still further until early in the

---

[56]*Id.* at 610. For other ministerial duties directed by the court, see United States v. Price, 116 U.S. 43 (1885) and United States v. Louisville, 169 U.S. 249 (1898).

[57]Decatur v. Paulding, 39 U.S. (14 Pet.) 497, 516 (1840).

[58]Reeside v. Walker, 52 U.S. (11 How.) 272, 290 (1850).

year. On December 22, 1972, without warning, Secretary Butz terminated the disaster loan program.[59] A federal judge in Minnesota distinguished between two types of secretarial duties: discretionary (declaring which areas are entitled to disaster assistance), and ministerial (processing applications after a designation has been made). Once the secretary designates the counties eligible for federal assistance, it is incumbent upon his department to accept loan applications and process them. The court declared that Butz had acted in excess of his authority and in an arbitrary, capricious manner.[60] The administration, declining to appeal the ruling, restored the program.

In other cases the distinction between executive and ministerial runs afoul of more complex considerations. Should public officers, for example, be immune from liability for their actions? The Federal Tort Claims Act of 1946 provides that, regarding tort claims, the United States, subject to certain limitations, shall be liable in the same manner and to the same extent as a private individual under like circumstances. But the act exempts several areas of governmental action. It does not apply to claims based upon an act (or omission) of a federal employee, "exercising due care, in the execution of a statute or regulation, whether or not such statute or regulation be valid, or based upon the exercise or performance or the failure to exercise or perform a *discretionary function or duty* . . . whether or not the discretion involved be abused."[61]

The subject of official immunity reached the Supreme Court in 1959, in *Barr v. Matteo*. The court weighed two conflicting values: the right of a citizen to be protected from oppressive or malicious actions on the part of federal officials, and the interest of the general public in shielding federal officials from harassment by vin-

[59]The initial announcement is reprinted in H. Rept. No. 15, 93d Cong., 1st Sess. 2 (1973).

[60]Berends v. Butz, 357 F.Supp. 143, 151, 157 (D. Minn. 1973). See National Treasury Employees Union v. Nixon, 492 F.2d 587 (D. C. Cir. 1974).

[61]60 Stat. 845, sec. 421, codified at 28 U.S.C. 2680 (1970). Emphasis supplied.

dictive or ill-founded damage suits. The court decided this particular suit (a libel action) by the narrow vote of five to four in favor of official immunity. The court believed that the threat of damage suits might inhibit the "fearless, vigorous, and effective administration of policies of government." Officials enjoy immunity whenever they perform "discretionary acts at those levels of government where the concept of duty encompasses the sound exercise of discretionary authority." The acts are privileged whenever taken "within the outer perimeter" of an official's line of duty.[62]

A dissenting opinion by Chief Justice Warren, joined by Justice Douglas, insisted that the court had balanced the wrong interests. Associating federal officials with the "public interest" had the effect of deterring public discussion of governmental conduct. Only brave citizens would venture to criticize government officials who were at liberty to respond with libelous remarks made immune from prosecution. Justice Brennan, in his dissenting opinion, asked: "Where does healthy administrative frankness and boldness shade into bureaucratic tyranny?"[63]

A federal court faced this issue in 1972. Agents of the Federal Bureau of Narcotics had entered an apartment without a warrant, arrested a man and manacled him in front of his wife and children, and threatened to arrest the entire family. The man brought suit to compensate for the humiliation, embarrassment, mental suffering, arrest without probable cause, and search without warrant.

The court, drawing support from a Supreme Court decision in 1970, held that even though the agents were carrying out their duties (making arrests in cases involving narcotics), and were acting within the "outer perimeter" of their line of duty, the act of making an arrest is not a discretionary function. As a result, agents

---

[62]Barr v. Matteo, 360 U.S. 564, 571, 575 (1959). The decision in *Barr* relied heavily on Learned Hand's opinion in Gregoire v. Biddle, 177 F.2d 579 (2d Cir. 1949).

[63]360 U.S. at 590. In 1977 an appellate court ruled that government officials are absolutely immune from civil lawsuits charging them with common-law offenses such as libel or slander they might commit in their official duties; Expeditions Unlimited Aquatic Enterprises, Inc. v. Smithsonian Institution (D.C. Cir. Sept. 16, 1977), 46 U.S.L.W. 2156.

are subject to damage suits based upon allegations of violations of constitutional rights. They can defend their actions by proving "good faith" and reasonable belief that the arrest and search are lawful and reasonable. Because the courts had recognized these defenses for law enforcement officials, Congress rewrote the Tort Claims Act in 1974 to decrease official immunity. Sovereign immunity is waived for claims arising out of "assault, battery, false imprisonment, false arrest, abuse of process, or malicious prosecution" by federal investigative and law enforcement officers.[64] In 1977 the Federal Bureau of Investigation was severely shaken by an indictment against one of its agents, John J. Kearney, in a suit involving mail opening and wiretapping.

A decision in 1975 put another dent in the principle of official immunity. Several officials of the Department of Housing and Urban Development (HUD), including some brokers under contract with HUD, were charged with negligence respecting the maintenance of a government-owned building. The plaintiffs claimed that they had told the officials repeatedly of hazardous conditions in the building but that the officials failed to take action. A fire in the HUD building caused the plaintiffs' building to burn down. Were the officials immune from liability for money damages?

A district court, relying on the exemption for discretionary actions provided in the Federal Tort Claims Act, recognized an immunity for ranking officials who engaged in planning and policy-making operations. It refused to extend immunity to lower-level administrators charged with carrying out the department's policy. This holding is ironic from the standpoint of hierarchy, for the

[64]Bivens v. Six Unknown Named Agents of Fed. Bur. of Narc., 456 F.2d 1339, 1345–1348 (2d Cir. 1972); Bivens v. Six Unknown Fed. Narcotics Agents, 403 U.S. 388 (1970). For 1974 statute see P.L. 93-253, 88 Stat. 50, and S. Rept. No. 588, 93d Cong., 1st Sess. (1973). Also on the doctrine of official immunity: Doe v. McMillan, 412 U.S. 306 (1973). In 1977 a federal appellate court held that a prosecutor, who allegedly committed perjury before a judge while serving as an investigative officer of the court, was entitled only to a qualified immunity; Briggs v. Goodwin (D.C. Cir. Sept. 21, 1977), 46 U.S.L.W. 2178. Compare to absolute immunity of prosecutor engaged in advocacy; Imbler v. Pachtman, 424 U.S. 409 (1976).

more "responsible" an official, the less vulnerable he is to civil actions.[65]

But even presidents and top officials may be held liable under other circumstances. In 1977 a district court ruled that former President Nixon, his aide H. R. Haldeman, and former Attorney General John Mitchell had to pay damages to Morton Halperin and four members of his family for an illegal wiretap on their home. The judgment awarded nominal damages (a total of five dollars) but established an important principle of accountability for high-ranking officials who violate the constitutional rights of citizens.[66]

EXECUTIVE PREROGATIVE

Charles McIlwain, tracing the slow and tortuous evolution of constitutionalism, stressed the opposition to *gubernaculum*—emergency or extraordinary powers available to the executive. Actions taken for "reasons of state" were solely within the king's province. In contrast was the concept of *jurisdictio*, which limited the king's discretion. An early challenge to *gubernaculum* appears in a seventeenth century speech in Parliament by Sir Benjamin Rudyard: "This by the way I will say of Reason of State, that, in the latitude by which it is used, it hath eaten out almost, not only the laws, but all the religion of Christendom." Another member of Parliament warned that to admit reason of state in a particular situation would "open a gap, through which Magna Charta, and the rest of the statutes, may issue out and vanish."[67]

The idea of *gubernaculum* carried forward in the form of the executive prerogative. John Locke anticipated ciircumstances in which the executive should be free to act in accordance with his

[65]Estrada v. Hills, 401 F.Supp. 429 (N.D. Ill. 1975). See Scott A. Mayer, "Immunity Denied to Federal Officials Failing to Perform Discretionary Duties," 35 *Fed'l Bar J.* 206 (1976).

[66]*Washington Post*, Aug. 6, 1977, at A1:6. The liability of Nixon, Haldeman, and Mitchell had been decided the previous year: Halperin v. Kissinger, 424 F.Supp. 838 (D.D.C. 1976).

[67]Charles Howard McIlwain, *Constitutionalism: Ancient and Modern* 126 (1947).

own perception of the public good. In governments where the legislative and executive powers are in distinct hands, "the good of the society requires that several things should be left to the discretion of him that has the executive power." Legislators could not foresee, and provide by laws, everything needed by the community. Cases arise where the executive official has to use power "for the good of the society" until legislators can assemble to pass laws. A strict and rigid observance of the laws, Locke reasoned, might do more harm that temporarily vesting in the executive power the responsibility to take action for the community's good. The power to act "according to discretion for the public good, without the prescription of the law and sometimes even against it, is that which is called prerogative . . ." Locke subjected the use of the prerogative to a few general restrictions. It had to be used for the good of the people "and not manifestly against it." But when disputes arose as to whether the power had been properly used, and when a legislative body depended upon the will of the executive for their convening, "there can be no judge on earth." The people had no other remedy "but to appeal to Heaven."[68]

A more secular safeguard emerged under the American system. Presidents could take the initiative, in the absence of law or even against it, but had to seek the legislature's sanction. Thomas Jefferson, remembered as a "strict constructionist" and a sharp critic of Hamilton's liberal interpretations of the Constitution, found a need as president to act without specific legislative authority. In 1807, after Congress had recessed, a British vessel fired on the American ship *Chesapeake*. Jefferson ordered military purchases for the emergency, reporting his actions to Congress after it convened. "To have awaited a previous and special sanction by law," he wrote, "would have lost occasions which might not be retrieved."[69] After leaving office he said that the observance of the written law is a high duty of a public official, but not the highest. The laws of self-preservation and national security claimed a higher priority: "To lose our country by a scrupulous adherence to written law, would be to lose the law itself, with life, liberty, property and all those

[68]John Locke, *Second Treatise on Civil Government*, Ch. XIV.
[69]Richardson, *Messages and Papers*, I, 416 (Oct. 27, 1807).

who are enjoying them with us; thus absurdly sacrificing the end to the means." The executive may act outside the law when necessity demands it, explain his actions, and ask the legislature for acquittance.[70]

Lincoln followed these procedures in his extraordinary Civil War actions. In April 1861, with Congress in recess, he issued proclamations calling forth state militias, suspending the writ of habeas corpus, and placing a blockade on the rebellious states. When Congress returned he explained that his actions, "whether strictly legal or not, were ventured upon under what appeared to be a popular demand and a public necessity, trusting then, as now, that Congress would readily ratify them."[71] This is precisely what the legislators did. Congress passed an act "approving, legalizing, and making valid all the acts, proclamations, and orders of the President, etc., as if they had been issued and done under the previous express authority and direction of the Congress of the United States."[72]

Edward S. Corwin, dean of presidential scholars, held conflicting opinions on the executive prerogative. He maintained that the framers' view of balanced government carried with it "the idea of a *divided initiative in the matter of legislation and a broad range of autonomous executive power or 'prerogative.'*" Yet the scope of that prerogative became the subject of spirited debate in 1951. After President Truman sent troops to Korea without congressional approval, such scholars as Henry Steele Commager and Arthur M. Schlesinger, Jr., defended his decision. Corwin rebuked the scholars (calling them the "high-flying prerogative men") and denounced the president's action and the justifications that accompanied it. Less than two decades later both Commager and Schlesinger had altered their philosophy of executive power, becoming vociferous critics of the claims of President Johnson to conduct the war in Southeast Asia.[73] In these cases the notion of

[70]Thomas Jefferson, *Writings* (Washington ed.), V, 542-545.

[71]Richardson, *Messages and Papers*, VII, 3225.

[72]12 Stat. 326.

[73]Edward S. Corwin, *The President* 14 (1957), emphasis in original. He discusses the meaning of "executive power" on pages 3–30. For a defense of

prerogative served as a convenient tag to justify actions favored by scholars.

The executive prerogative retains a following, even among those bitterly opposed to the Vietnam War. In 1969 the Senate Foreign Relations Committee admitted its ineptitude in the handling of the Gulf of Tonkin Resolution. In the future, the committee counseled, it would be better to have presidents take the action they regarded as necessary "without attempting to justify it in advance and leave it to Congress or the courts to evaluate his action in retrospect. A single unconstitutional act, later explained or pronounced unconstitutional, is preferable to an act dressed up in some spurious, precedent- setting claim of legitimacy."[74]

Truman's action, see Schlesinger's letter to *The New York Times*, Jan. 9, 1951, and Commager's article, "Presidential Power: The Issue Analyzed," *New York Times Magazine*, Jan. 14, 1951. Corwin replied to them in "The President's Power," *New Republic*, Jan. 29, 1951. By 1966 Schlesinger was counseling that "something must be done to assure the Congress a more authoritative and continuing voice in fundamental decisions in foreign policy": Arthur M. Schlesinger, Jr. and Alfred de Grazia, *Congress and the Presidency* 28 (1967). Commager meanwhile had also altered his view, for he told the Senate in 1967 that there should be a reconsideration of executive-legislative relationships in the conduct of foreign relations: *Changing American Attitudes Towards Foreign Policy*, hearings before the Senate Committee on Foreign Relations, 90th Cong., 1st Sess. 21 (1967). See also Commager's testimony in *War Powers Legislation*, hearings before the Senate Committee on Foreign Relations, 92d Cong., 1st Sess. 7–74 (1971). Schlesinger in 1973 stated that the "idea of prerogative was *not* part of presidential power as defined in the Constitution," although it "remained in the back of [the framers'] mind"; *The Imperial Presidency* 9 (1973), emphasis in original.

[74]S. Rept. No. 129, 91st Cong., 1st Sess. 32 (1969). See also James R. Hurtgen, "The Case for Presidential Prerogative," 7 *Toledo L. Rev.* 59 (1975), and Arthur S. Miller, *Presidential Power* 200–214 (1977).

3

Theory in a Crucible: The Removal Power

Occasionally a statement in the *Federalist Papers* is so wide of the mark, at such odds with events to come, that it has an abrupt and startling effect. So it is with the breezy claim of Alexander Hamilton, in Federalist 77, that the consent of the Senate "would be necessary to displace [public officials] as well as to approve."

The issue that Hamilton disposed of so nonchalantly divided the members of the First Congress. It overshadowed most of the matters that pressed upon the fledgling legislative body in 1789. From May 19 through June 24 the House of Representatives explored the removal power in all its nuances. The debate, occupying almost two hundred pages of the record, represents one of the most thorough expositions on the nature of implied powers. In contrast to many members of Congress today, who let constitutional issues slide by them to be disposed of by the courts (if at all), the members of the First Congress faced the constitutional issue with a deep sense of responsibility.

For more than a century it has been the custom of attorneys and scholars, discussing the removal issue in the First Congress, to write of four schools of thought: (1) the Senate must have equal participation; (2) removals may be made only by the constitutional process of impeachment; (3) Congress, since it creates an office, may attach to it any condition it decides proper for tenure and removal; (4) the power of removal belongs exclusively to the president as an incident to the executive power.[1]

[1]Ex parte Hennen, 13 Pet. 230, 233 (1839), argument of Mr. Coxe for plaintiff; George H. Haynes, *The Senate of the United States*, II, 786–787 (1938); Edward S. Corwin, *The President* 87 (1957).

Those four categories, while convenient for their simplicity and tidiness, fail to do justice to the wide-ranging nature of the debate, the complexity of the issues, or the shifting tide of opinion that advanced and receded each day as the deliberation continued. The debate merits close attention because of its instruction on constitutional power.[2]

THE "DECISION OF 1789"

James Madison began the debate by proposing three executive departments: Foreign Affairs, Treasury, and War. At the head of each department would be a secretary, to be appointed by the president with the advice and consent of the Senate, "and to be removable by the President." William Smith of South Carolina immediately protested against giving the president sole power of removal. Madison countered by saying that the removal power would make the president responsible for the conduct of departmental heads. His fellow Virginian, Theodorick Bland, wanted the removal power shared with the Senate to make it consistent with the Constitution's appointment process. If a deparmental head were found unfit for his office "the person must remain there," Smith said, just like a member of Congress, unless guilty of some crime. But the House rejected Bland's motion to add the words "by and with the advice and consent of the Senate." John Vining, opposing the motion, pointed out that the Senate could not serve as an impartial judge in impeachment proceedings if it had already rendered a judgment in a removal case. As the first day's debate drew to a close, the House by a "considerable majority" declared that the removal power lay with the president.

Two days later the House considered a resolution to make the heads of the three executive departments "removable by the President." Eleven members, Madison among them, were appointed to draw up a bill. When the House took up the topic on June 16, Wil-

[2]The House debate in 1789, on all three executive departments, appears in the *Annals of Congress*, I, 368–383 (May 19), 384–396 (May 20), 396 (May 21), 455–479 (June 16), 479–512 (June 17), 512–552 (June 18), 552–577 (June 19), 578–585 (June 22), 590–592 (June 24), 592–607 (June 25), 611–614 (June 27), 614–615 (June 30), and 615 (July 1).

liam Smith clarified his position by offering two choices: either the Constitution gave the president the power of removal (in which case it was nugatory for Congress to repeat it) or else it was not given to him (and therefore improper for Congress to confer). He also cautioned that competent people would be reluctant to accept a position and risk their reputation if the president could remove them at will. Smith wanted the language eliminated and the question left to the judiciary. This represents a fifth school of thought on the removal issue and is an early inclination, long before *Marbury* v. *Madison* (1803), of judicial review.

Madison, after taking a few days to reexamine the Constitution, conceded that it did not "perfectly correspond with the ideas I entertained of it from the first glance." Precisely how he had adjusted his opinion is not evident from his remarks. The Constitution, he said, vested the executive power in the president, subject to certain exceptions, such as the Senate's participation in the appointment process. He believed that Congress could not extend the exceptions or modify in any way the president's authority. Therefore it was improper to associate the Senate with the president in the removal process. Yet to strike the clause might imply that Congress doubted whether the president had the removal power. It was better, Madison concluded, to retain the language.

Other delegates objected to Congress's amending the Constitution by statutory construction whenever the document was silent on a question. Congressman Samuel Livermore acknowledged that Congress had authority to create an office and to attach to it whatever limitations and restrictions it thought appropriate, but he thought it very improper to reason that the power of giving birth to a creature permitted Congress to "bring forth a monster." Since he feared that a president might remove someone on mere caprice to make room for a favorite, he wanted every person "to have a hearing before he is punished." Here we have a sixth school: procedural due process.

On June 17 the House resumed debate on the motion to make the secretary of foreign affairs "removable by the President." Thomas Hartley, a representative from Pennsylvania, denied that officials had a property in their office and could be removed only for criminal conduct. That doctrine "may suit a nation which is strong in proportion to the number of dependents upon the Crown, but will be very pernicious in a Republic like ours." Some officers held their commissions during good behavior; others, like the secretary, served at the pleasure of the president. Was removal subject to the same limitations spelled out in the Constitution for impeachment? Congressman James Jackson asked: "Suppose the President should be taken with a fit of lunacy, would it be possible by such arguments to remove him? I apprehend he must remain in office during his four years. . . . madness is no treason, crime, or misdemeanor."

George Clymer of Pennsylvania had no doubt that the removal power was incident to the executive. Even if the Constitution had been silent on the power of appointment, he reasoned, the executive would have had that power as well. The Constitution mentioned appointment only to "give some further security against the introduction of improper men into office. But in cases of removal there is not such necessity for this check." One of the more active participants in the debate, Roger Sherman of Connecticut, said that an officer existed as a creature of Congress. Depending upon the statute creating the office, the person might hold office during good behavior, be elected every year, displaced for negligence of duty, or subjected to any other provision without calling upon the president or the Senate.

Madison abhorred this theory of government. He considered it fundamental that the Constitution vested the executive power in the president and required him to take care that the laws be faithfully executed. If the president wantonly removed a meritorious officer, that would "subject him to impeachment and removal from his own high trust." Madison wanted to protect the responsibility of the president: "Vest this power in the Senate jointly with the President, and you abolish at once that great principle of unity and responsibility in the Executive department, which was intended for the security of liberty and the public good."

Debate continued on June 18. The idea of deriving the removal power from the general nature of "executive power," as Madison had suggested, elicited a challenge from Alexander White of Virginia, who said that such a doctrine could be supported only by examples "brought from beyond the Atlantic." This is an amusing twist, for Madison advanced essentially the same argument in 1793 in trying to refute Hamilton in the celebrated Pacificus-Helvidius exchange.

Still another Virginian, John Page, objected to joining the Senate with the president in the removal power. In nine cases out of ten, he predicted, where the president was confident that someone must be removed, it would be impossible to produce the necessary evidence. Could the Senate proceed without evidence? If not, should such a man "be saddled upon the President, who has been appointed for no other purpose but to aid the President in performing certain duties?" James Jackson denied that the heads of departments were necessarily dependent upon the president. The Constitution itself "specifically points them out." Benjamin Goodhue blunted the force of that argument. He explained that while senators played an important role in confirming an officer, since they might be better acquainted with the nominee than the president, the man's *performance in office* could be judged better by the president. He would be more apt to learn of improper conduct by subordinates. To Livermore, Congress should not interfere with the executive departments by including language on removals: "Leave them to do their duty, and let us do ours."

June 19 arrived and the House still did not know whether to strike the words "to be removable by the President." Peter Silvester of New York helped crystallize the issue: Congress had to give its opinion either by declaration or by implication. If the Constitution lodged the removal power in the president, it was useless for Congress to interfere by making an express declaration. If the Constitution did *not* leave the power with the president, could Congress give it? While the Constitution did not expressly grant the power, neither was there anything "in contradiction to it." The problem was compounded, Sherman added, by the fact that the words "to be removable by the President" might imply that the president lacked the removal power and had to have it granted by law. The motion to strike the language was rejected twenty to thirty-four.

By June 22 the House was moving in the direction of treating the removal power by implication, not declaration. Benson moved that the bill provide that the chief clerk (second in command in the Foreign Affairs Department) take charge of all records whenever the secretary "shall be removed from office" by the president. His motion avoided the problem in the phrase "to be removable by the President," which appeared to be a grant of power by Congress. The new language displeased Smith who preferred that Congress express itself in "more candid and manly" terms by declaration, not implication, but Benson's motion carried, thirty to eighteen. Benson then moved to strike the phrase "to be removable by the President," which the House agreed to, thirty-one to nineteen.

When the Senate took up the bill and someone proposed to delete the president's power to remove the secretary of foreign affairs, a tie vote (nine to nine) resulted. Vice-president Adams broke the tie by voting against the motion.[3] A few days later, during House action on the bill to establish a War Department, Benson offered language to give the president removal power by implication. Although the identical principle and language were at issue, his motion carried by the smaller margin of twenty-four to twenty-two. On a motion in the Senate to strike the president's power to remove the Secretary of War, the effort failed by the close vote of nine to ten.[4]

The Foreign Affairs and War departments had been regarded as "executive departments," largely because of their origin and evolution during the Continental Congress. No such concession was made for Treasury.[5] One would have expected Congress, jealous of its control over finances during the preceding decade, to contest the president's power to remove the Secretary of the Treasury. The challenge came, but from the Senate, not the House. The Senate deleted the president's power to remove the secretary. Later on a motion that the Senate recede from its position and accept the House language, another tie vote occurred, ten to ten. Vice-president Adams cast the deciding vote for the motion.[6]

As a result of these actions, Congress passed legislation to adopt the same approach for the departments of Foreign Affairs, War, and Treasury. The subordinate officers would have charge and cus-

[3]*Journal of the First Session of the Senate* (Washington: Gales and Seaton, 1820), I, 142 (July 18, 1789).
[4]*Id*. at 51.
[5]Louis Fisher, *President and Congress* 86–87 (1972).
[6]*Journal of the First Session of the Senate*, I, 50, 62–63.

tody of all records whenever the secretary "shall be removed from office by the President of the United States."⁷

The fact that Congress recognized the president's freedom to remove departmental heads did not mean that the president could remove *all* administrative officials. Congress did not intend to vest the entire removal power with him. When Madison turned his attention to the tenure of the comptroller of the treasury, he said that it was necessary "to consider the nature of his office." Its properties were not "purely of an Executive nature," he said. "It seems to me that they partake of a Judiciary quality as well as Executive; perhaps the latter obtains in the greatest degree." Because of the mixed nature of the office, "there may be strong reasons why an officer of this kind should not hold his office at the pleasure of the Executive branch of the Government."⁸ Madison's insight would hold the attention of scholars and the courts more than a century later.

It is interesting to note that Hamilton retreated from his position in Federalist 77. In 1793 he offered a broad interpretation of executive power in his Pacificus essays. With the exception of the Senate's participation in the appointment of officers and in the making of treaties, and Congress's power to declare war and grant letters of marque and reprisal, Hamilton contended that "the *executive power* of the United States is completely lodged in the President. This mode of construing the Constitution has indeed been recognized by Congress in formal acts, upon full consideration and debate; of which the power of removal from office is an important instance."⁹

CONTROVERSIES FROM JACKSON TO CLEVELAND

Congress has authority to create an office and specify the term of office. May it also specify the manner in which an incumbent is re-

⁷1 Stat. 29, 50, 67.

⁸*Annals of Congress*, I, 611–612 (June 27, 1789).

⁹*The Works of Alexander Hamilton* (Lodge ed.), IV, 439, emphasis in original.

moved? This issue, presented here as an academic exercise, assumed solid form with Andrew Jackson in the White House. Jackson's predecessors had used the removal power with restraint. The opportunity for removals, however, expanded considerably in 1820 when Congress passed legislation that limited a large number of federal officers to a term of four years, also stipulating that they would be "removable from office at pleasure."[10] Supported by this legislative authority, and by his own philosophy favoring rotation of federal personnel, Jackson removed more officers than all of the presidents who preceded him (252 for Jackson compared to 193 for his predecessors).[11]

Congressional opposition to Jackson's policy came to a head in 1833, when he removed the secretary of the treasury for refusing to carry out his policy toward the Second United States Bank. At issue was more than the removal power. Congress regarded Treasury with proprietary interest, often treating the secretary as *its* agent. It had, for example, delegated to the secretary—not the president—the responsibility for placing government funds either in national banks or state banks. The Senate responded to Jackson's action by passing a resolution of censure: "*Resolved*, That the President, in the late Executive proceedings in relation to the public revenue, has assumed upon himself authority and power not conferred by the Constitution and laws, but in derogation of both."

Jackson, outraged that the Senate should censure him on the basis of unspecified charges, without an opportunity for him to be heard, and in circumvention of the formal constitutional procedure for impeachment, prepared a lengthy and impassioned protest. With great force he argued that the Constitution vested in the president the executive power, requiring him to take care that the laws be faithfully executed. That made him, he said, "responsible for the entire action of the executive department." Following this logic, the president had a right to employ agents of his own choice to aid him. When no longer willing to be responsible for their acts, he could remove them. Jackson regarded the secretary of the treasury as

[10]3 Stat. 582.
[11]George H. Haynes, *The Senate of the United States*, II, 793 (1938); Leonard D. White, *The Jacksonians* 317–321 (1954).

"wholly an executive officer."[12] Three years later the Senate ordered its resolution of censure expunged from the record.[13] Millard Fillmore, in his first annual message to Congress in 1850, expressed the view that in the case of "unfortunate" administrative appointments it would be proper for the president to exercise the power of removal.[14]

The removal power developed into a poisonous dispute during the administration of Andrew Johnson. Even before he took office, Congress had begun to trench upon the president's removal power. Legislation in 1863 created a comptroller of the currency to hold office for the term of five years "unless sooner removed by the President, by and with the advice and consent of the Senate." Two years later Congress passed legislation to permit military and naval officers, upon dismissal by the president, to apply for a trial.[15]

Congress continued this policy in 1867 by passing the Tenure of Office Act, which provided that every person holding civil office, with the advice and consent of the Senate, should be entitled to hold office until the president appointed a successor, with the advice and consent of the Senate. The bill further provided that the secretaries of state, treasury, war, navy , and interior, the postmaster general, and the attorney general should hold office during the term of the president who appointed them, and for one month thereafter, "subject to removal by and with the advice and consent of the Senate." During Senate recess the president could suspend an official. The president would have to report to the Senate, upon its return, the evidence and the reasons for the suspension. If the Senate concurred in his action the suspended officer would be removed. If the Senate refused to concur, the suspended officer would resume the functions of his office.[16]

Here was a frontal challenge to presidential control over his own officers. Johnson vetoed the bill, claiming that it violated the Con-

[12]Richardson, *Messages and Papers*, III, 1288–1312.

[13]*Register of Debates*, 24th Cong., 2d Sess. 379–418, 427–506 (1837); *S. Journal*, 24th Cong., 2d Sess. 123–124 (April 15, 1834).

[14]Richardson, *Messages and Papers*, VI, 2616 (Dec. 2, 1850).

[15]12 Stat. 666, sec. 1 (1863); 13 Stat. 489, sec. 12 (1865).

[16]14 Stat. 430.

stitution and the construction placed upon it by the debate of 1789. His message was well reasoned and fully documented.[17] But Congress, caught up in the fierce politics of that time, was not receptive to facts or argument. Both houses promptly overrode his veto.[18] Johnson had hoped that the disruptive voice in his cabinet, Secretary of War Edwin M. Stanton, would resign. He did not. As the months rolled by and the political crisis deepened, Johnson decided to suspend Stanton. The Senate returned from its recess and refused to concur in the suspension. Johnson upped the ante by *removing* Stanton, with the expectation that the constitutionality of the Tenure of Office Act would be tested in the courts. Yet because of the actions of Ulysses S. Grant, whom Johnson had installed as war secretary ad interim, and Lorenzo Thomas, Grant's successor, the tactic backfired. Stanton was able to regain his office. Johnson's strategy merely fanned the fire of impeachment that had been smoldering for a year, a movement that fell one vote short in the Senate.[19]

The political extravagance of Congress did not go unnoticed. President Grant, in his first annual message in 1869, recommended that Congress repeal the Tenure of Office Act. To him the law was inconsistent with efficient administration: "What faith can an Executive put in officials forced upon him, and those, too, whom he has suspended for reason?" Congress revised the act that year, softening the suspension section but retaining the Senate's involvement in the removal process.[20]

Congress continued to expand the Senate's role. Legislation in 1872 required the postmaster general and three assistant postmasters general to be appointed by the president, by and with the advice and consent of the Senate, and provided that they might be "removed in the same manner." In 1876 Congress required the

[17]Richardson, *Messages and Papers*, VIII, 3690–3694 (March 2, 1867).

[18]14 Stat. 430 (1867).

[19]Lately Thomas, *The First President Johnson* 484–618 (1968); Raoul Berger, *Impeachment* 252–296 (1973); Harold M. Hyman, "Johnson, Stanton, and Grant: A Reconsideration of the Army's Role in the Events Leading to Impeachment," 66 *Am. Hist. Rev.* 85 (1960).

[20]Richardson, *Messages and Papers*, IX, 3992; 16 Stat. 6 (1869).

Senate's advice and consent for the removal of all first-, second-, and third-class postmasters.[21]

A new confrontation between president and Congress occurred from 1885 to 1886, after Grover Cleveland suspended several hundred officials and refused to deliver certain papers and documents to the Senate. Cleveland declared that the power to remove or suspend executive officials was vested solely in the president by the Constitution, particularly by the "executive power" and "take care" clauses. He also noted that the law governing suspensions, as amended in 1869, did not justify the Senate's request for documents.[22] Congress repealed the Tenure of Office Act a year later.[23]

COURT INTERPRETATIONS FROM 1789 TO 1926

Myers v. *United States* (1926) represents the first full-scale judicial decision on the removal power, but the issue had been explored by courts throughout the nineteenth century. Chief Justice Marshall discussed it in *Marbury* v. *Madison*. In disposing of the case, Marshall observed that the president had discretion over an office until an appointment is made. Thereafter "his power over the office is terminated in all cases, where by law the officer is not removable by him. The right to the office is *then* in the person appointed, and he has the absolute, unconditional power of accepting or rejecting it."[24] Marshall also noted that Congress had given Marbury's office a tenure of five years and Marbury had a legal right to serve for

[21]17 Stat. 284, sec. 2; 19 Stat. 80, sec. 6.

[22]Richardson, *Messages and Papers*, X, 4960–4968 (March 1, 1886).

[23]16 Stat. 7, sec. 2 (1869); 24 Stat. 500 (1887). This incident is described in detail in Grover Cleveland, *The Independence of the Executive* 25–82 (1913).

[24]Marbury v. Madison, 5 U.S. (1 Cr.) 137, 162 (1803), emphasis in original. In Myers v. United States, 272 U.S. 52, 139–142 (1926), Chief Justice Taft stated that the president's removal power was not before the court in *Marbury*. Justice McReynolds, dissenting in the Myers case, argued (at 201–202) that *Marbury* had expressly repudiated the claim that the president could remove officials contrary to congressional directives.

that duration. This argument suggested that Congress can circumscribe the president's removal power by statute.

In 1839 the Supreme Court gave its first full attention to the nature of the removal power. The case, *Ex parte Hennen,* concerned a clerk of a federal court. After four years he was removed by a new judge, who, while praising the clerk's record, wanted to give the office to a personal friend. Justice Thompson, speaking for a unanimous court, said that the power to appoint a clerk had been vested exclusively in the lower court. The Supreme Court had no control over the appointment or removal, nor could it entertain any inquiry into the grounds for removal. If the judge had abused his power, the plaintiff was advised to seek relief elsewhere—just how or where the court did not say.[25]

In 1854 the court divided on a removal issue that came before it in the form of *United States* v. *Guthrie.* President Taylor had appointed Aaron Goodrich to be chief justice of the Supreme Court for the territory of Minnesota. The appointment was made in 1849 for four years. Two years later, after Taylor's death, President Pierce removed Goodrich. Goodrich went to court to recover the pay for his unexpired term of office. Here was a novel and sensitive issue: the president's removal power had been directed against a sitting judge (not a potential member of the judiciary, as in *Marbury*). Still, it was not such a direct clash between the president and the judiciary. Territorial judges were not judges within Article III of the Constitution. Goodrich served as judge of a "legislative court," established to carry out Article I duties, not a constitutional court.

Although the attorneys who argued the case spent considerable time examining the nature of the removal power, Justice Daniel, delivering the opinion of the court, rested his decision on narrower ground. The true question, he said, related neither to the tenure of the judicial office nor to the powers and functions of the president. Instead, it was a question whether a court could command the withdrawal of money from the Treasury to settle the claim. The particular facts of the case convinced the court that the administrative action was executive in nature, requiring judgment and discretion, and could not be reviewed and countermanded by the courts.

[25]Ex parte Hennen, 13 Pet. 230 (1839).

Justice Curtis filed a separate opinion, joined by Justices Nelson, Grier, and Campbell, agreeing that a writ of mandamus to the secretary of the treasury was not an available remedy. He expressed no opinion on any other question argued by attorneys.[26]

Justice McLean dissented. He did not agree with the reasoning that gave to the president the removal power as incident to the appointing power. Nevertheless, as applied to executive officers, he concluded that the removal power "has been, perhaps, too long established and exercised to be now questioned." But extending the president's removal power to judicial officers was another matter. The presidential duty to see that the laws are faithfully executed, and the president's responsibility over administrators, related to political, not judicial, officers of the government. The president's power to superintend the executive departments gave him no control over the actions of the judiciary. Justice McLean warned that whenever "any portion of the judicial power shall become subject to the executive, there will be an end to its independence and purity."[27] He regarded the payment of money to Goodrich as a ministerial act and therefore subject to mandamus proceedings.

Another removal case reached the Supreme Court in 1886. This one involved the discharge of a naval cadet engineer who sued for his pay in the Court of Claims. The court upheld his position without passing judgment on the president's removal power (the cadet had been removed by the secretary of the navy) or the authority of Congress to restrict that power. The Court of Claims stated that when Congress, by law, vests the appointment of officers in the heads of departments, "it may limit and restrict the power of removal as it deems best for the public interest." Since the naval officer had not been found deficient at any examination, and had not been dismissed for misconduct under the provisions of law, nor sentenced by court martial (also pursuant to law), he was still in office and entitled to the pay attached to it. The Supreme Court unanimously affirmed the judgment of the Court of Claims.[28]

A decision in 1897, *Parsons* v. *United States*, involved President

[26]United States v. Guthrie, 58 U.S. (17 How.) 284, 305.

[27]*Id.* at 310.

[28]United States v. Perkins, 116 U.S. 483, 485 (1886).

Cleveland's removal of a federal attorney. Parsons maintained that his commission, authorizing him to hold office for a four-year term as prescribed by law, had been illegally abridged by the president. The Supreme Court declined to answer the constitutional question. After reviewing the many precedents, including Congress's repeal of the Tenure of Office Act, it concluded in a unanimous decision that the president may remove an officer "when in his discretion he regards it for the public good, although the term of office may have been limited by the words of the statute creating the office"[29]

Another unanimous opinion by the Supreme Court, in *Shurtleff* v. *United States* (1903), dealt with President McKinley's removal of a customs official. Congress had specified "inefficiency, neglect of duty, or malfeasance in office" as the statutory grounds on which the president could remove such officers. McKinley's action had not been taken for any of these causes. The court held that Congress could restrict the president to specified causes, but only if the statute clearly eliminated his general power of removal. The removal power inhered in the right to appoint, "unless limited by Constitution or statute. It requires plain language to take it away."[30]

In 1922 the Supreme Court decided the case of *Wallace* v. *United States*, precipitated by President Wilson's dismissal of an officer from the Quartermaster Corps. The officer claimed that he had been wrongfully dismissed and applied unsuccessfully for trial by court-martial. He then brought suit in the Court of Claims to recover salary. Unsuccessful there, he turned to the Supreme Court. Chief Justice Taft, in a unanimous decision, reviewed the legislative restrictions that had been imposed upon the president's power to remove an army officer. He concluded that the restrictions did not apply, since the president had submitted the name of another officer to take the place of the one dismissed and the Senate had given its consent. Taft presumed that the Senate knew that its confirmation would fill the legal complement of such officers, and to that extent supported the president's removal.[31] This treatment allowed

[29]Parsons v. United States, 167 U.S. 324, 343 (1897).

[30]Shurtleff v. United States, 189 U.S. 311, 316 (1903).

[31]Wallace v. United States, 257 U.S. 541, 545–546 (1922).

Taft to duck some central issues. Could Congress, by statute, restrict the president's removal power? If the president violated those restrictions, why was the Senate's participation in the violation legally significant? Within a few years Taft had an opportunity to explore the removal issue more fully.

THE MYERS CASE AND ITS PROGENY

The Supreme Court's record on the removal power, though marked largely by unanimous holdings, contained many inconsistencies. The tension finally erupted into considerable discord in the celebrated case of *Myers* v. *United States* (1926). Since the litigation resulted from Woodrow Wilson's action, we need to know his earlier pronouncements on the removal power.

In 1920 Wilson opposed a section of the Budget and Accounting Bill, which reserved to Congress a role in the removal of the comptroller general and the assistant comptroller general. They could be taken from office by impeachment, concurrent resolution, "and in no other manner." A concurrent resolution, which requires the consent of the House and Senate, is not sent to the president for his signature. Wilson vetoed the bill, expressing his conviction that Congress lacked constitutional power to "limit the appointing power and its incident, the power of removal derived from the Constitution."[32] Congress revised the bill to require a joint resolution (which does go to the president) and President Harding signed the bill into law. But even as modified, the bill allows Congress to *initiate* a removal.[33]

Wilson's legal dispute resulted from the appointment of Frank S. Myers, postmaster at Portland, Oregon, to a four-year term in 1917. Prior to the expiration of the term the postmaster general removed him, an action concurred in by Wilson. This removal specifically violated the act of 1876, which required the Senate's advice and consent for the removal of all first-, second-, and third-class

[32]H. Doc. No. 805, 66th Cong., 2d Sess. (1920).
[33]42 Stat. 24, sec. 303 (1921).

postmasters. Myers brought suit in the Court of Claims to recover his salary.

Attorneys for Myers, in their presentation to the Supreme Court, argued that the appointment of postmasters derived from a statute passed pursuant to a power granted Congress by the Constitution ("to establish post offices and post roads"). Congress could therefore attach to that office any conditions it desired. Solicitor General Beck, arguing for the administration, maintained that the law of 1876 could be held unconstitutional "without assuming the absolute power of the President to remove any executive officer." A statute may, in creating an office, "limit the duration of the term thereof."[34]

Chief Justice Taft, writing for a six to three majority, opted for a broader interpretation of presidential power—too broad, in fact, to withstand scholarly analysis and subsequent court holdings. Taft even parted company with his own reasonable position in *Wallace* (1922), where he had held that "*at least in absence of restrictive legislation*, the President, though he could not appoint without the consent of the Senate, could remove without such consent in the case of any officer whose tenure was not fixed by the Constitution."[35] Taft now asserted that the president's power of removal was unrestricted, even in the presence of statutory limitations. From the congressional debates of 1789 he decided that there was not the "slightest doubt" that the power to remove officers appointed by the president and the Senate is "vested in the President alone."[36] This was a rash conclusion, for the record in 1789 reveals deep divisions among members of the House and close votes on the Senate side. Moreover, many of the legislators supported presidential power because the office in question was secretary of foreign affairs, an agent of the president and executive in nature.

Taft recognized that the court had, in the Shurtleff case, agreed that Congress might restrict the president's power by specifying causes for removal. He realized also that Congress, in establishing regulatory agencies (beginning with the Interstate Commerce Com-

[34]Myers v. United States, 272 U.S. 52, 61, 98 (1926).

[35]Wallace v. United States, 257 U.S. 541, 544 (1922). Emphasis added.

[36]Myers v. United States, 272 U.S. 52, 114 (1926).

mission in 1887), had specified causes for removal: inefficiency, neglect of duty, or malfeasance in office. Still, he held that the postmaster law of 1876 was "in violation of the Constitution and invalid."[37]

Justice Holmes penned the first of three dissents. To him the chief justice's arguments were "spider's webs inadequate to control the dominant facts." Justice McReynolds, in his dissent, identified many of the statutes that prescribed restrictions on removals. Protected by these restrictions were members of the Interstate Commerce Commission, the Board of General Appraisers, the Federal Reserve Board, the Federal Trade Commission, the Tariff Commission, and the Shipping Board, among others.[38]

The third dissenter, Justice Brandeis, conceded that the power to remove (or suspend) a high political officer "might conceivably be deemed indispensable to democratic government and, hence, inherent in the President." But he flatly denied that the president's ability to remove an inferior administrative officer, such as postmaster, was essential to the workings of government.[39]

Taft's decision provoked immediate criticism from the academic community. The most devastating rebuke came from Edward S. Corwin, whose monograph, *The President's Removal Power Under the Constitution*, appeared in 1927. Corwin did not object too strongly to the proposition that when an executive officer is appointed by the president, with the advice and consent of the Senate, the removal power belongs to the president alone. Such a conclusion, while "decidedly vulnerable on both historical and logical grounds, is not improbably supported by practical considerations."

What Corwin found intolerable was the more sweeping proposition that *any* executive officer could be removed by the president. Such a notion denied Congress any right to determine the tenure of an officer. A balance had to be reached, said Corwin, between the president's removal power and Congress's power to create an office under the "necessary and proper" clause. To Corwin, this balance depended on the nature of the office involved. For example, he be-

[37]*Id.* at 171, 176.
[38]*Id.* at 177, 181.
[39]*Id.* at 241, 247.

lieved that a member of the Interstate Commerce Commission did not exercise power that resulted from presidential authority, either constitutional or statutory. The commissioner's powers derived from a delegation by Congress of its own express power under the Constitution.[40] Corwin remarked that presidents had been able to live with a number of statutory restrictions on their removal power. Procedural safeguards existed for personnel in the classified civil service; they could not be removed "except for such cause as will promote the efficiency of said service and for reasons given in writing, and the person whose removal is sought shall have notice of the same and of any charges preferred against him." Federal employees had the right to join unions; no postal employee could be reduced in rank or dismissed for joining such an organization. Civil service employees had the right to petition Congress without fear of removal. Congress had passed many other statutes to specify the causes for removal from regulatory commissions. Corwin's reading of the debates of 1789 led him to reject Taft's conclusion that a vast majority of the members of the House believed that removal was an incident of the executive power. Instead, Corwin said, Congress found that those who held to that theory "were a fraction of a fraction, a minority of a minority."[41] Somewhere between Corwin and Taft, on the debates of 1789, lies the truth.

Corwin could not delineate with any precision the boundaries between executive-legislative prerogatives over the removal power. He asserted that Congress's power was not absolute, any more than the president's, for it was "conditioned in each case by the nature of the office being dealt with as shown particularly by the source and nature of its powers."[42] But who decides the "nature," and using what criteria?

[40]Edward S. Corwin, *The President's Removal Power Under the Constitution* v–viii (1927). This is reproduced with little change as "Tenure of Office and the Removal Power Under the Constitution," 27 *Colum. L. Rev.* 353 (1927).

[41]Corwin, *The President's Removal Power Under the Constitution*, at 4, 22–23.

[42]*Id.* at 66.

This problem reached the Supreme Court in 1935 in *Humphrey's Executor* v. *United States.* William E. Humphrey, nominated by President Hoover for the Federal Trade Commission (FTC) in 1931, had been confirmed by the Senate. The FTC Act provided that the president could remove a commissioner for "inefficiency, neglect of duty, or malfeasance in office." On July 25, 1933, President Roosevelt asked Humphrey to resign, explaining that the "aims and purposes of the Administration with respect to the work of the Commission can be carried out most effectively with personnel of my own selection." The following month he wrote Humphrey: "I do not feel that your mind and my mind go along together on either the policies or the administering of the Federal Trade Commission." After Humphrey refused to submit his resignation, Roosevelt removed him for policy reasons rather than those specified in the FTC Act.[43]

Justice Sutherland, delivering a unanimous opinion, described the FTC as charged with the enforcement of "no policy except the policy of the law. Its duties are neither political nor executive, but predominantly quasi-judicial and quasi-legislative."[44] "Quasi," of course, is no more precise a term than Corwin's "nature," but Sutherland felt confident that a distinction could be drawn between the executive duties of a postmaster (the Myers case) and the duties of a federal trade commissioner. The FTC "cannot in any proper sense be characterized as an arm or an eye of the executive."[45]

Corwin applauded the narrowing of Taft's holding, but did not like Sutherland's classification of the FTC. If a federal trade commissioner was not in the executive department, Corwin asked, "where is he? In the legislative department; or is he, forsooth, in the uncomfortable halfway situation of Mahomet's coffin, suspended 'twixt Heaven and Earth?" Instead of conjuring up a fourth branch, floating independently, Corwin wanted to preserve the existing three branches of government. He regarded all nonjudicial agencies established to carry out the law as being "executive" in the sense of the Constitution.[46] Justice Jackson, in a later case, also voiced ex-

[43]Humphrey's Executor v. United States, 295 U.S. 602, 618–619 (1935).
[44]*Id.* at 624.
[45]*Id.* at 627–628.
[46]Corwin, *The President* 93, 378–379 (1957).

asperation with the location of regulatory agencies in our tripartite system: "The mere retreat to the qualifying 'quasi' is implicit with confession that all recognized classifications have broken down, and 'quasi' is a smooth cover which we draw over our confusion as we might use a counterpane to conceal a disordered bed."[47]

In his closing paragraph, Sutherland admitted that there existed a "field of doubt" between *Myers* and *Humphrey's*: "we leave such cases as may fall within it for future consideration and determination as they may arise."[48] The "field of doubt" was soon in the courts because of a bitter, long-festering, and frustrating disagreement that threatened to paralyze the Tennessee Valley Authority (TVA). Arthur E. Morgan, chairman of the board of directors, was locked in a nasty feud with his fellow directors. He resisted President Roosevelt's effort to negotiate a settlement, claiming that Congress alone was the proper party to investigate the dispute. The president, after weeks of discussion, told Morgan to withdraw publicly the charges he had made against his colleagues or else resign. When Morgan chose to do neither, Roosevelt removed him.[49]

The TVA Act required that appointments and promotions be made on the basis of "merit and efficiency." Any member of the board of directors found by the president "to be guilty of a violation of this section shall be removed from office by the President." The act made board members subject to removal at any time by concurrent resolution. (Recall that Woodrow Wilson vetoed the Budget and Accounting Bill because it permitted removal by that very instrument.)

Morgan sought judicial relief, but his complaint was dismissed by a district court in Tennessee. While admitting that FDR's action was not specifically based on statutory considerations, the court did not find in the TVA Act a clear enough intent by Congress to limit the executive power over removals. Echoing the holding in the Shurtleff case, it stated that there had to be "plain language" in a statute to take away that power.[50]

[47]Fed. Trade Comm'n v. Ruberoid Co., 343 U.S. 470, 487–488 (1952).

[48]Humphrey's Executor at 632.

[49]For background on Morgan's removal see C. Herman Pritchett, *The Tennessee Valley Authority* 203–215 (1943).

[50]Morgan v. Tennessee Valley Authority, 28 F.Supp. 732 (E.D. Tenn. 1939).

The district court's opinion was upheld unanimously by an appellate court. Morgan's attorney argued that Congress deliberately intended to restrict the president's removal power by employing a concurrent (rather than joint) resolution for congressional removal. The court rejected this argument, insisting that Congress, if that had been its intention, could have expressed its will in unequivocal terms. Also, during the time that the case was pending in the district court, Roosevelt sent to the Senate the name of James P. Pope to succeed Morgan, and the Senate confirmed the appointment. Its action implied that at least one house of Congress did not oppose Morgan's removal. The circuit court also regarded TVA as predominantly an administrative arm of the executive branch and therefore distinguishable from the regulatory commission involved in *Humphrey's*. The Supreme Court denied certiorari (refusal to review a lower court's decision) for the Morgan case.[51]

More akin to the circumstances in *Humphrey's* was President Eisenhower's removal of a member of the War Claims Commission. The enabling statute, anticipating a short-lived agency, made no provision for removal. Eisenhower removed an official on the ground that the act should be administered "with personnel of my own selection." The Court of Claims dismissed the plaintiff's suit, but the Supreme Court, in *Wiener* v. *United States* (1958), unanimously reversed this decision. It held that the president had no power under the Constitution or the statute to remove a member from the War Claims Commission. The agency's task, said the Court, had an "intrinsic judicial character." Congress had explicitly rejected a legislative option that would have placed responsibility with the administration. Congress could not, therefore, have wanted to hang over the head of the commission "the Damocles' sword of removal" by a president for no other reason than that he

[51]Morgan v. Tennessee Valley Authority, 115 F.2d 990 (6th Cir. 1940), *cert. denied*, 312 U.S. 701 (1941). Arthur Larson, "Has the President an Inherent Power of Removal of his Non-Executive Appointees?" 16 *Tenn. L. Rev.* 259 (1940), did not agree that TVA was a predominantly executive agency. He concluded that the members of the TVA, the Securities and Exchange Commission, the Federal Communications Commission, the Federal Power Commission, and the Employees Compensation Commission could not be removed by the president under any circumstances.

wanted his own man. At the time the commission was abolished, the Senate still had not confirmed Eisenhower's nominee.[52]

DISLOYALTY DISMISSALS AND PROCEDURAL SAFEGUARDS

As a result of congressional action and various executive orders, federal employees have been removed from office on the charge that they represented a security risk. One of the more flagrant legislative efforts came in 1943, when the chairman of the House Un-American Activities Committee announced that thirty-nine Government employees were "irresponsible, unrepresentative, crackpot, radical bureaucrats" and affiliates of "Communist-front organizations." The House created a special subcommittee to examine his sensational allegations. The subcommittee subsequently accused three of the employees of engaging in "subversive activity." By way of an amendment attached to an appropriations bill, Congress prohibited the use of public funds for salaries to the three individuals. Counsel for Congress contended that congressional powers over appropriations were plenary and not subject to judicial review.[53] In *United States* v. *Lovett* (1946), however, the Supreme Court struck down that use of legislative power because it inflicted punishment without a judicial trial and therefore violated the Constitution's prohibition against bills of attainder.[54]

In 1950 Congress passed legislation to permit certain agencies to suspend civilian employees whenever "necessary in the interest of national security."[55] As later rewritten, the authority extended to the departments of State, Commerce, Justice, and Defense; the military departments; the Coast Guard; the Atomic Energy Commission (replaced in 1974 by the Energy Research and Development Administration and the Nuclear Regulatory Commission); the National Aeronautics and Space Administration; and "such other

[52]Wiener v. United States, 357 U.S. 349 (1958).
[53]89 Cong. Rec. 4583 (1943).
[54]United States v. Lovett, 328 U.S. 303 (1946).
[55]64 Stat. 476 (1950).

agency of the Government of the United States as the President designates in the best interests of national security." If the agency head determines that the "interests of national security permit," he may notify the employee of the reasons for the suspension.

Once suspended, an employee has access to procedural safeguards before being removed. An employee with a permanent or indefinite appointment, who has completed his probationary or trial period and who is a citizen of the United States, is entitled to these protections before removal: (1) a written statement of the charges within thirty days after suspension, stated as specifically as security considerations permit; (2) an opportunity to answer the charges and submit affidavits; (3) a hearing (at the employee's request) by an agency authority constituted for that purpose; (4) a review of the case by the agency head or designee prior to a decision adverse to the employee is made final; and (5) a written statement of the decision.[56]

Administrative actions can be challenged in the courts. An appellate court decision in 1950 concerned the removal of Dorothy Bailey from her federal job on the grounds of disloyalty. Although she was given notice, an opportunity for a hearing, and had access to an appeal, the agency did not permit her to confront and cross-examine her secret accusers. The court rejected her plea for trial-type procedures, concluding that compliance with the Sixth Amendment was not a prerequisite for dismissing civil service employees. "Even in normal times," observed the court, "and as a matter of ordinary internal operation, the ability, integrity and loyalty of purely executive employees is exclusively for the executive branch of Government to determine, except in so far as the Congress has a constitutional voice in the matter." The court also noted that disloyalty in the government service "under present circumstances" (the Cold War) was a matter of great public concern.[57]

Circuit Judge Edgerton, dissenting, demonstrated an appreciation for individual rights and procedural due process that would

[56]64 Stat. 476 (1950), modified by 80 Stat. 529 (1966) and codified at 5 U.S.C. 7532 (1970).

[57]Bailey v. Richardson, 182 F.2d 46, 51, 64 (D.C. Cir. 1950), aff'd per curiam by an equally divided Supreme Court, 341 U.S. 918 (1951).

later find expression in Supreme Court rulings. He noted that Bailey occupied a "wholly nonsensitive position," that the informants had not been identified to her or even to the Regional Loyalty Board responsible for investigating her case, and that the informants did not make their statements under oath. In contrast, Bailey had denied under oath any membership in or relationship or sympathy with the Communist party, any activities connected with it or with communism, and any affiliation with any organization that advocated the overthrow of the United States government. Judge Edgerton believed that the executive order that provided the standards for her dismissal required that employees should have an opportunity to cross-examine opposing witnesses. If secret accusers wanted to preserve their anonymity, the accused should be cleared or the proceedings dropped. While Edgerton agreed that most dismissals from government employment were not punitive, did not require a judicial trial, and were within the authority of the executive, to him the dismissal of Dorothy Bailey constituted punishment—not for wrong conduct but for "wrong views." Dismissal for disloyalty was punitive in nature, as in the Lovett case, and the right of confrontation and cross-examination was essential for nonsensitive positions. The government had not demonstrated that the suspicion of the disloyalty indicated a security risk: "*Appellant's dismissal for wrong thoughts has nothing to do with protecting the security of the United States.*"[58]

Corwin did not believe that federal employees dismissed for loyalty reasons were entitled to procedural safeguards. Even in cases of disloyalty it was "plausible doctrine that the President enjoys an overriding power of removal."[59] And what did Corwin use to document his position? None other than the majority opinion in the Myers case! The particular page of the decision cited by Corwin contains this statement by Chief Justice Taft: "The power to remove inferior executive officers, like that to remove superior executive officers, is an incident of the power to appoint them, and is in its nature an executive power." Corwin had excoriated the opinion when

[58]*Id.* at 70, emphasis in original.

[59]Corwin, *The President* 104 (1957), footnote omitted. Footnote 109, on page 385 of Corwin's work, refers to p. 161 of *Myers*.

it first appeared. Why did he exhume it three decades later to support his argument? In his own value system the stigma of disloyalty did not have consitutional significance for the removal issue. To him it was a "unique proposition" that a court should stand in judgment against the determination of an executive official that someone is disloyal.[60] But why was it "unique" for a court to insist on procedural standards and constitutional rights for those accused of betraying their country?

Within a few years the Supreme Court began to place restrictions on administrative removals of so-called security risks. A leading case involved Kendrick Cole, removed from his position with the Department of Health, Education and Welfare after an administrative investigation disclosed that he had associated with groups on the attorney general's "subversive list." The Supreme Court in *Cole* v. *Young* (1956) decided that the term "national security," as used in the statute supporting the removal, related only to activities directly concerned with the nation's safety. Whereas the federal government could summarily suspend employees who occupied a "sensitive" position, this power did not extend to other positions. In view of the "stigma attached to persons dismissed on loyalty grounds," the need for procedural safeguards seemed even greater than in other cases.[61] The court ruled that the administration's action did not conform to the governing statute and that Cole's discharge violated the procedures of the Veterans Preference Act (including the right to appeal to the Civil Service Commission).

Members of Congress tried to override the decision by specifically extending summary suspension powers to nonsensitive federal jobs, but the effort failed.[62] In other cases the Supreme Court insisted that individuals whose employment status had been jeopardized and injured by the federal government were entitled to confront and cross-examine their "faceless informers."[63] When ad-

[60]*Id.* at 108, 110.

[61]351 U.S. 536, 546 (1956).

[62]Walter F. Murphy, *Congress and the Court* 174–175, 218–219, 236 (1962).

[63]Peters v. Hobby, 349 U.S. 331 (1955); Service v. Dulles, 354 U.S. 363 (1957); Vitarelli v. Seaton, 359 U.S. 535 (1959); Greene v. McElroy, 360

ministrators felt legally unable to remove employees for loyalty reasons, they switched to grounds of "suitability" as established by civil service regulations.[64]

Through a series of holdings from the late 1960s to the early 1970s, the Supreme Court insisted that individuals could not be deprived of "property" or "liberty" without the protection of fundamental procedural safeguards, including notice and a hearing.[65] This pattern was interrupted in 1974 by *Arnett* v. *Kennedy*, when a sharply divided (five to four) court decided that a nonprobationary employee in the competitive civil service had been adequately protected by hearing procedures made available *after* his dismissal.[66]

The employee, Wayne Kennedy, claimed that the standards and procedures established by the Lloyd-LaFollette Act of 1912, as amended, interfered with his freedom of expression and denied him procedural due process of law. Lloyd-LaFollette permits the removal of employees in the classified civil service "for such cause as will promote the efficiency of the service." An employee is entitled to reasons given in writing; notice of the action and of any charges preferred against her or him; a copy of the charges and reasonable time to file a written answer to them, with affidavits; and a written decision on the answer at the earliest practicable date. The act specifically states that examination of witnesses, trial, or hearing, "is not required but may be provided in the discretion of the individual directing the removal or suspension without pay."[67] In addition to this statutory procedure, Kennedy had access to protections offered by Civil Service Commission and Office of Economic Opportunity regulations. Yet the court decided that he could be removed prior

U.S. 474 (1959); Cafeteria Workers v. McElroy, 367 U.S. 886 (1961). For further discussion see C. Herman Pritchett, *Congress Versus the Supreme Court* 96–106 (1961).

[64]H. Rept. No. 1637, 92d Cong., 2d Sess. 61 (1973).

[65]For example, Sniadach v. Family Finance Corp., 395 U.S. 337 (1969); Goldberg v. Kelly, 397 U.S. 254 (1970); Bell v. Burson, 402 U.S. 535 (1971); Lynch v. Household Finance Corp., 405 U.S. 538 (1972); and Perry v. Sindermann, 408 U.S. 593 (1972).

[66]Arnett v. Kennedy, 416 U.S. 134 (1974).

[67]37 Stat. 555, sec. 6 (1912), as amended by 62 Stat. 354 (1948), and codified at 5 U.S.C. 7501 (1970).

to a hearing. If reinstated at some later date, he would receive full back pay.

A concurring opinion by Justice Powell, joined by Justice Blackmun, formed the five to four majority. Justice Powell balanced the government's interest against that of the employee, giving particular weight to the government's interest in removing employees whose conduct "hinders efficient operation and to do so with dispatch." Requirement of a prior evidentiary hearing, Powell said, "would impose additional administrative costs, create delay, and defer warranted discharges."[68]

REMOVAL ACTIONS FROM NIXON TO CARTER

Although a large number of federal employees are formally protected from summary removal procedures, informal political pressures are sometimes used to force civil servants from office or place them in undesirable assignments. John M. McGee offended his superiors in the Navy Department during the late 1960s by talking about lax inspection procedures that permitted the theft of millions of gallons of fuel in Thailand. For his outspokenness the navy reprimanded him and denied him an in-grade salary increase.[69]

The air force meted out stiffer punishment to A. E. Fitzgerald, a procurement specialist. In response to Senator William Proxmire's question in 1968 about whether the C-5A cargo aircraft was running $2 billion above initial cost estimates, Fitzgerald called the figure "approximately right." The Pentagon, which had yet to acknowledge the cost overrun, took away Fitzgerald's civil service protection, assigned him menial tasks, searched into his private life for incriminating evidence, and eventually fired him. In 1973, after nearly four years of litigation, the Civil Service Commission ruled

[68]Arnett v. Kennedy, 416 U.S. 134, 168 (1974).

[69]115 Cong. Rec. S4461 (daily ed. May 1, 1969). See General Accounting Office, "Investigation in Thailand of the Systems for Distributing Petroleum, Oil, and Lubricants and for Processing Related Documentation," Report No. B-163928 (Jan. 9, 1969).

that Fitzgerald had been improperly dismissed and should be reinstated to his former position. In 1975 a federal judge ordered the Civil Service Commission to pay his legal fees of some $400,000.[70] During Fitzgerald's appeal the C-5A experienced other mechanical and financial embarrassments. Structural defects in the wings caused small cracks to appear. The expected life of the aircraft plummeted from 30,000 to 8,000 hours (from more than thirty years to less than ten). To stretch the life, the air force operated the aircraft at half the load capacity, and proposed in 1975 that the wings be modified at the cost of an additional billion dollars.[71]

Fitzgerald's case has certain parallels with that of Gordon Rule, a naval procurement official who antagonized his superiors. In testimony before the Joint Economic Committee in 1972, he delivered his views with customary bluntness and spent the next day in bed recovering from laryngitis. There he received a visit from an admiral who asked him to sign a request for retirement. Rule, who had received the navy's highest civilian award the previous year, refused. His superiors tried to detail him to a navy training school to update its curriculum (and had other pedestrian tasks in mind after that), but Rule fought successfully to retain his procurement responsibilities.[72]

The "Saturday Night Massacre" of 1973 catapulted the removal issue back into the courts. Archibald Cox, after pursuing presidential documents too assiduously for Mr. Nixon's safety, was dismissed as Watergate special prosecutor. As an official in the executive branch, he would normally have been subject to presidential

[70]The CSC examiner's ruling is reprinted at 119 Cong. Rec. S16997 (daily ed. Sept. 19, 1973). For the judicial order, see the *Washington Post*, Dec. 30, 1975, at A4:5. For more on the McGee and Fitzgerald incidents, see Senator William Proxmire, *Report from Wasteland* 25–47 (1970); *The Dismissal of A. Ernest Fitzgerald by the Department of Defense*, hearings before the Joint Economic Committee, 91st Cong., 1st Sess. (1969); and Fitzgerald v. Seamans, 553 F.2d 220 (D.C. Cir. 1977).

[71]*Department of Defense Appropriations, Fiscal Year 1976* (Part 5), hearings before the Senate Committee on Appropriations, 94th Cong., 1st Sess. 123–167 (1975).

[72]*The Acquisition of Weapons Systems* (Part 6), hearings before the Joint Economic Committee, 92d Cong., 2d Sess. 1821–1924, 2205–2244 (1973).

removal. But Nixon had relinquished that authority when the Justice Department released an order conferring an unusual degree of autonomy on the special prosecutor. The order gave Cox the "greatest degree of independence that is consistent with the Attorney General's statutory accountability . . . The Attorney General will not countermand or interfere with the Special Prosecutor's decisions or actions." According to the order from the Justice Department, the special prosecutor would not be removed "except for extraordinary improprieties on his part." Otherwise, he was to carry out his responsibilities "until such time as, in his judgment, he has completed them or until a date mutually agreed upon between the Attorney General and himself."[73]

Ralph Nader and several members of Congress brought suit against Robert H. Bork, the acting attorney general, for discharging Cox. The administration made no claim that Cox had been removed for "extraordinary improprieties." A district court did not agree with Bork that the congressional plaintiffs lacked standing. Nor was the controversy moot because Cox had returned to Harvard University and a new special prosecutor had been sworn in. The issue was still alive. Legislation had been introduced relating to Watergate and the new special prosecutor might be dismissed, as the court noted, "if he presses too hard . . ." The court held that Cox had been illegally discharged from office.[74]

The Carter administration has offered several proposals designed to insulate the Justice Department from political pressures. One idea is to prevent the removal of the attorney general except on a stated, rational basis. Carter's attorney general, Griffin Bell, explained in an interview: "We would like to put a system in place where anybody that is Attorney General would have a feeling of independence, even though he might not be completely independent under the Constitution."[75]

The Nixon administration lost the contest over Archibald Cox but was able to resist an effort by Congress to remove the director and deputy director of the Office of Management and Budget. Con-

[73]38 Fed. Reg. 14688 (1973).
[74]Nader v. Bork, 366 F.Supp. 104 (D.D.C 1973).
[75]*Washington Post*, Nov. 9, 1977, at A2:2.

gress wanted to abolish the two offices and reestablish them as subject to Senate confirmation. Nixon vetoed the bill in 1973 because it required the "forced removal by an unconstitutional procedure." He did not dispute the authority of Congress to abolish an office, but said that the exercise of such power "cannot be used as a backdoor method of circumventing the President's power to remove." Congress, after sustaining the veto, passed new legislation in 1974 that applied the confirmation process only to future OMB directors and deputy directors.[76]

Conspicuous conflicts over the removal power did not arise during the administration of Gerald Ford, but he was able to edge out of office a member of a regulatory commission, the Civil Aeronautics Board (CAB). During June 1974 the chairman of the board, Robert D. Timm, spent a weekend in Bermuda as a guest of United Aircraft Corporation. Other guests included four airline executives whose firms had cases pending before the CAB. After the trip received publicity in the press, and the House Commerce Committee conducted an investigation, Timm reimbursed United Aircraft for the expenses and disqualified himself from taking part in certain CAB proceedings. Additional congressional investigations revealed that he had made other trips with airline executives, often at their expense. By the end of the year the Ford administration announced that Timm would not be reappointed as chairman of CAB.[77] The next question was, should he remain on the board?

The issue gained momentum in the fall of 1975 after Timm severely criticized the proposals of some members of the Ford administration. White House officials asked him to resign. They also planned a hearing to decide on his removal. According to law, members of the CAB "may be removed by the President for inefficiency, neglect of duty, or malfeasance in office." Timm regarded

[76]P.L. 93–250, 88 Stat. 11 (1974). Veto message: *Public Papers of the Presidents, 1973*, at 539. See Louis Fisher, *Presidential Spending Power* 51–55 (1975).

[77]The account in this paragraph is drawn from thirty-two newspaper and magazine articles, the more prominent ones being the *Los Angeles Times*, July 13, 1974, at 8; *Wall Street Journal*, Aug. 21, 1974, at 13; *The New York Times*, Aug. 28, 1974, at 62; *Washington Star-News*, Sept. 19, 1974, at A8; and *Washington Star-News*, Dec. 20, 1974, at A1.

the hearing as unlawful, unauthorized, and a method of punishment for his positions on regulatory policy, particularly since he differed with the administration's policy. White House officials related the removal proceeding to Timm's "neglect of duty" and "inefficiency," in part stemming from the Bermuda trip. Although Timm denied all the charges, he resigned from office in December 1975.[78]

As originally justified, the removal power was intended to protect the unity and responsibility of the executive. Because of Congress's authority to create an office and attach conditions to it—especially regarding tenure and cause for dismissal—the removal power has been sharply curtailed over the years. Also, while the president remains theoretically responsible for the operation of the executive branch, this expectation has become increasingly unrealistic with the growth of the federal bureaucracy, the creation of agencies and commissions charged with legislative and judicial functions, civil service reform, and procedural safeguards (particularly in loyalty cases) imposed by the courts. With each development the president's removal power has suffered some shrinkage until it now applies, in general, only to major officials on whom he depends to carry out his policies.

The Humphrey case did not settle the removal issue, if indeed it can ever be resolved to anyone's satisfaction. Justice Sutherland suggested that Congress can limit the president's removal of a regulatory commissioner for certain causes and no others. But if Congress can specify the causes of "inefficiency, neglect of duty, or malfeasance in office," logically it may shorten the list still further, such as limiting it to malfeasance in office. Can this mean that a president may not remove a regulatory officer too inefficient to perform his duties, or one who patently neglects them? Might not there be valid reasons for removal other than those specified by statute? As counsel for the government told the Supreme Court in *Humphrey's*, "Faithful execution of the laws may require more than

[78]*Washington Star-News*, Sept. 9, 1975, at D7: 49 U.S.C. 1321(a) (2); *Washington Post*, Dec. 11, 1975, at C1; *Washington Star*, Dec. 11, 1975, at A3; *Aviation Week & Space Technology*, Dec. 15, 1975, at 28.

freedom from inefficiency, neglect of duty, or malfeasance in office."[79] Inconsistencies in statutes, unique circumstances, and congressional responses to a removal are some of the uncertainties that will keep the removal power undefined and undefinable.

[79]Humphrey's Executor v. United States, 295 U.S. 602, 616 (1935).

4

Vetoes: Presidential and Legislative

It has become customary to associate the veto with the executive. Historically, however, the veto has played a more general role in government. Roman tribunes uttered "veto" to protect the plebs from injustice at the hands of the patricians.[1] In the seventeenth century Poland adopted a *liberum veto*, which permitted a single deputy of the legislature to exclaim "I disapprove." During the time of Alexander Hamilton, the New York constitution lodged the veto power in a council of revision consisting of the governor, chancellor, and judges of the supreme court.[2] The Articles of Confederation (1777) granted to each state a veto over any amendment to that charter. The framers of the American Constitution gave serious consideration to the idea of a joint revisionary power, to be shared by the president and the Supreme Court. They thought that joining the executive and the judiciary for this purpose would help preserve their independence against Congress.[3]

The veto, as an instrument to prevent or postpone governmental action, is exercised today on many fronts: the executive veto provided in the Constitution, the ability of courts to strike down legislative and executive actions as invalid, the veto of the vice-president when he votes No on a tie vote, Senate vetoes of treaties and appointments, and vetoes by Congress that take the form of concurrent resolutions, simple resolutions, and committee decisions.

[1]Charles J. Zinn, *The Veto Power of the President* 1 (1951), a committee print for the use of the House Committee on the Judiciary.

[2]Federalist 73, and Charles C. Thach, Jr., *The Creation of the Presidency* 35–41 (1923).

[3]Farrand, *Records*, I, 105, 108, 139; II, 77.

THE PRESIDENTIAL VETO

The framers gave short shrift to the proposal for an absolute executive veto. They had only to recall the very first charge leveled against King George III in the Declaration of Independence: "He has refused his Assent to Laws, the most wholesome and necessary for the common good." James Wilson and Alexander Hamilton maintained that an absolute veto was acceptable for the American presidency, since there was little danger it would be "too much exercised," but delegates at the Philadelphia convention rejected such speculation. The proposal failed of adoption, ten states voting against it and not a single one in favor. The president received a qualified veto, subject to an override by a two-thirds majority of each house of Congress.[4]

Some of the Antifederalists, espousing a literalist view of the separation doctrine, regarded the executive veto as an encroachment upon the legislature. One critic of the Constitution called it "a political error of the greatest magnitude, to allow the executive power a negative, or in fact any kind of control over the proceedings of the legislature."[5] To this kind of criticism Hamilton replied, in Federalist 73, that the veto was necessary to protect the president against the "depredations" of the legislature: "He might gradually be stripped of his authorities by successive resolutions or annihilated by a single vote. And in the one mode or the other, the legislative and executive powers might speedily come to be blended in the same hands."

The Purpose of the Veto

Hamilton identified one of the principal objectives of the veto: to protect the executive from legislative encroachment. Use of the

[4]Farrand, *Records*, I, 96–104. George Reed of Delaware later proposed that the president be given an absolute veto; his motion was rejected, one to nine (*id*. at II, 200). The delegates voted on August 15 to require a three-fourths majority for an override, voting six to four (*id*. at II, 301), but reversed themselves on September 12 by an identical vote in support of the two-thirds requirement (*id*. at II, 582–583, 585–587).

[5]Anonymous "William Penn" writing in the (Philadelphia) *Independent Gazetteer*, Jan. 3, 1788, cited by Morton Borden, ed., *The Antifederalist Papers* 210 (1965).

veto for other reasons has produced periodic waves of hysteria. As recently as the administration of Gerald Ford, critics claimed that he had used the veto unconstitutionally. Edward Pessen, professor of history at Baruch College, concluded that the veto power exercised by Ford, Nixon, Johnson, and almost all the presidents since Andrew Jackson has been "utterly at odds" with the intentions of the framers. According to Pessen, the veto should be rarely exercised. Madison and Hamilton, he said, believed that the veto would be used for limited purposes: "protection of the integrity of the Presidential office and rejection of flagrantly unconstitutional legislation."[6]

Charles L. Black, Jr., professor of law at Yale University, also insists that President Ford misused the veto. This power may be applied "only rarely, and certainly not as a means of systematic policy control over the legislative branch, on matters constitutionally indifferent and not menacing the President's independence." According to Black, the early vetoes mainly protected the integrity of the president's office.[7] These studies advance two basic propositions: the veto should be used sparingly; and it should be used primarily to protect the president's office. Neither assertion is well founded.

As to the frequency of vetoes, the framers could not have anticipated the vast range of activities to be carried out by the federal government, the outpouring of legislation that resulted, and the great mass of private bills. On a single day in 1886 President Cleveland received nearly 240 private bills granting new pensions for veterans, increasing their benefits, or restoring old names to the list. Many of the bills were so indefensible that they invited a veto.[8] Congress adopted the practice of keeping separate lists of public and private bills. While congressional efforts to override vetoes of

[6]Edward Pessen, "The Arrogant Veto," *The Nation*, Aug. 30, 1975, at 133–137.

[7]Charles L. Black, Jr., "Some Thoughts on the Veto," reprinted in 122 Cong. Rec. E390–392 (daily ed. Feb. 3, 1976); *id.* at E454–455 (Feb. 4, 1976); *id.* at E501–502 (Feb. 5, 1976); published in 40 *Law & Contemp. Prob.* 87 (1976).

[8]Richardson, *Messages and Papers*, X, 5001–5002 (May 8, 1886).

public bills are common, Congress often concedes vetoes of private bills without a vote.[9]

Nor did the framers foresee the emergence of party politics or the resulting potential for different parties to control Congress and the White House and the encouragement this situation would give to vetoes. Congress has also provoked numerous vetoes by passing hundreds of measures in the closing days of a session.[10] A favorite device used by Congress to enhance its power consists of tacking irrelevant amendments ("riders") onto appropriations bills. Since appropriations are necessary for the operation of the government, members hope to gain safe passage for a legislative idea that might not survive on its own merits. Rutherford B. Hayes vigorously opposed this tactic, which he regarded as a coercive measure designed to strip him of the veto power.[11] After a series of vetoes he prevailed, but succeeding presidents continued to receive omnibus bills that were amalgams of disparate elements. These are some of the factors that explain the growth of presidential vetoes.

What of the second proposition: that vetoes should be used primarily to protect the president's office? Justice White, in a 1976 opinion, claimed that the veto's principal aim was not to provide "another check against poor legislation" but rather to protect the executive against legislative encroachments.[12] Some delegates to the Philadelphia convention, including Elbridge Gerry, did regard the veto primarily as an instrument to defend the executive branch, not the general interest. But Madison viewed the power in more generous terms. The veto existed "to restrain the Legislature from encroaching on the other co-ordinate Departments, or on the rights of the people at large; or from passing laws unwise in their principle, or incorrect in their form . . ."[13] Hamilton, in Federalist 73, de-

[9]Clarence A. Berdahl, "The President's Veto of Private Bills," 52 *Pol. Sci. Q.* 505 (1937).

[10]John D. Long, "The Use and Abuse of the Veto Power," 4 *The Forum* 253 (1887).

[11]Richardson, *Messages and Papers*, IX, 4475, 4488, 4494 (April 29, May 29, and June 23, 1879); T. Harry Williams, ed., *Hayes: The Diary of a President* 193–234 (1964).

[12]Buckley v. Valeo, 424 U.S. 1, 285 (1976).

[13]Farrand, *Records*, II, 586; I, 139. See also II, 74, 587, and IV, 81.

fended the veto as necessary not only to protect the president but also to furnish "an additional security against the enaction of improper laws. It establishes a salutary check upon the legislative body, calculated to guard the community against the effects of faction, precipitancy, or of any impulse unfriendly to the public good, which may happen to influence a majority of that body." The veto would protect the community from the passage of "bad laws, through haste, inadvertence, or design." This larger view of Madison and Hamilton prevailed.

It is interesting that Gerald Ford's critics placed such heavy emphasis on the use of the veto to protect the president's office. The historical record is quite to the contrary. George Washington vetoed two bills—the first on constitutional grounds (an apportionment bill) and the second because he thought the bill so carelessly drafted and so unwise in substance that it should not become law.[14] Neither bill affected the president's office. Professor Black suggested that the second bill, involving the military, "may have been seen as a dangerous weakening of the country's military force, connected with the Commander-in-Chief power, so that the veto may well be thought to fall within the category of defense of the presidential office."[15] This supposition rests on too many "may's." The evidence is straightforward: Washington thought it a bad bill.

John Adams and Thomas Jefferson did not use the veto power. The next president, James Madison, relied on it five times for regular (as opposed to pocket) vetoes. Four were for constitutional reasons (one involving trials in district courts, one having to do with internal improvements, and two concerning church-state separation); the fifth bill, which regarded the national bank, seemed to Madison too poorly designed to accomplish its purpose.[16] Professor Black states that Madison vetoed the bank bill because it failed to provide adequately for circulating money in time of war: "Perhaps, without stretching too much, such a veto may (like Washington's second veto) be connected with protection of the

[14]Richardson, *Messages and Papers*, I, 116, 203.

[15]122 Cong. Rec. E391 (daily ed. Feb. 3, 1976).

[16]Richardson, *Messages and Papers*, II, 496, 569, 474, 475, 540 (in order of my discussion).

President's role as Commander-in-Chief, and with the effective execution of that power."[17] Again, too much stretching.

During this initial period of twenty-eight years, covering four presidents and seven administrations, there were seven regular vetoes, five of them for constitutional reasons. Only one affected the independence of the executive: the district courts bill, which Madison vetoed in part because he thought it usurped his appointment powers.[18]

Ironically, the critics of the Ford administration borrowed unwittingly from Whig theories of the nineteenth century. Increased use of the veto by Presidents Jackson and Tyler had produced three basic complaints: (1) since the veto was rarely overridden it amounted to an absolute veto, contrary to the framers' intent; (2) the veto was originally granted to bolster a weak executive, who was now able to defend himself by other means; and (3) the veto's limited purpose (to defend the Constitution) had been ignored by presidents. Members of Congress tried to reduce the vote needed for an override from two-thirds to a simple majority. All such proposals failed.[19]

During this period a number of chief executives recorded their philosophy on the veto power. In 1841 President William Henry Harrison recommended a restrained use of the veto, for it was "preposterous" to believe that the president could better understand the wishes of the people than their own representatives. He conceded that presidents were more independent of sectional pulls, however, and might have to veto legislation of a strongly local nature. Harrison justified vetoes to protect the Constitution, defend the people from hasty legislation, and preserve the rights of minorities from the effects of combinations.[20]

Harrison's successor, John Tyler, exercised the veto too frequently for his opponents in Congress, who introduced a resolution to impeach him. Among the grounds was this: "I charge him with the high crime and misdemeanor of withholding his assent to laws un-

[17]122 Cong. Rec. E391 (daily ed. Feb. 3, 1976).

[18]Richardson, *Messages and Papers*, II, 496.

[19]Edward Campbell Mason, *The Veto Power* 133–137 (1890).

[20]Richardson, *Messages and Papers*, III, 1866.

dispensable [*sic*] to the just operations of government, which involved no constitutional difficulty on his part; . . ."[21]

The Democratic party held a less restricted view of the veto power. President Polk, in a detailed analysis in 1848, denied that the obligations of the president were "in any degree lessened by the prevalence of views different from his own in one or both Houses of Congress." The president had to do more than check hasty and inconsiderate legislation. If Congress, after full deliberation, agreed to measures which the president regarded as "subversive of the Constitution or of the vital interests of the country, it is his solemn duty to stand in the breach and resist them."[22] The Democratic platforms of 1844, 1848, 1852, and 1856 placed the party on record as being "decidedly opposed" to taking from the president his qualified veto power to suspend the passage of bills that lacked a two-thirds majority in each house. The veto power, claimed the platforms, had saved the American people from the "corrupt and tyrannical domination" of the United States Bank and the "corrupting system of general interest improvements."[23]

Zachary Taylor, who followed Polk in the White House, adhered to the Whig interpretation. He viewed the veto as "an extreme measure, to be resorted to only in extraordinary cases, as where it may become necessary to defend the executive against the encroachments of the legislative power or to prevent hasty and inconsiderate or unconstitutional legislation."[24] The personal opinion of the president "ought not to control the action of Congress upon questions of Domestic policy; nor ought his opinion & objections to be interposed when questions of Constitutional power have been settled by the various Departments of government and acquiesced in by the people." On such subjects as the tariff, the currency, and internal improvements "the will of the people as expressed through their Representatives in Congress ought to be . . . carried out and

---

[21]Cong. Globe, 27th Cong., 3d Sess. 144 (1843).

[22]Richardson, *Messages and Papers*, VI, 2512 (Dec. 5, 1848).

[23]Kirk H. Porter and Donald Bruce Johnson, *National Party Platforms* 4, 11, 17, 24 (1956).

[24]Richardson, *Messages and Papers*, VI, 2561 (Dec. 4, 1849).

respected by the Executive."[25] In essence, this is the position of Democrats who criticized Ford's veto record. How chagrined they would be to know that they walk in the footsteps of Zachary Taylor!

Other Issues

Ambiguities about the veto power have required clarification through a number of judicial decisions. Did the Constitution require two-thirds of the total membership of each house for an override or merely two-thirds of a quorum (that is, a majority of its members)? The Supreme Court announced in 1919 that two-thirds of a quorum would suffice.[26] Could a president sign a bill after Congress recessed? Yes, as decided in 1899.[27] Could he sign a bill after a final adjournment of Congress? Yes again, as a result of a 1932 decision.[28]

Most of the controversies over the veto power remained within the political arena. James Monroe alarmed some members of Congress in 1817 by signaling in advance his opposition to contemplated legislation. He announced his "settled conviction" that Congress lacked constitutional authority to appropriate money for internal improvements.[29] A House committee, established to review his message, reacted with indignation. The committee's report said that the president's message should not be permitted to have any influence on Congress's disposition to legislate on the subject. Nothing should restrain the ability of Congress to express its will. If Congress, deferring to the president's opinion, refrained from action, "it might happen that the opinion of the President would prevent the enaction of a law, even though there should be the Constitutional majority of two-thirds of both Houses in its favor." Such

[25]Taylor's first "Allison letter," April 22, 1848, to his brother-in-law, John Stadler Allison, reprinted in Arthur M. Schlesinger, Jr., ed., *History of American Presidential Elections*, II, 913–914 (1971).

[26]Missouri Pac. Ry. Co. v. Kansas, 248 U.S. 277 (1919).

[27]La Abra Silver Mining Co. v. United States, 175 U.S. 423 (1899).

[28]Edwards v. United States, 286 U.S. 482 (1932).

[29]Annals of Congress, 15th Cong., 1st Sess. 18 (1817).

a practice should not go uncontested, for otherwise the presidential veto "would acquire a force unknown to the Constitution, and the legislative body would be shorn of its power from a want of confidence in its strength, or from indisposition to exert it."[30] Today such "interference" by the president is commonplace.

Other practices broadened the scope of presidential action. The Constitution provides for three forms of action: the president may sign a bill, veto it, or allow it to lapse by using a "pocket veto" (see pp. 96–99). Custom soon extended the range of choice, such as letting a bill become law without the president's signature. Grover Cleveland took this course in 1894 to dissociate himself from the Wilson-Gorman Tariff Act. To veto the bill would have offended his party (in control of both houses and therefore responsible for the measure) and yet Cleveland did not want his name on the bill. To him it contained provisions "which are not in line with honest tariff reform, and it contains inconsistencies and crudities which ought not to appear in tariff laws or laws of any kind."[31]

The Item Veto

Given the omnibus nature of modern legislation, should presidents be allowed to veto individual items of a bill? Before reaching that question, let us first recognize that such a power has already been exercised in various forms.

Andrew Jackson sparked a controversy in 1830 when he signed a bill and simultaneously sent to Congress a message that restricted the reach of the statute.[32] The House, which had recessed, was powerless to act on the message. A House report later interpreted his action as constituting, in effect, an item veto of one of the bill's provisions.[33] President Tyler continued the custom by advising the House in 1842 that, after signing a bill, he had deposited with the secretary of state "an exposition of my reasons for giving to it my sanction." He expressed misgivings about the constitutionality and

[30]*Id.* at 451–452.
[31]Robert McElroy, *Grover Cleveland*, II, 116 (1923).
[32]Richardson, *Messages and Papers*, III, 1046 (May 30, 1830).
[33]H. Rept. No. 909, 27th Cong., 2d Sess. 5–6 (1842).

policy of the entire act.[34] A select committee of the House issued a spirited protest, claiming that the Constitution gave the president only three modes of action upon receiving a bill: a signature, a veto, or a pocket veto. To sign a bill and add extraneous matter in a separate document could be regarded "in no other light than a defacement of the public records and archives."[35]

A more obvious form of item veto developed with public works legislation, when presidents decided to carry out certain projects while ignoring others. Senator Stephen Douglas of Illinois explained how an appropriations act of 1857 had failed to benefit his state. President Buchanan, after quarreling with representatives from Illinois, had penalized them by withholding funds from their districts. The funds had been scheduled for post offices and other public buildings.[36] In 1876, while signing a river and harbor bill, President Grant objected to particular projects and announced that he would refuse to spend funds on projects that were "of purely private or local interest."[37]

This selective enforcement of the laws has received support from influential legislators. In 1896 Senator John Sherman, second-ranking Republican on the Finance Committee, expressed regret that Cleveland had vetoed a river and harbor bill. Sherman regarded the appropriations bill as permissive in nature: "If the President of the United States should see proper to say, 'That object of appropriation is not a wise one; I do not concur that the money ought to be expended,' that is the end of it. There is no occasion for the veto power in a case of that kind."[38]

The practice of impounding funds, which gained momentum particularly under Franklin D. Roosevelt, allowed presidents to negate part of an appropriations act. Most of the impoundments by Roosevelt, Truman, Eisenhower, and Kennedy were directed at military programs. Lyndon Johnson moved against domestic pro-

[34]Richardson, *Messages and Papers*, V, 2012 (June 25, 1842).

[35]H. Rept. No. 909, 27th Cong., 2d Sess. (1842).

[36]Cong. Globe, 36th Cong., 2d Sess. 1177 (1861).

[37]Richardson, *Messages and Papers*, IX, 4331 (Aug. 14, 1876).

[38]28 Cong. Rec. 6031 (1896).

grams, but only temporarily, for he backtracked in the face of opposition from Congress and the states. The spate of Nixon's impoundments caused Congress to pass the Impoundment Control Act of 1974. The statute directs the president to report on two types of impoundments: a permanent cancellation of funds (rescission), which requires the approval of both Houses of Congress within forty-five days of continuous session; and a temporary withholding of funds (deferral), which can be disapproved by either house at any time.[39] This legislation contains a modified form of item veto, for it permits the president to sign an entire bill and later express disagreement with some portion of it.

Presidents have also discriminated against sections of authorization bills. Woodrow Wilson signed a merchant marine bill in 1920, ignoring one section that he found unconstitutional. On the basis of advice from the State Department, Wilson refused to carry out the provisions of the section:

> The action sought to be imposed upon the Executive would amount to nothing less than the breach or violation of said treaties, which are thirty-two in number and cover every point of contact and mutual dependence which constitute the modern relations between friendly States. Such a course would be wholly irreconcilable with the historical respect which the United States has shown for its international engagements and would falsify every profession of our belief in the binding force and the reciprocal obligation of treaties in general.[40]

President Nixon, upon signing a military authorization bill in 1971, said that one of the sections (the "Mansfield Amendment" dealing with Southeast Asia) did not represent the policy of his administration. He regarded the section as "without binding force or effect."[41] A federal court in 1972 disputed his position: "No executive statement denying efficacy to the legislation could have

[39]P.L. 93–344, 88 Stat. 332 (1974). See Louis Fisher, *Presidential Spending Power* 147–201 (1975).

[40]Richardson, *Messages and Papers*, XVII, 8871–8872 (Sept. 24, 1920).

[41]*Public Papers of the Presidents, 1971*, 1114 (1971).

either validity or effect." Nixon's statement, said the court, was "very unfortunate."[42] In 1976 President Ford signed a defense appropriations bill which required, for certain executive actions, the approval of the Appropriations and Armed Services committees of both houses. Characterizing the procedure as a legislative encroachment upon the constitutional powers of the executive branch, Ford said that he would treat it "as a complete nullity." He adopted the same position toward a one-house veto provision in a veterans' bill. The provision, "a nullity, is severable from the balance of the bill."[43]

How do those actions square with the Constitution? Some writers argue that a separate veto of a rider might be upheld in the courts if the rider bore no relationship to the legislation. A crucial question is what constitutes a "bill" under Article I, Section 7 of the Constitution, which empowers the president to sign, or to return with his objections, "every bill which shall have passed the House of Representatives and the Senate." If Congress tried to attach a reapportionment measure to a foreign assistance act (actually attempted in 1964), would the president be faced with one bill or two? May he sign the basic legislation and veto the rider? To some the answer is Yes. Others maintain that such a power might undermine the policy-setting role of Congress and violate the separation of power doctrine.[44]

Legislation has been introduced over the years to grant the president an item veto. Generally the proposals are limited to disapproval of an appropriation; occasionally they cover provisions (riders) in an appropriations bill and also items in an authorization bill. Some scholars argue that this power could be extended to the president by mere statute, simply by defining "bill," although most commentators agree that a constitutional amendment would be required. A combination is possible: a constitutional amendment to

[42]DaCosta v. Nixon, 55 F.R.D. 145, 146 (1972).

[43]*Wkly Comp. Pres. Doc.*, XII, 172 (Feb. 10, 1976), and *id.* at 1519 (Oct. 15, 1976). See also *Wkly Comp. Pres. Doc.*, XII, 1104 (July 1, 1976).

[44]For a supporting view see Richard A. Givens, "The Validity of a Separate Veto of Nongermane Riders to Legislation," 39 *Temp. L. Q.* 60 (1965); in opposition is Richard A. Riggs, "Separation of Powers: Congressional Riders and the Veto Power," 6 *U. Mich. J. L. Reform* 735 (1973).

permit Congress, by statute, to vest the power in the president. The advantage here is that Congress could withdraw the power by statutory action rather than initiate another constitutional amendment. Withdrawal would be even easier by allowing Congress to act by concurrent resolution, which is not subject to a veto.

These are intriguing questions, worthy of discussion, but it is extremely unlikely that Congress will ever consent to item-veto authority. The idea does have wide public support, since it appears to offer hope for increased economy and efficiency in government: it appears ideally suited to combat "logrolling" and "pork-barrel" politics in Congress. Closer examination, however, takes much of the emotional appeal from the campaign for an item veto.

First, it is argued that over forty states have granted their governors an item veto. This argument carries weight if Congress wants to pattern itself after state legislatures and if presidential power can be equated with gubernatorial power. Neither position is attractive or realistic.

Second, it is widely assumed that logrolling is a peculiar trait of the legislature, yet it is no less characteristic of the executive branch. The Blue Ribbon Defense Panel, in its report to President Nixon in 1970, concluded that the frequent unanimity of the Joint Chiefs could not be interpreted simply as subjugation of particular service views. Such unanimity could just as "cogently support a conclusion that the basis of such recommendations and advice is mutual accommodation of all Service views, known in some forums as 'log rolling,' and a submergence and avoidance of significant issues or facets of issues on which accommodations of conflicting Services views are not possible."[45] Also, Congress is not unique in wanting to place disparate elements in the same package to enhance prospects for passage. Administrations do the same. For example, they combine economic and military assistance in the same bill for fear that neither part will stand well on its own.

Third, to allow the president to veto a portion of a bill may upset the original design of the legislation. Deletion of some sections may

[45]*Report to the President and the Secretary of Defense on the Department of Defense by the Blue Ribbon Defense Panel* 33 (July 1, 1970).

make the remainder contrary to legislative intent, in terms not only of technical and substantive questions but of political balance as well.

Fourth, the availability of an item veto would probably make Congress more irresponsible. To satisfy constituent demands, even of the most indefensible nature, a member need only add extraneous material to a bill with the understanding among his colleagues that the president could disapprove the offensive amendment. Instead of adopting a reform that would control logrolling, the problem would be exacerbated.

Fifth, item-veto authority would increase the stature of the president's budget. When first initiated under the Budget and Accounting Act of 1921, the executive budget was nothing more than a proposal to be amended (up or down) as Congress decided. The final judgment lay with Congress, subject to presidential veto. But the president, armed with an item veto, could strike from an appropriations bill the programs that Congress had added or augmented. Rarely could Congress attract a two-thirds majority in each house to override him. Administration officials who advocate item-veto authority have been very candid in admitting that congressional initiatives and add-ons would be vulnerable. As Budget Director Percival F. Brundage told the House Judiciary Committee in 1957: "the authority to veto an appropriation item would include authority to reduce an appropriation—but only to the extent necessary to permit the disapproval of amounts added by Congress for unbudgeted programs or projects, or of increases by Congress of amounts included in the budget."[46] The president's budget should be a starting point, not a fixed ceiling, for congressional action (see pp. 175–183).

Sixth, and most important, presidents could use item-veto authority to control the votes of members. A particular project in their district or state could be held hostage in return for the member's support of a nominee or some other interest of the White House. In the words of Senator Paul H. Douglas:

[46]*Item Veto*, hearing before the House Committee on the Judiciary, 85th Cong., 1st Sess. 24 (1957).

With item veto power, a partisan President could punish certain areas which had not supported him by withholding funds for their projects, for example, or force Senators to approve nominees to the executive branch who were repugnant to them under the threat of losing funds for certain projects, or force approval of questionable legislation under the same threat.[47]

The Pocket Veto

The Constitution provides that any bill not returned by the president "within ten Days (Sundays excepted)" shall become law "unless the Congress by their Adjournment prevent its Return, in which Case it shall not be a Law." This instrument, known as the "pocket veto," was first used in 1812 by President Madison. From Madison through Andrew Johnson, presidents who used the pocket veto generally prepared a memorandum explaining the basis for their disapproval. This practice, after lapsing from Grant through Hoover, was reinstated by Franklin D. Roosevelt.[48]

Uncertainty over the meaning of the Constitution led to the Pocket Veto Case of 1929. A bill had been presented to President Coolidge less than ten days prior to an end-of-the-session adjournment (lasting from July to December). The Supreme Court unanimously upheld the pocket veto, concluding that the adjournment prevented the president from returning the bill. The court thus clarified that "adjournment" did not refer merely to final adjournment at the end of a Congress. The critical issue was not whether an adjournment was final or interim but whether it "prevented" the bill's return. The court also decided that "ten Days" meant calendar days, not legislative days.[49]

Other questions were resolved by *Wright* v. *United States* (1938). In this controversy the Congress did not adjourn. The Senate alone had recessed for three days, a period the court considered so short

[47]*Id.* at 94.

[48]Clement E. Vose, "The Memorandum Pocket Veto," 26 *J. Pol.* 397 (1964).

[49]The Pocket Veto Case, 279 U.S. 644 (1929). See Abram R. Serven, "The Constitution and the 'Pocket Veto,'" 7 *N.Y.U.L. Q. Rev.* 495 (1919).

that the Senate could act with "reasonable promptitude" on the veto. This decision meant that adjournment by "the Congress," constitutionally, referred to both houses. Also important was the fact that the secretary of the Senate functioned during the recess and was able to receive (and did receive) the bill. As a more general point the court noted that the veto procedure served two fundamental purposes: (1) to give the president an opportunity to consider a bill presented to him; and (2) to give Congress an opportunity to consider his objections and override them. Both objectives required protection. To allow the concept of a pocket veto to expand without limit would create a kind of absolute veto emphatically rejected by the framers.[50]

There the matter rested until December 14, 1970, when the Family Practice of Medicine Bill was presented to President Nixon. It had passed by such overwhelming majorities (64 to 1 in the Senate and 346 to 2 in the House) that a veto would have met an almost certain override. Both houses adjourned on December 22 for the Christmas holidays. The Senate returned December 28, the House the following day. Not counting December 27 (a Sunday), the Senate was absent for four days and the House for five. Despite the shortness of that interval, and the fact that the Senate had designated its secretary to receive messages from the President, Nixon returned the bill on December 26 as a pocket veto.[51]

Unlike the 1929 case, the one that resulted in this instance involved a short adjournment *during* a session rather than a lengthy adjournment at the end of a session. This distinction was of pivotal importance to the courts. In 1973 a federal district court held that the Christmas adjournment had not prevented Nixon from returning the bill to Congress as a regular veto. The bill therefore became law, said the court, on December 25, 1970.[52]

[50]Wright v. United States, 302 U.S. 583, 589–590, 596–597 (1938). Since Congress did not attempt to override the president, his action was treated as a regular veto, not a pocket veto, after the ten-day period. For an attorney general's opinion upholding a pocket veto (after Congress had adjourned in 1943 for two months), see 40 Ops. Att'y Gen. 274 (1943).

[51]*Public Papers of the Presidents, 1970*, at 1156.

[52]Kennedy v. Sampson, 364 F.Supp. 1075, 1087 (D.D.C. 1973).

The manner in which an appellate court upheld this decision the next year cast doubt on pocket vetoes during *any* intrasession adjournment, no matter how long. Circuit Judge Tamm stated that an intrasession adjournment of Congress "does not prevent the President from returning a bill which he disapproves so long as appropriate arrangements are made for the receipt of presidential messages during the adjournment."[53] This reasoning could be carried a step further. Because of the brief interval between the first and second sessions (it can be less than an intrasession adjournment), it is logical to prohibit *inter*session pocket vetoes as well. This reasoning restricts the use of the pocket veto to one occasion: final adjournment at the end of the second session.

The Nixon Administration did not carry this case to the Supreme Court.[54] But what was left hanging as a legal issue was soon resolved by a political accommodation. The Ford administration, communicating its views through House Minority Leader John Rhodes, decided not to use the pocket veto during intersession adjournments. As Rhodes announced: "he will either sign it or veto it in the ordinary way, which would preserve the right of this House and of the other body to either sustain or override those vetoes when we come back after the sine die adjournment."[55]

The determination of Senator Edward Kennedy to settle the matter in the courts resulted in an announcement from the Justice Department on April 13, 1976. It stated that President Ford would use the return veto rather than the pocket veto during intrasession and intersession recesses and adjournments of Congress, provided that the house of Congress to which the bill was returned had specifically authorized an officer or other agent to receive return vetoes during the period.[56]

The Family Practice of Medicine Act is remembered for its legal significance, not for its impact on programs. It was printed as a public law in 1975 (P.L. 91–696) and backdated to December 25,

[53]Kennedy v. Sampson, 511 F.2d 430, 437 (D.C. Cir. 1974). See also *Public Papers of the Presidents, 1970,* at 441, and the final paragraph at 442.

[54]Arthur John Keeffe, with John Harry Jorgenson, "Solicitor General Pocket Vetoes the Pocket Veto," 61 *Am. Bar Assn J.* 755 (1975).

[55]121 Cong. Rec. H13071 (daily ed. Dec. 19, 1975).

[56]122 Cong. Rec. S5912 (daily ed. April 26, 1976).

1970—the expiration of the ten-day period. Congress had appropriated the token sum of $100,000 for the program, but the money was impounded during the litigation. After the administration decided not to appeal the case further, it released the money for obligation. But officials at the Department of Health, Education and Welfare (HEW) estimated that it would cost $300,000 to set up the administrative machinery called for by the act. With the concurrence of the appropriations committees, HEW reprogramed the $100,000 to a similar activity under Title VII of the Public Health Services Act.[57]

THE LEGISLATIVE VETO

The legislative process usually follows the customary route: Congress passes a bill and presents it to the president for his signature or veto. The Constitution calls for this procedure. It provides that "Every Order, Resolution, or Vote to which the Concurrence of the Senate and House of Representatives may be necessary (except on a question of Adjournment)" shall be presented to the president. An early exception to the Presentation Clause was the adoption of constitutional amendments in the form of resolutions and their referral directly to the states (rather than to the president) for ratification. The Supreme Court upheld this procedure in *Hollingsworth* v. *Virginia* (1798).[58]

From an early date Congress also passed simple resolutions (adopted by either house) and concurrent resolutions (adopted by both houses) for internal housekeeping matters. Since these were not regarded as "legislative in effect," there was no need to present them to the president. A Senate report in 1897 concluded that "legislative in effect" depended not on the mere form of a resolution but on its substance. If it contained matter that was "legislative in its character and effect," it had to be presented to the president.[59]

---

[57]Interview with HEW budget official. The $100,000 had been made available in a supplemental appropriation bill in 1973 (P.L. 93–50, 87 Stat. 106). The impoundment was reported as D75-87 in 1974; H. Doc. No. 386, 93d Cong., 2d Sess.

[58]Hollingsworth v. Virginia, 3 Dall. 378 (1798).

[59]S. Rept. No. 1335, 54th Cong., 2d Sess. 8 (1897).

Nevertheless, simple and concurrent resolutions gradually evolved into instruments for controlling executive actions. An important conceptual breakthrough occurred in the nineteenth century when executive officials realized that the legislative effect of such resolutions could be changed fundamentally by having their use sanctioned in a public law. In 1854 Attorney General Cushing stated that a simple resolution could not coerce a departmental head "unless in some particular in which a law, duly enacted, has subjected him to the direct action of each; and in such case it is to be intended, that, by approving the law, the President has consented to the exercise of such coerciveness on the part of either House."[60] Specific examples were not long in coming. In 1905 Congress relied on concurrent resolutions to direct the secretary of war to make investigations in rivers and harbors matters. Two years earlier Congress resorted to simple resolutions to direct the secretary of commerce to make investigations and to issue reports.[61]

Reorganization Authority

The development of legislative vetoes is closely associated with the delegation of reorganization authority to the president. Franklin D. Roosevelt asked for authority in 1937 to reorganize the executive branch, subject to disapproval by a *joint* resolution of Congress (a form of legislative action that must be presented to the president for his signature). Although FDR stated that he would, "in the overwhelming majority of cases," withhold his veto from congressional disapprovals, legislators did not like the idea of having to locate a two-thirds majority in each house to override him. In effect they would have delegated authority by majority vote but could retrieve it only with a two-thirds majority. Partly because of this concern, Congress did not enact a reorganization bill in 1938.[62]

---

[60] 6 Ops. Att'y Gen. 680, 683.

[61] 33 Stat. 1147, sec. 2 (1905); 32 Stat. 829, sec. 8 (1903). See *Hinds' Precedents,* II, §§1593-1594.

[62] 83 Cong. Rec. 4487 (1938). See also Doyle W. Buckwalter, "The Congressional Concurrent Resolution: A Search for Foreign Policy Influence," 14 *Midwest J. Pol. Sci.* 434, 438-440 (1970) and Donald G. Morgan, *Congress and the Constitution* 189 (1966).

The next year members of Congress proposed that reorganization plans be subject to disapproval by a concurrent resolution. Would such a resolution be "legislative in effect"? If so, it would have to be presented to the president. Congressman Edward Cox argued that the concurrent resolution was merely a condition attached to the reorganization authority delegated to the president. If he objected to the feature he could exercise his veto power. Otherwise, by signing the bill, he would indicate a willingness to abide by the condition.

The House Select Committee on Government Organization defended the concurrent resolution procedure by pointing to a recent Supreme Court decision, *Currin* v. *Wallace*, which had upheld a delegation of authority to the secretary of agriculture to designate tobacco markets. No market could be designated unless two-thirds of the growers voting in a referendum favored it.[63] To the committee it seemed absurd "to believe that the effectiveness of action legislative in character may be conditional upon a vote of farmers but may not be conditioned on a vote of the two legislative bodies of the Congress."[64]

As enacted in 1939, the Reorganization Act authorized the president to submit plans for executive reorganization. The plans would take effect after sixty days unless Congress, within that time, disapproved them by concurrent resolution. Extension of the authority in 1949 permitted disapproval by a single house. Congress renewed the president's reorganization authority periodically until 1973, when it lapsed because of opposition to President Nixon. Congress restored the authority in 1977, but only after a major challenge from Congressman Jack Brooks, who believed that the constitutional process could be preserved by requiring Congress to vote affirmatively on each reorganization plan. As passed, however, the legislation retained the one-house veto.[65]

The Justice Department, having objected to previous legislative

[63]49 Stat. 732, sec. 5 (1935) and Currin v. Wallace, 306 U.S. 1 (1939).

[64]H. Rept. No. 120, 76th Cong., 1st Sess. 6 (1939). See 84 Cong. Rec. 2477 (1939).

[65]53 Stat. 561 (1939), 63 Stat. 203 (1949), and 91 Stat. 29 (1977). See remarks of Congressman Brooks at 123 Cong. Rec. H2667–2668 (daily ed. March 29, 1977).

vetoes on the grounds that they trespassed upon presidential authority, made an exception for reorganization authority. The attorney general argued that since the decision to present a plan lay solely with the president, this freedom not to act was an equivalent to a presidential veto.[66] Judging from the record of the executive branch on reorganization authority—proposing a joint resolution in 1938, acceding to a concurrent resolution of disapproval the next year and a simple resolution a decade later—it appears that the Justice Department can construct whatever argument is necessary to obtain reorganization authority for the president.

The debate on the 1977 legislation was not characterized by analytic rigor. Attorney General Griffin Bell claimed that the reorganization statute "does not affect the rights of citizens or subject them to any greater governmental authority than before. It deals only with the internal organization of the executive branch, a matter in which the President has a peculiar interest and special responsibility." His statement is so unrealistic that it does not require a rebuttal. The House Committee on Government Operations, when it reported out the bill, acknowledged the substantive impact of reorganization on the people. It added a new congressional intention that "appropriate means should be provided by the President for citizen advice and participation in executive reorganization. This intention recognizes the vital role that citizens and the public (those ultimately most affected) should play in Government reorganization."[67] But if the issue is "vital," why should Congress not go on record by an affirmative vote?

For many members of Congress it was sufficient that Jimmy Carter had promised, during the 1976 campaign, to reorganize the federal government. To deny him that authority, they reasoned, would torpedo a solemn pledge to the people. Still, a campaign promise should not relieve legislators of the responsibility for deciding whether a delegation of authority is constitutional or pru-

[66]Attorney General Bell's opinion, January 31, 1977, reprinted in *Providing Reorganization Authority to the President*, hearings before the House Committee on Government Operations, 95th Cong., 1st Sess. 40–41 (1977).

[67]H. Rept. No. 105, 95th Cong., 1st Sess. 6, 11 (1977).

dent. Members used other arguments to evade the constitutional question. They said that the issue was already in the courts and would be resolved there.[68] But the courts might not be able to decide the matter, or might decide it in a manner unsatisfactory to Congress. Members have a duty to express their own views regarding the constitutionality of their actions. When joining Congress each takes an oath of office that reads in part: "I do solemnly swear (or affirm) that I will support and defend the Constitution of the United States against all enemies, foreign and domestic; that I will bear true faith and allegiance to the same; that I take this obligation freely, without any mental reservation or purpose of evasion, and that I will well and faithfully discharge the duties of the office on which I am about to enter." This duty cannot be set aside lightly by legislators who say they are not lawyers, or, if lawyers, are not constitutional scholars. To swear to defend a document and then claim ignorance of its contents is an empty exercise.

Members of Congress also supported the 1977 legislation because the attorney general had upheld the constitutionality of the reorganization bill. In addition to the fact that the attorney general is an assistant to the president and may issue self-serving opinions, this deference to the Justice Department stands in sharp contrast to the attitude of Congress during the Watergate period.

Committee Vetoes

A committee veto obligates an executive agency to submit its program to designated committees before placing the program in operation. Committee vetoes actually predate the legislative vetoes of the reorganization acts. Legislation in 1867 placed the following restriction on appropriations for public buildings and grounds: "To

[68]In Clark v. Valeo, an appellate court decided that the issue of a one-house legislative veto of regulations issued by the Federal Election Commission was not ripe for judicial determination; 45 U.S.L.W. 2349 (decided Jan. 21, 1977), affirmed by the Supreme Court on June 6, 1977, *sub. nom.* Clark v. Kimmitt, 45 U.S.L.W. 3785. In Atkins v. United States, the Court of Claims rejected a challenge brought by 140 federal judges who contested the procedures of the Federal Salary Act, including its provision for a one-house veto; 45 U.S.L.W. 2560 (decided May 18, 1977).

pay for completing the repairs and furnishing the executive mansion, thirty-five thousand dollars: *Provided*, That no further payments shall be made on any accounts for repairs and furnishing the executive mansion until such accounts shall have been submitted to a joint committee of Congress, and approved by such committee."[69] Such were the sad straits of Andrew Johnson.

President Wilson vetoed a bill in 1920 because it provided that no government publication could be printed, issued, or discontinued unless authorized under regulations prescribed by the Joint Committee on Printing. Wilson said that Congress had no right to endow a joint committee or a committee of either House "with power to prescribe 'regulations' under which executive departments may operate."[70]

The executive branch continued to object to committee involvement in administrative matters. In 1933 Attorney General William Mitchell regarded as unconstitutional a bill that authorized the Joint Committee on Internal Revenue Taxation to make the final decision on any tax refund that exceeded $20,000.[71] Interestingly, it took a dollar threshold, not a committee veto, to precipitate the constitutional objection. Previous legislation had allowed the Joint Committee on Internal Revenue Taxation to decide all tax refunds over $75,000.[72]

Every president from Truman to Ford expressed opposition to committee vetoes. Frequently presidents signed bills with the statement that they would not abide by a committee-veto provision. Nevertheless, the committee veto has become a fixture in an increasing number of statutes.[73]

---

[69]14 Stat. 469 (1867).

[70]H. Doc. No. 764, 66th Cong., 2d Sess. 2 (1920).

[71]37 Ops. Att'y Gen. 56 (1933). In 1955 Attorney General Herbert Brownell held that the committee veto engrafted executive functions onto legislators and usurped power confided to the executive branch; 41 Ops. Att'y Gen. 230 (1955), reprinted in 60 *Dick. L. Rev.* 1 (1955). See also Ops. Att'y Gen. 300 (1957).

[72]See 76 Cong. Rec. 2448 (1933). The Joint Committee now reviews all refunds in excess of $200,000.

[73]For example, *Public Papers of the Presidents, 1955*, 688; *id., 1956*, 649–650; *id., 1963*, 6; *id., 1963–64*, I, 104; *id. 1965*, II, 1083; *id., 1972*,

In addition to committee vetoes provided by statute, Congress has evolved a complex set of committee and subcommittee vetoes detailed in nonstatutory sources, chiefly committee reports and departmental directives and instructions. Most activity in this area consists of agency proposals to reprogram funds from one appropriation account to another. Depending on the amount of money involved and the nature of the transaction, prior approval by committees and subcommittees may be required.[74]

Constitutionality

Whatever legal misgivings Presidents have about the legislative veto procedure in reorganization acts, they acquiesce in this type of conditional legislation. They realize that Congress will not delegate such authority without attaching strings to it. By this reasoning a constitutional issue is reduced to practical proportions. Presidents who want the authority have to take the conditions that go with it. Harvey C. Mansfield cut through the constitutional complications by making this astute observation about the legality of reorganization authority: "There the question has rested, 'no tickee, no washee.'"[75] The Nixon administration never uttered a word of protest when the Impoundment Control Act of 1974 authorized the president to defer the spending of funds, subject to a one-house veto. It wanted the authority and accepted the condition.

President Roosevelt regarded the Lend Lease Act of 1941 as unconstitutional because Congress reserved to itself the opportunity to terminate the president's authority by concurrent resolution. The political situation, however, did not permit him to disclose his sentiment. Long-standing political enemies were already on record as opposed to the concurrent resolution feature as unconstitutional; to reveal his attitude would associate the president with the wrong

---

627–628, 686–688; *Wkly Comp. Pres. Doc.*, XII, 172 (Feb. 10, 1976) and 1104 (July 1, 1976). See also H. Lee Watson, "Congress Steps Out: A Look at Congressional Control of the Executive," 63 *Calif. L. Rev.* 983 (1975).

[74]Louis Fisher, *Presidential Spending Power* 75–98 (1975).

[75]Harvey C. Mansfield, "Reorganizing the Federal Executive Branch: The Limits of Institutionalization," 35 *Law & Contemp. Prob.* 461, 464 (1970).

group. His attorney general, Robert H. Jackson, later explained: "to make public his views at that time would confirm and delight his opposition and let down his friends. It might seriously alienate some of his congressional support at a time when he would need to call on it frequently."[76]

That the legislative veto parts company with the procedures set forth in the Constitution is obvious. But so do many other practices. The Senate delegates much of its power over appointments to individual members through the custom of "senatorial courtesy." Legislative actions by the executive branch do not always come to Congress for review; often they are accomplished unilaterally by executive order, proclamation, or agency rulemaking. As Justice White noted in 1976, the legislative veto (even by a single house) "no more invades the President's powers than does a regulation not required to be laid before Congress."[77]

Legislative and committee vetoes upset the tidy neatness of separated powers. For those who conceive of two entirely separate branches with distinct responsibilities and functions—one branch to legislate and the other to execute—legislative vetoes are plainly offensive. But the procedure can be compatible with some of the larger purposes of the separation doctrine, particularly when used to prevent the accumulation of power in one branch or when used to reinforce the system of checks and balances. The two-house veto is rarely if ever exercised. It represents a warning that if the executive branch tries to go it alone and fails to cultivate legislative support, the policy may fail. The mere threat of its use serves a major purpose.

Practical considerations also carry weight. Congress may not want to delegate authority it can recover only by passing a new law. If the new law is vetoed, Congress has to find a two-thirds majority in each house to override the president. Congress concludes that it will not delegate certain powers unless it can withdraw the authority by a one-house or two-house veto. It may also prefer to subject administrative actions to the review of designated commit-

---

[76]Robert H. Jackson, "A Presidential Legal Opinion," 66 *Harv. L. Rev.* 1353, 1356–1357 (1953).
[77]Buckley v. Valeo, 424 U.S. 1, 284 (1976).

tees, so that it can call upon the expertise of its committees. Furthermore, to attach strings to delegated authority protects Congress from the charge that it abdicates its powers.

Congress incorporated a legislative veto in the War Powers Resolution of 1973. It had been unable to stop the Vietnam War that spring, even though a majority in each house opposed the president's policy. A majority was not enough, Congress discovered, for each effort by Congress to end the war encountered a veto from President Nixon. A lower court concluded that the failure of Congress to override the president should not be taken as legislative authority to continue the war. Said Judge Judd: "It cannot be the rule that the President needs a vote of only one-third plus one of either House in order to conduct a war, but this would be the consequence of holding that Congress must override a Presidential veto in order to terminate hostilities which it has not authorized."[78] To insist that every legislative action must be presented to the president and made subject to his veto would allow the president to conduct a war with minority backing. That cannot be the intention of the Constitution.

The legislative veto becomes of concern when Congress uses it not for the purpose of retaining control over its own powers, which it may temporarily delegate, but to control actions and responsibilities that are executive in nature. Here Congress attempts to control what the president claims belongs to him under the Constitution. As the Senate Foreign Relations Committee acknowledged in 1976: "The legislative veto could not be used to invade areas of plenary presidential prerogative, such as the pardon power (article II, section 2, clause 1) or the recognition power (article II, section 3). It could not be employed to oversee the finest details of the day-to-day administration of the Federal Government."[79]

Suppose the president enters into an armistice with a foreign country. Could Congress veto such an action by passing a concurrent or simple resolution, as contemplated by pending legislation on executive agreements? (See chapter 8.) What happens if Con-

[78]Holtzman v. Schlesinger, 361 F.Supp. 553, 565 (E.D. N.Y. 1973), reversed by Holtzman v. Schlesinger, 484 F.2d 1307 (2d Cir. 1973) after stays by the Supreme Court, 414 U.S. 1304, 1321 (1973).

[79]S. Rept. No. 605, 94th Cong., 2d Sess. 14 (1976).

gress, under the War Powers Resolution, passes a concurrent resolution to order the president to withdraw troops—whereupon he determines that their presence is needed to protect American lives? Congress may pass such resolutions, but the president may also conclude that his obligations under the Constitution cannot be circumscribed by two-house vetoes. However obscure and ill-defined the realm of foreign affairs and national security, it is vastly different from reorganization authority, which is congressionally based, and granted and withheld as Congress decides.

A different issue is involved in the effort by Congress to control administrative rulemaking. In recent years members of Congress have charged that administrators promulgate hundreds of regulations, sometimes with criminal sanctions, that Congress never intended. Various bills have been introduced to curb this bureaucratic activity. The use of legislative vetoes in this area raises profound and disturbing questions regarding the integrity of the administrative process, a subject explored separately on pages 136–138).

5

Administrative Duties

The president carries the title of "chief executive." He is obligated under the Constitution to "take Care that the Laws be faithfully executed." In shorthand fashion we refer to his realm as "the administration." But, formalities aside, administration ranks low on the list of priorities for presidents and those who study presidents.

However, the record is not totally bleak. An administrative duty preoccupied the First Congress: its first major constitutional debate on the presidency involved the power of removal. Delegation of reorganization authority has also aroused heated debates. President Nixon raised management to a high level of visibility by shifting his tactics from legislative action to administrative action. What he could not do through legislation, because of congressional opposition, he tried to accomplish administratively by impounding funds, dismantling programs, issuing regulations, shifting personnel, and controlling the civil service.[1]

This chapter concentrates on two administrative functions: first, the appointment power, including the Senate's advice and consent; and second, the capacity of administrators to legislate through proclamations, executive orders, and rulemaking. These powers remain a source of sharp dispute.

APPOINTMENTS

The British monarch not only appointed officers but created the offices as well. The framers rejected this model by giving Congress

[1]Richard P. Nathan, *The Plot That Failed: Nixon and the Administrative Presidency* (1975).

the power to create offices and by joining the Senate with the executive in making appointments. The Constitution allows Congress to vest the appointment of "inferior officers" in the president alone, in the courts, or in departmental heads. For all other offices (except temporary appointments during Senate recess) the president nominates an individual and seeks the advice and consent of the Senate.

The initial draft presented at the Philadelphia convention (the Virginia Plan) lodged in Congress the responsibility for choosing an executive and the members of a national judiciary. The executive would have had the power "to appoint to offices in cases not otherwise provided for" by the Constitution. James Wilson, one of the ablest members of the convention, objected to the appointment of judges by a legislature: "Experience shewed the impropriety of such appointmts. [sic] by numerous bodies. Intrigue, partiality, and concealment were the necessary consequences. A principal reason for unity in the Executive was that officers might be appointed by a single, responsible person." To vest such power in a single person, others feared, would be "leaning too much toward Monarchy."[2]

James Madison proposed a compromise: let the Senate (not as numerous as the House, yet more numerous than the executive) appoint the judges. His plan was agreed to in mid-June. A month later delegates remained divided on the issue. Some worried that the executive, armed with the power to appoint, might favor one region of the country over another. Others, such as Luther Martin of Maryland, argued that the Senate would be "best informed of characters & most capable of making a fit choice." Madison modified his position by suggesting that the executive appoint judges with the concurrence of some fraction of the Senate. To him this had the advantage of uniting the responsibility of the executive with the security afforded by Senate opposition to "incautious or corrupt" nominations. On July 21, however, the convention voted to have judges appointed solely by the Senate. The delegates followed a different approach for appointments to the executive branch. The executive retained power "to appoint to offices in cases not otherwise provided for" in the Constitution.[3]

[2]Farrand, *Records*, I, 21, 63, 119.
[3]*Id.* at I, 119–128, 232–233; II, 41–44, 80–83, 121.

As the debate continued, the delegates moved away from the concept of a congressional choice over the president and judicial officers. The idea of three separate and distinct branches took shape, as well as the system of using electors from the states to choose the president.

In early September the convention gave the president authority to nominate and—by and with the advice and consent of the Senate—appoint ambassadors, other public ministers and consuls, judges of the Supreme Court, and all other federal officers. A few days later the Convention agreed to empower the president to fill all vacancies that "may happen" during the Senate's recess. It also added "and which shall be created by Law" (to prevent appointments to positions unauthorized by Congress) and reserved to Congress the right to vest the appointment of inferior officers in the president, the courts, or departmental heads.[4]

Nomination

In *Marbury* v. *Madison* Chief Justice Marshall called the nomination process the "sole act of the president" and "completely voluntary."[5] This principle was buttressed in 1871 by Attorney General Akerman, who reviewed a proposal that permitted a civil service board to designate a single person for appointment. To him it was "inadmissible" to have a method of selection that gave no room for the exercise of judgment and will by the president. To require the president to appoint a person judged by examiners as the fittest was no different in constitutional principle from insisting that "he shall appoint John Doe to that office."[6]

The Civil Service Act of 1883 recognized the president's prerogative over nominations by restricting appointments to those "among" the highest grades in competitive examinations. The first rules promulgated by President Arthur provided that four names would be considered for each vacancy. In 1888 the number was changed to three. Present law provides that a nominating or ap-

---

[4]*Id.* at II, 498–499, 533, 539, 627–628.
[5]Marbury v. Madison, 5 U.S. (1 Cr.) 137, 155 (1803).
[6]13 Op. Att'y Gen. 516 (1871).

pointing official will be furnished at least three names from the top of the list of eligibles for each vacancy.[7]

The president's exclusive authority to nominate has been curbed by a number of developments. In creating an office Congress may stipulate the qualifications of appointees. Justice Brandeis once prepared a long list of requirements that Congress had placed on the president's selection of nominees. These included citizenship; being a resident of the United States, a state, a particular state, a particular district, a particular territory, the District of Columbia, or a particular foreign country; specific professional attainments or occupational experience; test by examinations; requirements of age, sex, race, property, or habitual temperance in the use of intoxicating liquors; selection on a nonpartisan basis; and representation by industrial or geographic criteria.[8]

The mere fact that the president sends forth a name for consideration does not obligate the Senate to act promptly. Particularly at the end of a president's term, Congress may prefer to let his successor do the nominating. In 1976 dozens of nominations sent to Congress by President Ford were sidetracked in committee, left there to die quietly. The jobs included judges, U.S. attorneys, U.S. marshals, and regulatory commissioners.[9]

While there is some discretion on the part of the Senate, the president cannot decline to nominate. Once an office is authorized by Congress it must be filled. A president may frustrate this purpose for a time—as Franklin D. Roosevelt did in the 1930s by delaying the nomination of a comptroller general—but at some point the name must go forward.

This principle was underscored in 1973 by a court decision against President Nixon. His budget recommended the rescission of $18 million in Indian education funds.[10] The administration im-

---

[7]5 U.S.C. 3317-3318 (1970). See 22 Stat. 404 (1883) and Civil Service Commission, *Biography of an Ideal: A History of the Federal Civil Service* 47 (1973).

[8]Myers v. United States, 272 U.S. 52, 265–274 (1926).

[9]*Washington Post*, Aug. 26, 1976, at A5, and Oct. 3, 1976, at A8.

[10]*Budget of the United States Government, Fiscal Year 1974, Appendix,* at 1074.

pounded money pending congressional action on the rescission request. Private parties brought suit to require the president to appoint members to the National Advisory Council on Indian Education. A district court acknowledged that the president had discretion as to appointment but "he apparently has no discretion to decide if the Council should or should not be constituted."[11] On May 4, 1973, President Nixon appointed fifteen individuals to the council. Further orders by the same judge forced the release of the $18 million and required the appointment of the Deputy Commissioner of Indian Education.[12]

The selection of a nominee is supposedly a presidential matter. As Alexander Hamilton stated in Federalist 66, there would be "no exertion of *choice* on the part of the Senate. They may defeat one choice of the Executive, and oblige him to make another; but they cannot themselves *choose*—they can only ratify or reject the choice of the President." But this is by no means the practice. Senators from the same party as the president often "nominate" judges, United States attorneys, and marshals who serve from their state. The president is then placed in the position of giving his "advice and consent." If he and his advisers object to a senator's recommendation, they can offer suggestions in the hope of receiving a more acceptable name. Criteria can be established by executive officials to guide the Senate's choice. Teddy Roosevelt entered the White House declaring: "The Senators and Congressmen shall ordinarily name the *man*, but I shall name the *standard;* and the men have got to come up to it."[13]

Beginning with the Truman administration, the American Bar Association exerted influence on the selection of federal judges. It formed a special committee to determine the professional qualifications of judicial candidates. Acting only on names submitted by the attorney general, the committee informs the chairman of the Senate

[11]Minnesota Chippewa Tribe v. Carlucci, 358 F.Supp. 973, 975–976 (D.D.C. 1973). This was Civ. Action No. 175–73.

[12]Minnesota Chippewa Tribe v. Carlucci (Civ. Action No. 628-73, D.D.C. 1973), memorandum form.

[13]George H. Haynes, *The Senate of the United States*, II, 741, n. 1 (1938).

Judiciary Committee whether in its judgment the candidate is "qualified," "well qualified," "exceptionally well qualified," or "not qualified."[14] In 1977 President Carter sought greater independence from the Senate by establishing thirteen panels to recommend nominees to the appellate courts.[15] The president's constitutional authority to nominate is protected by requiring the panels to recommend five candidates for each vacancy. This arrangement is politically feasible (with regard to the Senate's stake in the procedure) because appellate courts overlap several states. Nominations for district courts, located within a state, are still strongly influenced by individual senators. Some senators have established commissions of their own to name candidates for district courts as well as U.S. attorneys.[16]

All of these factors crowd upon the president's constitutional authority to nominate. But some actions are plainly forbidden. While statutory qualifications may curb a president's discretion, they may not eliminate it altogether. In the words of Attorney General Akerman: "this right to prescribe qualifications is limited by the necessity of leaving scope for the judgment and will of the person or body in whom the Constitution vests the power of appointment." Nor may Congress, as the Supreme Court noted in 1947, violate the Bill of Rights by enacting legislation to provide that "no Republican, Jew or Negro shall be appointed to federal office."[17]

In 1976 the Supreme Court reviewed a lower court decision that upheld the power of Congress to appoint four members to the Federal Election Commission. All six voting members (including two

[14]Joel B. Grossman, *Lawyers and Judges: The ABA and the Politics of Judicial Selection* 62–81 (1965).

[15]*Wkly Comp. Pres. Doc.*, XIII, 214–215, 810–811 (Feb. 14 and May 24, 1977).

[16]Leo Rennert, "Cranston's Continuing Conflict Over Distribution of the Spoils," *California Journal*, June 1977, at 193–195; statement of Senator John Heinz (in concert with Senator Richard Schweiker) concerning Pennsylvania system, 123 Cong. Rec. S9812-9816 (daily ed. June 15, 1977); Wilson Morris, "Va. Tries to Improve System for Picking Judges," *Washington Post*, June 28, 1977, at C1.

[17]13 Op. Att'y Gen. 516, 520 (1871); United Public Workers v. Mitchell, 330 U.S. 75, 100 (1947).

nominated by the president) required confirmation by the majority of *both* houses. The lower court reasoned that Congress possessed constitutional authority (by way of the "necessary and proper" clause) to appoint the members to carry out appropriate legislative functions, even though the commission performed "quasi-executive" and "quasi-judicial" functions as well.[18]

The Supreme Court reversed this judgment. While it agreed that the "necessary and proper" clause empowered Congress to create the commission, the language could not be read so expansively as to permit Congress to appoint its members. The clause had to be read in concert with other constitutional provisions. Congress could not, merely by concluding that a measure was "necessary and proper," pass a bill of attainder or an ex post facto law. Nor could it violate other portions of the Constitution, such as the Appointments Clause, especially when a commission created by Congress was designed to discharge more than legislative functions. The powers conferred upon the Federal Election Commission could be exercised only by "Officers of the United States," appointed pursuant to Article II, Section 2, Clause 2. For the court this meant either one of two constitutional options: nomination by the president, subject to the advice and consent of the Senate; or vesting the appointment power in the president alone, in the courts of law, or in departmental heads.[19]

Temporary and Extralegal Appointments

The Constitution explicitly authorizes the president to fill all vacancies that may occur during a Senate recess. Commissions granted during that period "shall expire at the end of their next session." The scope of "recess appointments" has contracted ever since Congress evolved into basically a year-round institution. Other practices, however, give the president more latitude.

Presidents have dispatched agents on diplomatic missions without seeking the advice and consent of the Senate.[20] Since the ap-

[18]Buckley v. Valeo, 519 F.2d 821, 890–892 (D.C. Cir. 1975).

[19]Buckley v. Valeo, 424 U.S. 1, 134–143 (1976).

[20]*The Constitution of the United States of America*, S. Doc. No. 82, 92d Cong., 2d Sess. 521–523 (1973).

pointments were of a temporary nature, it could be argued that they did not satisfy the legal meaning of an "office," including such qualities as tenure and duration.[21] But Congress can use its appropriations power to rein in such activities. Teddy Roosevelt created a stir by appointing extralegal, unsalaried commissions to study social and economic issues. When he asked Congress for $25,000 to publish a commission study, Congress retaliated by prohibiting the appointment of commissions that lacked legislative authority. Although Roosevelt protested that Congress had no right to pass such restrictions and threatened to ignore the proscription, he had to seek private funds to publish the study.[22]

His cousin, Franklin D. Roosevelt, created agencies by executive order and used appropriations to finance agency activities that lacked legislative support. Congress passed the "Russell Rider" in 1944 to prohibit the use of any appropriation for an agency unless Congress specifically authorized it.[23] Toward the end of the administration of Lyndon Johnson, Congress prohibited the use of funds for interdepartmental boards, commissions, councils, committees, or similar groups that did not have prior and specific congressional approval. This prohibition has been repeated each year in appropriations bills.[24]

President Nixon precipitated a court battle in 1973 by trying unilaterally to dismantle the Office of Economic Opportunity (OEO). He requested no funds for OEO, and planned to parcel out its functions to other departments and agencies. Presiding over the dismemberment was Howard J. Phillips, who served as acting director. This designation circumvented a statute that called for the advice and consent of the Senate. The administration asserted that the president had constitutional power to appoint officers of the

[21]What constitutes an "office" is examined in United States v. Hartwell, 73 U.S. (6 Wall.) 385 (1868) and United States v. Germaine, 99 U.S. (9 Otto.) 508 (1879).

[22]*The Works of Theodore Roosevelt,* XX, 416–417; 35 Stat. 1027, sec. 9 (1909).

[23]58 Stat. 387, sec. 213 (1944), codified at 31 U.S.C. 696 (1970). See 90 Cong. Rec. 6021–6039 for legislative history.

[24]Action under Johnson had its origin in 1968; see S. Rept. 1275, 90th Cong., 2d Sess. 2-3 and H. Rept. No. 1348, 90th Cong., 2d Sess. 8. For current language see P.L. 94-363, 90 Stat. 979, sec. 608 (1977).

United States without Senate confirmation, drawing that power from the president's obligation under Article II, Section 3 to "take Care that the Laws be faithfully executed." It was a bizarre argument: the administration ignored a number of laws in order to do what no law permitted.

A district court denied that the president possessed such inherent (or derivative) power. The appointment was invalid because it did not satisfy the statute (requiring the Senate's advice and consent), nor was it made during a Senate recess.[25] As an emergency measure to permit OEO to function, the court allowed Phillips's successor, Alvin J. Arnett, to assume control as acting director. Arnett was later nominated, and confirmed, as OEO director.

A different dilemma arose on February 15, 1972, when John Mitchell announced his resignation as attorney general effective March 1, 1972. President Nixon submitted Deputy Attorney General Richard Kleindienst's name to Congress as his nominee for attorney general. On March 1, 1972, Kleindienst assumed the duties of attorney general; on June 8 he was confirmed. During this interim he authorized several wiretaps. The question was whether the wiretaps were valid, since Kleindienst had served for more than the thirty days permitted under the Vacancies Act. A district court upheld the wiretaps on the ground that Kleindienst, serving either as acting attorney general or as deputy attorney general, had authority to act as he did. Important for the court was the fact that his name had been sent to the Senate for confirmation even before he assumed the duties of attorney general: "Had the President been dilatory in sending a name to Congress, perhaps a different situation would be present."[26]

Senate Participation

On the question of nominations and appointments, the president and the Senate were originally on a completely equal footing. In an

[25]Williams v. Phillips, 360 F.Supp. 1363 (D.D.C. 1973). The D.C. Court of Appeals denied Phillips's motion for a stay, pending appeal, because he failed to show sufficient likelihood of success on the merits; Williams v. Phillips, 482 F.2d 669 (D.C. Cir. 1973). See Lois Reznick, "Temporary Appointment Power of the President," 41 *U. Chi. L. Rev.* 146 (1973).

[26]United States v. Lucido, 373 F.Supp. 1142, 1151 (E.D. Mich. 1974).

early communication to the Senate, President Washington stated that just as he had "a right to nominate without assigning his reasons, so has the Senate a right to dissent without giving theirs." Washington not only sought the advice of the Senate on nominations, but also depended on the judgment of friends in other quarters. Recommendations by members of the House of Representatives, excluded by the Constitution in the appointments process, carried considerable weight.[27]

During the first year of Washington's administration, the Senate rejected Benjamin Fishbourn as naval officer at Savannah, Georgia. It was rumored that the two senators from that state opposed the nomination because they had someone else in mind for the post. Washington, stung by this rebuff, advised the Senate that prior to voting down a nominee it should first inquire as to the qualifications and reasons in support of the nomination.[28]

In 1813 President Madison bridled at a Senate resolution that authorized a *committee* to confer with him on a nomination of a minister to Sweden. He declined to meet with it on the ground that the Constitution recognized only two types of action: the Senate could request information from the president or it could designate a committee to communicate with a department head. The appointment of a committee of the Senate "to confer immediately with the Executive himself appears to lose sight of the coordinate relation between the Executive and the Senate which the Constitution has established, and which ought therefore to be maintained."[29] Madison's successors have not reacted with such ruffled dignity at the thought of meeting with committees or individual senators.

Senatorial Courtesy   It has become an accepted practice to defer to senators' judgments about the merits of appointees from their own states. "Senatorial courtesy" is consistent with the expectation of the framers that senators would be well suited to determine the fitness of a candidate from their constituency. Madison, in the First

---

[27]*Writings of Washington* (Fitzpatrick ed.), XXX, 374. See Roy Swanstrom, *The United States Senate, 1789-1801*, S. Doc. No. 64, 87th Cong., 1st Sess. 93-95, 101-102 (1962), and also Dorothy Ganfield Fowler, "Congressional Dictation of Local Appointments," 7 *J. Pol.* 25 (1945).

[28]*Writings of Washington* (Fitzpatrick ed.), XXX, 370-371.

[29]Richardson, *Papers and Messages*, II, 516 (July 6, 1813).

Congress, noted that senators had been joined with the president in the appointment power because they were, "from their nature, better acquainted with the character of the candidates than an individual." A few weeks later Congressman Benjamin Goodhue drove home the same point by observing that it was "more probable that the Senate may be better acquainted with the characters of the officers that are nominated than the President himself."[30]

To come within the scope of senatorial courtesy, a nominee must be from the state of the senator and the appointment must be to a federal position within that state (instead of to a national office, such as the cabinet). The custom is further refined by requiring that the objecting senator be from the same party as the president. While a number of nominations have been defeated on the grounds of personal objection, or because they are "personally offensive" to a senator, senatorial courtesy has not prevailed in every instance.[31]

The reach of senatorial courtesy is broader than its formal dimensions. In 1970 Senator Barry Goldwater blocked an appointment to a national office (the State Department) that was not even subject to Senate advice and consent. Goldwater advised the secretary of state that the individual, Arthur J. Olsen, was "personally obnoxious" because of an article he had written in 1964 linking Goldwater—at that time the Republican candidate for president—with right-wing elements in Germany. The Nixon administration, warned by Goldwater that there would be "trouble," withdrew the appointment.[32] Senators from the opposite party can also bargain for power over patronage. During the Nixon years, Senators Alan Cranston and John Tunney of California (both Democrats) were able to work out an agreement that gave every third federal judgeship in that state to a Democrat.[33]

Supreme Court Nominees   The Senate is especially vigilant in reviewing nominations to the Supreme Court, rejecting approximate-

[30]*Annals of Congress*, I, 380 (May 19, 1789) and 534 (June 18, 1789).

[31]Floyd Riddick, *Senate Procedure: Precedents and Practices*, S. Doc. No. 21, 93d Cong., 1st Sess. 563–564 (1974).

[32]*Washington Post*, Aug. 31, 1970, at Al, and September 1, 1970, at A2.

[33]Nina Totenberg, "Will Judges be Chosen Rationally?" 60 *Judicature* 93, 95 (1976).

ly one out of five. Many of the rejections stem from partisan considerations, not individual qualifications.[34] Despite this record, the Senate's rejection of two of President Nixon's nominations to the court seemed to many senators a bold, if not unconstitutional, course of action. No matter how poorly the president may have made his selections, members of the Senate appeared uncertain and uncomfortable in exercising their prerogative. Acceptance of the third name submitted by President Nixon seemed inevitable. Why this uneasiness and sense of impropriety? After all, a senator is not obligated to vote for a nominee who appears unsuited for the office.

A recent Senate study tries to sharpen the criteria for Supreme Court nominees. The study regards lawyers with broad experience in their discipline, including political experience, as best suited to handle the responsibilities thrust upon members of the court. Senators, for their part, are justified in considering not merely a nominee's political and constitutional philosophy but also other appointments by the president, particularly when the balance of views on the court is at stake.[35]

Executive Officials   More circumspect and deferential is the Senate's behavior toward cabinet officers and other departmental positions. Broad support is given to the doctrine that the president is entitled to a cabinet of his own choice. To some senators this kind of submissive attitude is offensive and degrading. Senator Charles McC. Mathias, Jr., asked in 1977:

> Does it simply mean that after the President has had an opportunity to exercise the broad and plenary power to choose from among 215 million Americans, that we then merely have to ascertain whether his choice is a convicted felon or a com-

[34]Henry K. J. Abraham, *Justices and Presidents* 8 (1974) and William F. Swindler, "The Politics of 'Advice and Consent,'" 56 *Am. Bar. Asso. J.* 533 (1970).

[35]Senate Committee on the Judiciary, *Advice and Consent on Supreme Court Nominations*, 94th Cong., 2d Sess. (Comm. Print 1976); 121 Cong. Rec. S20602 (daily ed. Nov. 20, 1975); and 117 Cong. Rec. S17788-17793 (daily ed. Nov. 8, 1971).

mitted lunatic, and if we find that that is not the case, we then have to automatically grant confirmation? Well, I would say certainly not.[36]

The Senate's reluctance to contest presidential choices for departmental officials was anticipated by Alexander Hamilton, writing in Federalist 76: "as their dissent might cast a kind of stigma upon the individual rejected, and might have the appearance of a reflection upon the judgment of the Chief magistrate, it is not likely that their sanction would often be refused, where there were not special and strong reasons for the refusal." Joseph Story, one of the more distinguished commentators on the Constitution, correctly predicted that Senate rejections would be rare: "The more common error, (if there shall be any) will be too great a facility to yield to the executive wishes, as a means of personal, or popular favour."[37] If the nomination can be killed outright, senators may encourage each other to mass for the attack. But a senator may hesitate to step forward against a nominee who faces only minimal opposition. If the assault is likely to fall short, it may be prudent not to try— better not to attack a bear at all than merely to wound it.

Although the record demonstrates that the Senate only infrequently rejects a nomination to an executive position, statistics do not reveal the candidates who are eliminated as a result of a preliminary canvass among senators, people who decline an offer rather than submit to the glare of Senate publicity, and those who are not even seriously considered by the executive branch because of the likelihood of Senate opposition.

The Senate is in the process of reexamining its responsibility for reviewing nominees to executive offices. To defer to the president, on the principle that he has a right to select his own assistants, makes a nullity of the Senate's advice-and-consent role. Department heads and their assistants are not mere staff support for the president. They are called upon to administer programs that Congress has enacted into law. A lack of interest by an administrator, or overt hostility to a legislative program, can undercut the policies

[36]123 Cong. Rec. S1295 (daily ed. Jan. 25, 1977).
[37]Joseph Story, *Commentaries*, III, §1526 (1833).

that Congress has taken pains to announce as national goals. Administrators so disposed can shatter agency morale and create uncertainty for career personnel, who may not know whether they are supposed to implement, or sabotage, the statutory objectives. The idea that political appointees are subordinate to congressional purposes was stressed long ago by Joseph Story. Offices in a republican government "are established, and are to be filled, not to gratify private interests and private attachments; not as a means of corrupt influence, or individual profit; not for cringing favourites, or court sycophants; but for purposes of the highest public good; to give dignity, strength, purity, and energy to the administration of the laws."[38] Roger Sherman, who had been a signer of the Declaration of Independence, member of the Continental Congress, and delegate to the Philadelphia convention, offered this advice in 1789 while serving as a representative to the First Congress: "The executive magistrate is to execute the laws. The senate, being a branch of the legislature, will naturally incline to have them duly executed, and, therefore, will advise to such appointments as will best attain that end."[39]

Nevertheless, there is not even agreement at the present time that a nominee for a cabinet post needs expertise or experience for the task about to be assumed. This issue arose in 1973 when the Senate was considering the nomination of James T. Lynn, an attorney with very limited background in housing matters, to be secretary of housing and urban development. The issue reappeared in 1975, when Carla Anderson Hills was nominated to the same post. Some members objected to her lack of experience in the housing field, while other claimed that expertise might create a conflict of interest and suggested that inexperience might even be an asset.[40] Nor is there any agreement as to the right of the Senate to judge someone not simply on the basis of competence and integrity but also on philosophical grounds, particularly when there is doubt that the nominee's views and attitudes are in concert with the statutory mission.

[38]*Id.* at §1524.

[39]*The Works of John Adams* (Charles Francis Adams ed.), VI, 440.

[40]119 Cong. Rec. 2783-2795 (1973); 121 Cong. Rec. S3049-3056 (daily ed. March 5, 1975).

Ambassadors In recent years the Senate has been pushing for higher standards of professionalism for ambassadorial appointments. The Foreign Relations Authorization Act of 1975 provides that it is the sense of Congress that the position of United States ambassador to a foreign country "should be accorded to men and women possessing clearly demonstrated competence to perform ambassadorial duties." No individual should be accorded the position of ambassador "primarily because of financial contributions to political campaigns." In 1976 the Senate voted to require that 75 percent of ambassadorial positions be filled by professionals from the Foreign Service. As enacted, however, this provision became a sense-of-Congress statement that a greater number of ambassadorial positions should be occupied by career Foreign Service personnel.[41]

Regulatory Agencies The record of regulatory appointments has been criticized for decades. Recent studies conducted by the Senate conclude that neither the White House nor the Senate has demonstrated a sustained commitment to high-quality appointments to regulatory agencies.[42] In the face of such evidence the Senate is adopting a more assertive attitude. In 1973, for the first time in decades, it rejected by a recorded vote a nominee to a regulatory agency when it turned down the nomination of Robert H. Morris to the Federal Power Commission. No one questioned Morris's ability or integrity. At issue was his close association with the industry he would have to regulate. A majority of the Senate believed that members on the commission were already too industry-oriented and insufficiently attentive to consumer interests.[43]

[41]P.L. 94-141, 89 Stat. 757, sec. 104 (1975); P.L. 94-350, 90 Stat. 829, sec. 120 (1976) and H. Rept. No. 1302, 94th Cong., 2d Sess. 37 (1976). See *The Senate Role in Foreign Affairs Appointments,* prepared for the Senate Committee on Foreign Relations, 92d Cong., 1st Sess. (Comm. Print 1971).

[42]*Appointments to the Regulatory Agencies,* printed for the use of the Senate Committee on Commerce, 94th Cong., 2d Sess. (Comm. Print April 1976). *Study on Federal Regulations: The Regulatory Appointments Process* (Volume I), Senate Committee on Government Operations, 95th Cong., 1st Sess. (Comm. Print Jan. 1977).

[43]119 Cong. Rec. 19492–19508 (1973). The previous month a number of

Since then the Senate Commerce Committee has refused to recommend the confirmation of other nominees to regulatory agencies. The individuals, Senator Warren Magnuson said, "failed to meet minimum standards of qualifications for the post to which they were recommended." The committee adopted five reforms by (1) placing the background and financial statements submitted by nominees on the public record; (2) tightening the requirements for disclosing potential conflicts of interest; (3) reviewing the financial statements and biographies of nominees to identify potential conflicts of interest; (4) providing at least seven days' notice of hearings on nominees; and (5) relying on written interrogatories to develop a record on the nominees' depth of knowledge, policy commitments, and regulatory philosophy.[44]

The Senate's responsibility for confirming presidential nominees, although fixed firmly in the Constitution, remains unsettled in its application. The Senate was not meant to be a passive participant. Delegates to the Philadelphia convention believed that the Senate would be knowledgeable about nominees and capable of voting wisely. Yet for the most part it has acted cautiously, uncertain of the scope of its own constitutional power. The source of this uncertainty is not the Constitution. Nowhere in that document, or its history, is there an obligation on the part of the Senate to approve a nomination. On the contrary, the burden should be on the president to select and submit a nominee with acceptable credentials.

Senators Abraham Ribicoff, Charles Percy, and Jacob Javits introduced legislation in 1977 to create an Office on Nominations charged with the responsibility of assisting the Senate in its confirmation of nominees for executive departments and agencies, independent regulatory commissions, United States courts, and other officers. Ribicoff conceded that in too many cases confirmation hearings are pro forma proceedings, with advice and consent frequently exercised in a "casual fashion" while Percy criticized the "undue deference" accorded to presidential submissions.[45]

---

senators registered strong opposition to the nomination of William L. Springer to the FPC; *id.* at 16265–16281.

[44]122 Cong. Rec. S3882 (daily ed. March 22, 1976).

[45]123 Cong. Rec. S14415-14418 (daily ed. Sept. 8, 1977).

ADMINISTRATIVE LEGISLATION

Presidents are obligated under the Constitution to take care that the laws be "faithfully executed." The often conflicting and ambiguous passages within a law must be interpreted by executive officials to construct the purpose and intent of Congress. As important as intent is the extent to which a law is carried out. President Taft once remarked: "Let any one make the laws of the country, if I can construe them."[46]

To carry out the laws, administrators must issue rules and regulations of their own. The courts long ago appreciated this need. The Eliason decision of 1842, concerning regulations issued by the secretary of war, declared that rules and regulations "must be received as the acts of the executive, and as such, be binding upon all within the sphere of his legal and constitutional authority."[47] In a later decision the courts upheld regulations issued by the Treasury Department, partly because they were based upon general statutory authority given to executive departments to "prescribe regulations" for the conduct of their operations.[48] Current law authorizes the head of an executive department or military department to prescribe regulations "for the government of his department, the conduct of its employees, the distribution and performance of its business, and the custody, use, and preservation of its records, papers, and property."[49]

These duties, primarily of a "housekeeping" nature, relate only distantly to the citizenry. Many regulations, however, bear directly on the public. It is here that administrative legislation must be restricted in its scope and application. While administrative regulations are entitled to respect, "the authority to prescribe rules and regulations is not the power to make laws, for no such power can be delegated by the Congress."[50] Agencies cannot legally ignore or

[46]William Howard Taft, *Our Chief Magistrate and His Powers* **78** (1916).

[47]United States v. Eliason, 41 U.S. (16 Pet.) 291, 301 (1842).

[48]Boske v. Comingore, 177 U.S. 459 (1900).

[49]5 U.S.C. 301 (1970).

[50]Lincoln Electric Co. v. Commissioner of Int. Rev., 190 F.2d 326, 330 (6th Cir. 1951). See also American Broadcasting Co. v. United States, 110

depart from the policies and procedures they have promulgated.[51] Substantive policies have to be published in the Federal Register or the Code of Federal Regulations, not in internal agency manuals.[52]

Presidential Proclamations

Proclamations by the president take two forms. Some are merely declaratory in effect, such as those issued by President Carter during 1977 to designate Earth Week, Law Day, National Farm Safety Week, and other issues of general interest. Other proclamations have substantive impact.

A prime example of the latter was the "New Economic Policy" as unveiled by President Nixon in 1971. In part it involved a 10 percent surcharge placed on articles imported into the United States. The stated purpose was to assure that American products would not be at a disadvantage because of "unfair exchange rates."[53] The more immediate concern was a deterioration of the American balance of payments. A month later a study group of the Council of the General Agreement on Tariffs and Trade (GATT) called the surcharge incompatible with the GATT and an "inappropriate" means of remedying the U.S. balance of payments deficit.[54]

Importers immediately filed appeals with the Customs Bureau. When their petitions proved unsuccessful they turned to the United States Customs Court for relief, contending that the surcharge went beyond the scope of any authority delegated to the president by Congress. The Customs Court, in 1974, agreed with the importers and declared the surcharge invalid. It said "the Proclamation, in

---

F.Supp. 374, 384 (S.D. N.Y. 1953), *aff'd*, 347 U.S. 284 (1954); and Independent Meat Packers Ass'n v. Butz, 526 F.2d 228, 234-235 (8th Cir. 1975), *cert. denied*, 424 U.S.966 (1976).

[51]Vitarelli v. Seaton, 359 U.S. 535 (1959); Note, "Violations by Agencies of Their Own Regulations," 87 *Harv. L. Rev.* 629 (1974).

[52]Morton v. Ruiz, 415 U.S. 199 (1974).

[53]*Public Papers of the Presidents, 1971*, at 889. Proclamation 4074, 36 Fed. Reg. 15724 (1971). The surcharge was terminated Dec. 20, 1971: Proclamation 4098, 36 Fed. Reg. 24201 (1971).

[54]Philip C. Jones, "Attacks on the United States Import Surcharge Under Domestic and International Law: A Pragmatic Analysis," 6 *J. Int'l L. & Econ.* 269 (1971-72).

fact, arrogated unto the President a power beyond the scope of any authority delegated to him by the Congress."[55] Had this decision stood, the federal government would have had to repay about $500 million it had collected.[56]

A year later, however, the United States Court of Customs and Patents Appeals reversed the decision. While the appeals court subscribed to the theory that the president did not possess any undelegated power to regulate commerce or to set tariffs, and that no such inherent power existed for the president, it concluded that he had acted within the power delegated to him by the Trading With the Enemy Act (TWEA). Neither Proclamation 4074 nor the administration's legal defense (opinion of the General Counsel of the Treasury, September 29, 1971) had made reference to the TWEA. Furthermore, nothing in the TWEA specifically authorized or prohibited the imposition of a surcharge. The appeals court was not surprised that Congress "did not *specify* that the President could use a surcharge in a national emergency. Having left the battlefield, it would hardly do to dictate all the weapons to be used in the fight." It was also "self-evident" to the court that the surcharge had overtones of foreign relations and foreign policy. Foreign exchange rates, international monetary reserves, balances of payments, and trade barriers had become increasingly intertwined. The court relied on the Curtiss-Wright case of 1936 to argue that Congress could delegate more broadly in foreign affairs than in domestic affairs.[57] This reliance was misplaced. *Curtiss-Wright* involved a

[55]Yoshida Int'l Inc. v. United States, 378 F.Supp. 1155, 1167 (Cust. Ct. 1974).

[56]*Washington Post*, July 9, 1974, at A1:5.

[57]United States v. Yoshida Intern., Inc., 526 F.2d 560, 576, 580–582 (Ct. Cust. & Pat. App. 1975). See page 572 and note 13 for lack of inherent presidential power to regulate commerce or to set tariffs. In a separate action (Alcan Aluminum Corp. v. United States), challenging the appellate court decision in *Yoshida*, the Supreme Court denied certiorari; 429 U.S. 986 (1976). Background is provided by David Pollard and David A. Boillot, "The Import Surcharge of 1971: A Case Study of Executive Powers in Foreign Commerce," 7 *Vand. J. Transnat'l L.* 137 (1973). See also Jay G. McMains, ". . . Import Surcharge of 1971 is Invalid . . . ," 15 *Va. J. Int'l L.* 649 (1975) and Hal S. Scott, "The United States Response to Common Market Trade Preferences and the Legality of the Import Surcharge," 39 *U. Chi. L. Rev.* 177 (1972).

specific delegation of authority to prevent arms shipments to other regions. The Trading With the Enemy Act, as the court acknowledged, did not specifically delegate authority to impose a surcharge. Moreover, imposition of a surcharge is peculiarly within the province of Congress to levy tariffs and regulate foreign commerce.

Executive Orders

A more far-reaching instrument for administrative legislation is the executive order. No one knows how many have been issued. In the early years they were not numbered. In 1907 the State Department began assigning each order a number and filing it in chronological order. By January 10, 1978, the numbered series had reached 12,034. This quantity is understated, since an administration—when it discovers executive orders from prior decades—has to shoehorn them into the existing series by using letters or fractions (for example, Executive Order 106½, Executive Order 103A).[58] Estimates of the unnumbered executive orders range from 15,000 to as high as 50,000.[59]

President Roosevelt resorted to executive orders in June 1941—before Pearl Harbor and America's entry into World War II—in seizing North American Aviation's plant in California. He based his action not on statutory authority but on the general powers vested in him "by the Constitution and laws of the United States, as President of the United States of America and Commander in Chief of the Army and Navy of the United States." He invoked these same powers when he seized shipbuilding companies, a cable com-

[58]On the numbering of executive orders see *Presidential Executive Orders*, comp. by W.P.A. Historical Records Survey (2 vols., 1944), at viii.

[59]*Executive Orders and Proclamations: A Study of a Use of Presidential Power*, printed for the use of the House Committee on Government Operations, 85th Cong., 1st Sess. 37 (1957). A partial list of unnumbered orders appears in *List and Index of Presidential Executive Orders (Unnumbered Series), 1789-1941*, New Jersey Historical Records Survey, Work Projects Administration (1943). Under Title 3 of the *Code of Federal Regulations*, five-year compilations are published containing the full text of all proclamations and executive orders issued from 1936 to the present.

pany, a shell plant, and almost 4,000 coal companies. Not until 1943 did Congress pass the War Labor Disputes Act to provide statutory authority for presidential seizure of plants, mines, and other facilities.[60]

Also beginning with Franklin Roosevelt, presidents used executive orders to articulate and implement an antidiscrimination policy. Roosevelt threatened to withhold contracts from employers who failed to satisfy equal employment provisions in federal contracts. His executive order prohibited discrimination in the employment of workers in "defense industries or government because of race, creed, color, or national origin." Presidents Truman and Eisenhower continued this policy, while Kennedy threatened to cancel contracts as a means of forcing compliance with federal equal employment standards. Shortly after Kennedy issued his order, the comptroller general stated that "So far as we are aware the propriety of [nondiscrimination] clauses . . . has never been seriously questioned by any responsible administrative or judicial tribunal; nor has the Congress seen fit to proscribe the use of such clauses by appropriate legislation." Another order, issued by President Johnson, established the administrative structure for carrying out the nondiscrimination clause.[61]

The comptroller general challenged the nondiscrimination policy of the Nixon administration. Under the "Philadelphia Plan," contractors had to set specific goals for hiring members of minority groups as a condition for working on federally assisted projects. The comptroller general announced in 1969 that the plan conflicted with the Civil Rights Act of 1964, which prohibited setting up any kind of preferential treatment on the basis of race, color, or na-

---

[60]See John L. Blackmun, Jr., *Presidential Seizure in Labor Disputes* (1967).

[61]Executive Order (hereafter E.O.) 8802, 6 Fed. Reg. 3109 (1941); E.O. 10308, 16 Fed. Reg. 12303 (1951); E.O. 10479, 18 Fed. Reg. 4899 (1953); E.O. 10925, 26 Fed. Reg. 1977 (1961); E.O. 11246, 30 Fed. Reg. 12319 (1965). The comptroller general's decision appears at 40 Comp. Gen. 593, Dec. B-145475 (1961). See James E. Remmert, "Executive Order 11,246: Executive Encroachment," 55 *Am. Bar Asso. J.* 1037 (1969) and Ruth H. Morgan, *The President and Civil Rights: Policy-Making by Executive Order* (1970).

tional origin. To the comptroller general it was immaterial whether one designated the hiring commitment a "goal" or "quota." Whatever the name given it, the practice itself violated the 1964 act.[62] The secretary of labor disagreed. He said that interpretation of the Civil Rights Act had been vested by Congress in the Department of Justice; the department had approved the plan as consistent with the act. The secretary also claimed that the comptroller general had failed to recognize executive orders "as an independent source of law."[63] Various elements in Congress declared their opposition to the plan. A Senate subcommittee charged in 1971 that it was a "blatant case of usurpation of the legislative function by the executive branch."[64]

Federal courts upheld the legality of the plan as well as the executive order that placed it in operation. This use of presidential power was supported partly on the chief executive's implied power—as it relates to economical procurement policy—to assure that "the largest possible pool of qualified manpower be available for the accomplishment" of federal projects.[65]

Also encroaching on Congress's prerogative of the purse was an executive order by President Kennedy in 1961 establishing the Peace Corps.[66] Seven months went by before Congress appropriated funds for the agency.[67] In the meantime, Kennedy financed the agency by drawing upon contingency funds made available by the Mutual Security Act.[68]

[62]49 Comp. Gen. 59 (1969).

[63]115 Cong. Rec. 23740 (1969); 42 Op. Att'y Gen., No. 37 (Sept. 22, 1969).

[64]See *Congressional Oversight of Administrative Agencies: The Philadelphia Plan*, report of the Senate Judiciary Committee made by its Subcommittee on Separation of Powers, 92d Cong., 1st Sess. 13 (Comm. Print 1971).

[65]Contractors Ass'n of Eastern Pa. v. Secretary of Labor, 442 F.2d 159, 171 (3d Cir. 1971), *cert. denied*, 404 U.S. 854 (1971). See also Contractors Ass'n of Eastern Pa. v. Secretary of Labor, 311 F.Supp. 1002 (E.D. Pa. 1970); and Robert P. Schuwerk, "The Philadelphia Plan: A Study in the Dynamics of Executive Power," 39 *U. Chi. L. Rev.* 723 (1972).

[66]E.O. 10924, 26 Fed. Reg. 1789 (1961).

[67]75 Stat. 721 (1961).

[68]H. Rept. No. 1115, 87th Cong., 1st Sess. 66 (1961).

Another controversial executive order involved the Subversive Activities Control Board (SACB), established by President Truman in 1950 to investigate communist activities. The board had jurisdiction to identify and require the public registration of "communist-action" and "communist-front" organizations. Once stigmatized in this fashion, members of such organizations became subject to various penalties. A series of court decisions held that the registration feature violated the Fifth Amendment prohibition against self-incrimination. Congress rejuvenated the board in 1968 by authorizing it to determine, through hearings, whether individuals and organizations were communist. The following year an appellate court declared that the new procedure violated the First Amendment freedom of association. After the Supreme Court refused to review this decision, the board faced extinction.[69]

The SACB gained a new lease on life in 1971 when President Nixon issued an executive order expanding the board's power and field of inquiry.[70] Senator Sam Ervin, challenging the order, introduced a resolution stating that the president had no power "to alter by Executive order the content or effect of legislation enacted by Congress."[71] The Senate adopted Ervin's amendment to prohibit the use of appropriated funds to implement the president's order.[72] Congressman Don Edwards attempted to instruct House conferees to accept the Ervin amendment, but his motion was tabled.[73]

The dispute continued the next year when the House passed a bill to legitimate the executive order.[74] Senator Proxmire offered an

[69]The SACB, created by 64 Stat. 997 (1950), was rejuvenated by 81 Stat. 765 (1968). For court cases on SACB, see Communist Party of the United States v. Subversive Activities Control Board, 367 U.S. 1 (1961); Albertson v. Subversive Activities Control Board, 382 U.S. 70 (1965); United States v. Robel, 389 U.S. 258 (1967); and Boorda v. Subversive Activities Control Board, 421 F.2d 1142 (D.C. Cir. 1969), *cert. denied,* 397 U.S. 1042 (1970).

[70]E.O. 11605, 36 Fed. Reg. 12831 (1971).

[71]S. Res. 163, 92d Cong., 1st Sess. (1971) and 117 Cong. Rec. 30248 (1971).

[72]117 Cong. Rec. 25898–25902 (1971).

[73]*Id.* at 27305–27312. A Proxmire amendment, to delete $450,000 for the SACB, was rejected 41–47; *id.* at 25888–25898.

[74]118 Cong. Rec. 19075–19103 (1972).

amendment to delete $450,000 from SACB (its entire budget.)[75] During debate on the amendment, Senator Ervin remarked that the board had held hearings on 111 cases the previous year, devoting about 48 seconds to each case. "That is all they did last year," Ervin said, "except draw their breath and their salaries."[76] After the Senate adopted the Proxmire amendment, House and Senate conferees compromised by providing the board with $350,000 but expressly prohibiting it from using any of the funds to carry out the president's order.[77] Beginning with the fiscal 1974 budget, the administration did not even bother to request funds for SACB.

Executive orders are a source of law only when they draw upon the constitutional powers of the president or powers expressly delegated by Congress. Actions that exceed these bounds have been struck down by the courts. The major example is the Steel Seizure Case of 1952, which held that President Truman's attempt to seize the steel mills of the nation had no basis in statute or in the Constitution.[78] When departmental policies are contrary to due process they have been held invalid, as in *Cole* v. *Young* (1956), where the Supreme Court decided that the standard prescribed by an executive order—directed against "disloyal" civilian employees in the Department of Health, Education, and Welfare—did not conform to statutory provisions.[79]

Procedural Controls

Because of the ubiquity and necessity of administrative regulations, they must be reconciled to the rule of law. Agencies are not, like

[75]*Id.* at 21053–21074.

[76]*Id.* at 21063–21064.

[77]86 Stat. 1131, 1134 (1972). See *President Nixon's Executive Order 11605 Relating to the Subversive Activities Control Board,* hearing before the Senate Committee on the Judiciary, 92d Cong., 1 Sess. (1971).

[78]Youngstown Co. v. Sawyer, 343 U.S. 579 (1952).

[79]Cole v. Young, 351 U.S. 536, 555 (1956). Other executive orders were struck down in Little v. Barreme, 2 Cr. 170 (1804); United States v. Symonds, 120 U.S. 46 (1887); Panama Refining Co. v. Ryan, 293 U.S. 388, 433 (1935); and Kaplan v. Johnson, 409 F.Supp. 190, 206 (N.D. Ill. 1976). For an example of a court upholding the legality of an executive order, see

legislatures, representative bodies. They are not created to formulate and express a will. It is their duty to carry out the will announced by the legislative body. Agency officials should have greater expertise than legislators because of their opportunity to specialize, but this capability introduces a weakness to the administrative process: narrowness of view. Procedures are needed to bring forth, in systematic fashion, the full information and facts required for fair and intelligent rulemaking.[80]

Procedural safeguards are basic to the maintenance of a legal system. Yet throughout the nineteenth century and well into the twentieth, due process in administrative matters depended on voluntary agency actions and scattered statutory directives. It is remarkable that not until recent decades were administrative regulations required to be published in a central document. The House Judiciary Committee in 1935 spoke of "utter chaos" regarding the publication and distribution of administrative rules and pronouncements. The furious legislative pace of the Roosevelt administration exacerbated an already strained and deficient system. In his first fifteen months in office Franklin D. Roosevelt issued 674 executive orders. In its first year the National Recovery Administration issued 2,998 administrative orders. Departmental officials sometimes were unaware of their own regulations. At one point the government brought an indictment and took an appeal to the Supreme Court before discovering that the regulation on which the proceeding was based had not been promulgated.[81]

Congress passed legislation in 1935 to provide for the custody of federal documents and their publication in a "Federal Register." Included among the documents to be published are all presidential proclamations and executive orders that have general applicability and legal effect, and all documents or orders that prescribe a penal-

---

State ex rel. Kaser v. Leonard, 102 P.2d 197, 129 A.L.R. 1125, 1136 (1940).

[80]*Report of the Attorney General's Committee on Administrative Procedure*, S. Doc. No. 8, 77th Cong., 1st Sess. 101-102 (1941).

[81]H. Rept. No. 280, 74th Cong., 1st Sess. 1-2 (1935). See Erwin N. Griswold, "Government in Ignorance of the Law—A Plea for Better Publication of Executive Legislation," 48 *Harv. L. Rev.* 198 (1934).

ty. Based partly on the statutory authority vested in him by the Federal Register Act, President Roosevelt issued an executive order in 1936 that centered in the Bureau of the Budget the responsibility for reviewing all proposed executive orders and proclamations.[82]

Additional steps were needed to improve the process for drafting rules. In a major study published in 1937 for the Brownlow Committee, James Hart supported the use of advisory committees as one way to put before administrators the views of organized (and unorganized) interests. Other basic procedural safeguards to be used in the formulation of regulations were notice of a proposed regulation, formal hearings, publication of draft regulations, informal conferences with groups affected, and progression from voluntary to mandatory standards.[83] The Walter-Logan Bill, vetoed by President Roosevelt in 1940, represented the first general legislative effort to impose a uniform standard of procedures for administrative agencies. Roosevelt vetoed it partly because he believed that legislation should await the report of the Attorney General's Committee on Administrative Procedure, which was released in 1941.

These studies, reinforced by congressional hearings, culminated in the Administrative Procedure Act (APA) of 1946, a landmark effort to guarantee fairness by establishing procedures and uniform standards for rulemaking. Some of the major features of the act include adequate notice to the parties concerned, an opportunity for interested persons to participate in rulemaking by submitting material, and publication of the rule not less than thirty days prior to its effective date. The APA relies on the doctrine of separated powers by prohibiting investigative or prosecuting personnel from participating in the agency's decision. Judicial review is available. Courts may hold unlawful any agency action found to be "arbitrary, capricious, an abuse of discretion, or otherwise not in accordance with law" and "contrary to constitutional right, power, privilege, or immunity."[84]

[82]49 Stat. 500, sec. 5 (1935). Roosevelt's Executive Order 7298, Feb. 18, 1936, appeared too early for the first volume of the *Federal Register.* It is reprinted in James Hart, "The Exercise of Rule-Making Power," *The President's Committee on Administrative Management* 355 (1937).

[83]Hart, *President's Committee* at 339–342.

[84]60 Stat. 237, sec. 10(e) (1946); 5 U.S.C. 500–706 (1970). See *Adminis-*

Critics of the APA claimed that it mistakenly tried to apply an adversary model to administrative procedures. By placing agency activity in a "judicialized strait jacket," they said, the act "sabotaged" the administrative process.[85] But agencies have managed to live with the act without serious disability. For three decades it has survived with little change.

The APA did not provide for ongoing studies to improve and modify administrative rulemaking. This deficiency was corrected in 1954 when President Eisenhower established an administrative conference to study the changes needed in administrative procedures. President Kennedy formed another temporary conference in 1961. Finally, in 1964 President Johnson created a permanent body called the Administrative Conference of the United States to study and make recommendations on the "efficiency, adequacy, and fairness of the administrative procedure used by administrative agencies in carrying out administrative programs." The conference has since offered a number of recommendations to improve the administrative process.[86]

As another safeguard, Kenneth Culp Davis suggests that administrators should use their rulemaking power to clarify legislative standards and justify their decisions. This procedure would narrow the opportunity for arbitrary executive action.[87] But Judge J. Skelly Wright, responsible for reviewing some of the rulemaking activity by agencies, finds that the absence of rules by Congress too often means that the agency is at the "mercy of the pressures brought to

---

trative Procedure Act: Legislative History, S. Doc. No. 248, 79th Cong., 2d Sess. (1946).

[85]Frederick A. Blachly and Miriam E. Oatman, "Sabotage of the Administrative Process," 6 *Pub. Adm. Rev.* 213 (1946) and Foster H. Sherwood, "The Federal Administrative Procedure Act," 41 *Am. Pol. Sci. Rev.* 271 (1947).

[86]78 Stat. 616, sec. 6 (1964). For recent recommendations of the conference see 40 Fed. Reg. 27925 (1975). See also Randy H. Hamilton and Judy Kelsey, "The Administrative Conference of the U.S.," 29 Pub. Adm. Rev. 286 (1969).

[87]Kenneth Culp Davis, *Discretionary Justice* (1969) and "A New Approach to Delegation," 36 *U. Chi. L. Rev.* 713 (1969).

bear on it, its decisions little more than the resulting vector produced by conflicting political and economic forces."[88]

Legislative Veto of Regulations

The growth of agency rulemaking prompted Congress, in the Legislative Reorganization Act of 1946, to make its celebrated plea that each standing committee exercise "continuous watchfulness" over the execution of laws. Senator Robert LaFollette remarked that when Congress "yields up that rulemaking power and delegates it to an executive agency, it is part of the responsibility of Congress to keep informed as to whether the power is being exercised as it intended it should be."[89]

Criticism of agency rulemaking, a constant issue over the next few decades, reached a shrill pitch in the 1970s. Constituents reported various "horror stories" of administrative regulations that seemed to them a product of confusion, caprice, and plain harassment. Members of Congress vented this frustration by introducing a spate of bills directed at "faceless bureaucrats" who overstep their authority. The general objective was to give Congress veto power over agency rules and regulations.

In 1976 the House of Representatives voted 265 to 135 in favor of the Administrative Rulemaking Reform Act. Although far in excess of a majority, the vote fell short of the two-thirds needed under the parliamentary procedure used ("suspension of the rules"). The legislation is designed to permit Congress, by concurrent resolution, to disapprove agency rulemaking. Also, either house could adopt a resolution directing an agency to reconsider a rule.[90]

Rulemaking represents a fusion of two qualities: legislative (agency regulations have the force of law) and executive (agencies carry out the laws passed by Congress). The debate in 1976 highlighted a number of issues, practical as well as constitutional. Should Congress attempt to review the thousands of regulations issued each year? Does it have the staff, the expertise, and the time? More is involved than simply reading a regulation, which in itself

[88]J. Skelly Wright, "Beyond Discretionary Justice," 81 *Yale L. J.* 575, 577 (1972), footnote omitted.

[89]92 Cong. Rec. 6446 (1946).

[90]122 Cong. Rec. H10666–10719 (daily ed. Sept. 21, 1976).

can be a demanding assignment. To determine the fairness and reasonableness of a regulation, members and their staffs would have to study the entire record that supports it. The Federal Trade Commission estimated that one of its rules was the subject of four years of study and produced a public record of some 30,000 pages.[91]

Yet Congressman Walter Flowers, a principal supporter of the Administrative Rulemaking Reform Act, did not contemplate that "we would have a rerun or a rehash of all of the intricate rulemaking hearings and consideration that we have in the agencies. Congress is clearly not set up to do that; have no fear of that."[92] Still, if Congress does not examine the hearing record and does not intend to make an independent study of its own, on what would it base a decision to disapprove a regulation—hunches and political pressures?

To have Congress disapprove a regulation would also add substantively to the legislative history of an act. Statements on the floor or in committee reports, as part of the process of overturning a regulation, would supplement everything that preceded the public law. In this way Congress could selectively "amend" an act without permitting the president any participation.[93]

While the reform would permit Congress to pass judgment on regulations issued by agencies, it might also encourage Congress to legislate with even fewer guidelines. Advocates for vague delegation could always argue that Congress would be in a position at a later date to review regulations to make sure that they squared with congressional intent. But if a statute is vague, and if the legislative history supplies inadequate or conflicting directives, who is to say that the agency is departing from the legislative purpose? Nor would courts, through their review of agency rules, be any better prepared to determine the appropriateness of a regulation. If Congress believes that agencies are departing from legislative intent it would do better to draft statutes in more explicit language.

A second issue concerns the coverage of the Administrative Rule-

[91]*Congressional Review of Administrative Rulemaking*, hearings before the House Committee on the Judiciary, 94th Cong., 1st Sess. 465 (1975).

[92]122 Cong. Rec. H10673 (daily ed. Sept. 21, 1976).

[93]John R. Bolten, *The Legislative Veto: Unseparating the Powers* 23 (1977).

making Reform Act. With few exceptions, all agency regulations would be subject to legislative review and legislative veto. Is agency abuse so widespread that all regulations should be scrutinized by Congress? Is there in fact abuse, or does the problem originate in the lack of clear and understandable legislative standards? A less ambitious approach would be to apply the legislative veto more selectively to agencies that require special attention. In 1974, when it appeared that the General Services Administration (GSA) might improperly dispose of President Nixon's tape recordings and other materials, Congress passed legislation to subject regulations issued by the Administrator of the General Services to a one-house veto.[94] In 1977 the Supreme Court offered this judgment on the statute: "whatever are the future possibilities for constitutional conflict in the promulgation of regulations respecting public access to particular documents, nothing in the Act renders it unduly disruptive of the Executive Branch and, therefore, unconstitutional on its face."[95]

Even without reliance on a legislative veto, as with GSA regulations, Congress can act rapidly through the regular legislative process to disapprove an agency regulation. On May 9, 1977, the Department of Housing and Urban Development (HUD) promulgated a regulation that created an uproar in Congress. The regulation sought to define family groups eligible for public housing. HUD defined "stable family relationships" broadly enough to include unmarried couples, but because of ambiguities the definition could also cover homosexual couples—a result unintended by HUD. On June 15, 1977, the House voted to nullify the regulation and this nullifying provision was enacted into law.[96]

[94]P.L. 93-526, 88 Stat. 1695, sec. 104 (1974).

[95]Nixon v. Administrator of General Services, 45 U.S.L.W. 4917, 4922 (June 28, 1977).

[96]123 Cong. Rec. H5931–5932 (daily ed. June 15, 1977) and P.L. 95–119, 91 Stat. 1089, sec. 408 (1977).

6

Power over Knowledge: Seeking and Withholding Information

The Constitution does not explicitly grant Congress the power to investigate; neither does it give the president the privilege of withholding information. Yet the Supreme Court has held that the exercise of both powers, when essential for the proper functioning of each branch, is implied in the Constitution. The court announced in 1927 that a legislative body "cannot legislate wisely or effectively in the absence of information respecting the conditions which the legislation is intended to affect or change . . ." Investigation is a prerequisite for intelligent lawmaking.[1] And in 1974 the Supreme Court decided that the president's interest in withholding information for the purpose of confidentiality is implied in the Constitution: "to the extent this interest relates to the effective discharge of a President's powers, it is constitutionally based."[2]

These implied powers meet head-on whenever Congress, in an attempt to carry out its investigative function, is denied information by a president who invokes executive privilege. Which power should yield? It would be satisfying to discover a formula that is both unequivocal and trustworthy, but too much depends on individual circumstances. To subordinate one branch to another would destroy their coequal status and profoundly affect the operation of

---

[1]McGrain v. Daugherty, 273 U.S. 135, 175 (1927).
[2]United States v. Nixon, 418 U.S. 683, 711 (1974).

separated powers. We are left with a search for general boundaries and guideposts that satisfy constitutional principles as well as practical realities.

CONGRESSIONAL INVESTIGATIONS

Congress uses its investigative power for four main purposes: to enact legislation, to oversee the administration of programs, to inform the public, and to protect its integrity, dignity, reputation, and privileges.

The House ordered its first major investigation on March 27, 1792, by appointing a committee to inquire into the ill-fated expedition of Major General St. Clair, whose troops suffered disastrous losses to the Indians. The committee was empowered "to call for such persons, papers, and records, as may be necessary to assist their inquiries." According to the account of Thomas Jefferson, President Washington convened his cabinet to consider the extent to which the House could call for papers. The cabinet considered, and agreed

> first, that the House was an inquest, and therefore might institute inquiries. Second, that it might call for papers generally. Third, that the Executive ought to communicate such papers as the public good would permit, and ought to refuse those, the disclosure of which would injure the public: consequently were to exercise a discretion. Fourth, that neither the committee nor House had a right to call on the Head of a Department, who and whose papers were under the President alone; but that the committee should instruct their chairman to move the House to address the President.

The cabinet agreed that there was not a paper "which might not be properly produced." The committee examined papers furnished by the executive branch, listened to explanations from departmental heads and other witnesses, and received a written statement from

General St. Clair.[3] Yet the potential for executive privilege had been established. The president could refuse papers "the disclosure of which would injure the public."

The first use of the investigative power to protect the dignity of the House occurred in 1795. William Smith, a representative from South Carolina, told the House that a Robert Randall had confided to him a plan to obtain from Congress a grant of some 20 million acres, to be divided into forty shares. More than half would be set aside for members of Congress who supported the scheme. Congressman William Murphy had also been approached by Randall on the attempted bribery. One of Randall's associates, Charles Whitney, contacted Congressman Daniel Buck to curry his favor. The House adopted a resolution to direct the sergeant at arms, upon the order of the Speaker, to apprehend Randall and Whitney.[4]

On January 6, 1796, the House passed a resolution stating that Randall had been guilty of contempt and a breach of House privileges by attempting to corrupt the integrity of its members. He was brought to the bar, reprimanded by the Speaker, and recommitted to custody. The case against Whitney was handled differently, since he had attempted to bribe a member-elect. The House discharged Whitney from custody without charging him with contempt, and a week later voted to release Randall.[5]

The first committee witness punished for contempt of the House was Nathaniel Rounsavell, a newspaper editor charged with divulging sensitive information to the press. Although he admitted to a select committee that he was the source of the published account (which concerned secret House debates on a proposed embargo), and that he had derived part of it from a conversation between members of the House, he refused to identify the members or say where the conversation had taken place. Placed in the custody of

[3]*Writings of Thomas Jefferson* (Mem. Ed. 1903), I, 303–305. See *Annals of Congress*, 2d Cong., 1-2 Sess. 493–494, 1113.

[4]*Annals of Congress*, 4th Cong., 1st Sess. 155–170.

[5]*Id.* at 171–245, *passim*. For further details on Congress's power to punish for contempt, see *Hinds' Precedents*, II, §§1597–1640.

the sergeant at arms and brought before the bar of the House to be interrogated, he once again declined to identify the legislators.

On the following day, still in custody, Rounsavell prepared a letter in which he disclaimed any intention of showing disrespect to the House. He described the conversation of the members as inadvertent and explained that he withheld information from the committee only because it might incriminate those who had committed no crime. Only with prior knowledge, obtained from other sources, had he been aware that the subject under discussion was an embargo. At that point John Smilie of Pennsylvania rose to identify himself as the member from whom Rounsavell had obtained the information. Smilie considered the published information "of no importance." If the House wanted a victim, he said, he offered himself in place of Rounsavell.

Some means had to be found to discharge Rounsavell without compromising the rights and dignity of the House. The Speaker put to him the question: "Are you willing to answer such question as shall be propounded to you by order of the House?" Rounsavell answered in the affirmative. The House then moved that the editor, having purged himself of contempt, be discharged from confinement. The motion carried without opposition.[6]

Judicial Review

The British Parliament regarded its use of the contempt power and its determination of its privileges as wholly immune from the review of the courts. Not so with Congress. The authority of Congress to punish citizens for contempt of its authority or for a breach of its privileges, the Supreme Court has ruled, "can derive no support from the precedents and practices of the two Houses of the English Parliament, nor from the adjudged cases in which the English courts have upheld these practices."[7]

[6]*Annals of Congress*, 12th Cong., 1st Sess. 1255–1274. Additional cases where the House punished witnesses for contempt are described in *Hinds' Precedents*, III, §§1666–1701.

[7]Kilbourn v. Thompson, 103 U.S. 168, 189 (1881). See also Marshall v. Gordon, 243 U.S. 521, 533–541 (1917) and Watkins v. United States, 354 U.S. 178, 192 (1957).

The power of Congress to investigate became the subject of judicial scrutiny in *Anderson v. Dunn* (1821). The controversy arose when Congressman Lewis Williams advised the House that a Colonel John Anderson had offered him $500 in return for certain favors and considerations. The House issued a warrant directing the sergeant at arms to take Anderson into custody. After being brought to the bar and interrogated by the Speaker, Anderson was declared guilty of contempt and in violation of the privileges of the House. The Speaker reprimanded him and discharged him from custody.[8]

Three questions were placed before the Supreme Court. Did the House have authority to issue the warrant? Was issuance of a warrant exclusively a judicial power? Did the Constitution require a jury trial for all crimes? The Supreme Court upheld the action of the House as a valid exercise in self-preservation. Without the power to punish for contempt, the House would be left "exposed to every indignity and interruption that rudeness, caprice, or even conspiracy, may meditate against it." However, the power to punish for contempt was limited: the House had to exercise the least possible power adequate to the end proposed (in this case the power of imprisonment) and the duration of imprisonment could not exceed the life of the legislative body (that is, imprisonment had to terminate with adjournment).[9]

Because of this latter restriction, an individual could violate the dignity of the House in the closing days of a Congress and be punished only during that period. Partly for that reason, as well as a desire to delegate such matters to the courts, Congress passed legislation in 1857 to enforce the attendance of witnesses on the summons of either house. Failure to appear, or refusal to answer pertinent questions, could lead to indictment as a misdemeanor in the courts.[10]

[8]*Annals of Congress*, 15th Cong., 1st Sess. 580–583, 592–609, 777–790 (1818).

[9]Anderson v. Dunn, 6 Wheat. 204, 228 (1821). The Senate, a continuing body, is not limited by the expiration of a Congress; McGrain v. Daugherty, 273 U.S. 135, 181–182 (1927).

[10]11 Stat. 155 (1857), amended by 12 Stat. 333 (1862). For legislative history and the use of this statute see Allen B. Morehead, "Congressional In-

The contempt power was narrowed by *Kilbourn* v. *Thompson* (1881). The House of Representatives had summoned Hallet Kilbourn to answer certain questions and produce papers relating to a real-estate partnership. For refusing to comply with the congressional directive he was judged guilty of contempt and imprisoned for forty-five days. The Supreme Court recognized that Congress possessed a number of judicial powers. It could punish its members for disorderly behavior or for failure to attend its sessions. The House could also decide cases of contested elections and determine the qualifications of its members. It exercised the sole power of impeachment of officers of the government and in some cases might even fine or imprison a contumacious witness. But neither house possessed a general power to punish for contempt.[11] The constitutional right of a person to life, liberty, or property, unless taken by due process of law, meant "a trial in which the rights of the party shall be decided by a tribunal appointed by law, which tribunal is to be governed by rules of law previously established."[12] In this case the congressional investigation involved a matter pending in the courts and was thus judicial, not legislative, in nature.

McGrain v. *Daugherty* (1927) adopted a more generous view of investigations used to obtain information for a legislative function. A Senate committee, investigating the Teapot Dome scandal, issued a subpoena commanding Mally S. Daugherty to give testimony and bring certain records. He refused to appear for either purpose. The Supreme Court faced this issue: did either house of Congress have the power to compel a private individual to appear before it, or one of its committees, to give testimony needed for the exercise of its legislative function? The court decided that the Senate had ordered the investigation for a legitimate object; that the witness had wrongfully refused to appear and testify; and that

vestigations and Private Persons," 40 *So. Cal. L. Rev.* 189, 203–211 (1967). The 1857 law, as amended, was upheld by the Supreme Court; In re Chapman, 166 U.S. 661 (1897). The 1857 law, amended in 1938 (52 Stat. 942), is codified at 2 U.S.C. 192–194 (1970).

[11]Kilbourn v. Thompson, 103 U.S. 168, 190 (1881).

[12]*Id.* at 182. The contempt power was also limited by Marshall v. Gordon, 243 U.S. 521, 545–546 (1917), which held that a letter written to a House committee chairman, while ill-tempered, was not of such character as to threaten the ability of the House to carry out its legislative authority.

the Senate was entitled to have him give testimony pertinent to the inquiry, either at its bar or before a committee.[13]

Protection of Individual Rights

The investigative power is interpreted broadly by the courts to permit Congress to carry out its legislative functions. Zealous or careless investigations, however, can violate individual freedoms protected by the Constitution. In 1957 the Supreme Court declared that the Bill of Rights is applicable to congressional investigations: "Witnesses cannot be compelled to give evidence against themselves. They cannot be subjected to unreasonable search and seizure. Nor can the First Amendment freedoms of speech, press, religion, or political belief and association be abridged." Strong words, yet later in the same decision the court used meeker language to warn that Congress cannot "unjustifiably encroach" upon First Amendment rights.[14] How far can Congress go?

The Supreme Court has tried to draw boundaries to circumscribe the reach of congressional investigations. In *Kilbourn* (1881) the court stated that congressional investigations must relate to some legislative purpose. Congress cannot conduct "fruitless" investigations into the personal affairs of individuals (fruitless in the sense that the investigation "could result in no valid legislation on the subject to which the inquiry referred"). Later the court rendered a judgment more sympathetic to Congress. It declared a presumption in favor of a legislative purpose. Thus, *McGrain* in 1927 decided that a "potential" for legislation is sufficient. It is enough that the subject is one on which Congress can legislate and "would be materially aided by the information which the investigation was calculated to elicit."[15]

---

[13]McGrain v. Daugherty, 273 U.S. 135, 180 (1927).

[14]Watkins v. United States, 354 U.S. 178, 188, 198–199. For an earlier decision, sustaining an abridgment of First Amendment rights by the House Committee on Un-American Activities, see Barsky v. United States, 167 F.2d 241 (D.C. Cir. 1948), *cert. denied*, 334 U.S. 843 (1948).

[15]Kilbourn v. Thompson, 103 U.S. 168, 194–195 (1881) and McGrain v. Daugherty, 273 U.S. 135, 177 (1927). When a resolution defines the scope of an investigation, the committee cannot go beyond the legislative instruction; United States v. Rumely, 345 U.S. 41 (1953).

Congressional investigations must respect the Fifth Amendment right that protects individuals against self-incrimination. In the Quinn and Emspak decisions in 1955 the Supreme Court reversed the convictions of individuals who had refused to testify before a House committee regarding their alleged membership in the Communist party. The court ruled that even indirect and ambiguous references to the Fifth Amendment will afford witnesses the privilege against self-incrimination.[16] But Congress may, through a majority vote of either house or a two-thirds vote of a committee or subcommittee, request a federal court to issue an order that compels witnesses to testify. By surrendering the Fifth Amendment right witnesses are given partial immunity (their testimony may not be used against them in any criminal case).[17]

By the early 1950s it was evident that the investigative process had taken a turn for the worse. Most frequently attacked for violating individual rights and freedoms were the House Un-American Activities Committee (HUAC) and the Permanent Investigations Subcommittee of the Senate Government Operations Committee, chaired by Joseph R. McCarthy. Members of Congress, bar associations, and civic and political action groups drafted codes of fair procedure. Beginning in 1953 the House Rules Committee held hearings on suggested codes of rules for the committees, and in 1955 the House adopted a set of procedures for committee investigations.[18] Those procedures are now part of the House rules. Each committee may fix the number of its members to constitute a quorum for the purpose of taking testimony and receiving evidence, but the number cannot be less than two. The Supreme Court

[16]Quinn v. United States, 349 U.S. 155 (1955); Emspak v. United States, 349 U.S. 190 (1955).

[17]For immunity procedure see 18 U.S.C. 6001–6005 (1970). Its use as a substitute for the Fifth Amendment has been upheld in Ullmann v. United States, 350 U.S. 422 (1956), which supported the Immunity Act of 1954 (68 Stat. 745); Kastigar v. United States, 406 U.S. 441 (1972); and Application of U.S. Senate Select Com. on Pres. Cam. Act., 361 F.Supp. 1270 (D.D.C. 1973).

[18]*Legislative Procedure*, hearings before the House Committee on Rules, 83d Cong., 2d Sess. (1953). See Edward J. Heubel, "Congressional Resistance to Reform: The House Adopts a Code for Investigating Committees," 1 *Midwest J. Pol. Sci.* 313 (1957).

had earlier held that testimony received from a witness before a committee that lacked a quorum could not be regarded as perjury. Under such circumstances the committee is not a "competent tribunal." In the Senate, one-member committees (or subcommittees) may constitute a quorum for the purpose of receiving testimony and even taking sworn testimony.[19]

Due process was at issue in *Watkins* v. *United States* (1957). A labor organizer, convicted of contempt of Congress, described for HUAC his past participation with the Communist party. He even agreed to identify current members of the party. But he objected to committee questions about those who had left the movement. Watkins did not "take the Fifth Amendment." Instead, he considered such questions irrelevant to the committee's work. He believed that the committee had no right to expose people publicly because of their past activities.

The Supreme Court sided with Watkins. Fundamental fairness demanded that a witness be given adequate guidance in deciding the pertinency of questions. Somewhere in the resolution authorizing the investigation, the remarks of the chairman or members of the committee, or the nature of the proceeding, a witness had to have an opportunity to make a reasonable judgment as to a question's pertinence. The court ruled that, unless the subject matter appears with "undisputable clarity, it is the duty of the investigative body, upon objection of the witness on grounds of pertinency, to state for the record the subject under inquiry at that time and the manner in which the propounded questions are pertinent thereto." Because HUAC failed to do that, Watkins's conviction violated the Due Process Clause of the Fifth Amendment.[20]

The tone of the decision, containing reprimands aimed at Con-

[19]House Rule XI, §709. Christoffel v. United States, 338 U.S. 84 (1949). For Senate practices see *Rules Adopted by the Committees of Congress*, compiled by the Joint Committee on Congressional Operations, 94th Cong., 1st Sess. 225–304 (Comm. Print June 1975). See Senate Rule XXV, §5(b).

[20]Watkins v. United States, 354 U.S. 178, 214–215 (1957). In 1927 the court had held, on the basis of prior decisions, that a witness "rightfully may refuse to answer where the bounds of the power are exceeded or the questions are not pertinent to the matter under inquiry"; McGrain v. Daugherty, 273 U.S. 135, 176 (1927).

gress—together with other decisions handed down during that period—produced a groundswell of resistance from legislators. Bills of various content were introduced to curb the court.[21] In the face of this political pressure the Supreme Court liberalized its attitude on the investigative power two years later.

This case involved Lloyd Barenblatt, a college professor who refused to answer certain questions put to him by a subcommittee of HUAC. He maintained that (1) the compelling of testimony by the subcommittee was neither legislatively authorized nor constitutionally permissible because of vagueness in the character of authority given to the parent committee; (2) he had not been adequately apprised of the pertinency of the subcommittee's questions; and (3) the questions he refused to answer infringed on rights protected by the First Amendment. He expressly disclaimed reliance on the Fifth Amendment privilege against self-incrimination.

The Supreme Court, sharply divided on a five to four vote, rejected all three contentions. Borrowing language from the Watkins case, the court decided that pertinency had been made to appear with "undisputable clarity." As to the constitutional question, the court acknowledged that in some circumstances the First Amendment protects an individual from being compelled to disclose his associational relationships. But the judiciary had to balance competing private and public interests. In this case the court struck the balance in favor of the government's interest in self-preservation. Justice Black, in a biting dissent, objected to the balancing test because the interest of a solitary individual is not likely to outweigh the alleged interest of the government. To him the real interest in an individual's right to remain silent is the "interest of the people as a whole in being able to join organizations, advocate causes and make political 'mistakes' without later being subjected to governmental penalties for having dared to think for themselves.[22]

[21]For this period see Walter F. Murphy, *Congress and the Court* (1962) and C. Herman Pritchett, *Congress Versus the Supreme Court* (1961).

[22]Barenblatt v. United States, 360 U.S. 109, 144 (1959). Contemporary law provides that individuals summoned to testify before Congress shall be deemed guilty of a misdemeanor when they refuse to answer "any question pertinent to the question under inquiry." 2 U.S.C. 192 (1970).

When the activities of an organization do not raise questions of subversion, at least directly, the rights of association are more likely to find protection in the courts. This is the teaching of *NAACP v. Alabama* (1958). Although the case occurred at the state level, and involved an attempt by the state's attorney general (not a legislature) to obtain an organization's membership list, the principles announced give greater support to the rights to freedom of speech, assembly, and association. Balancing still occurs, but here the individual is on firmer ground.[23]

The potential conflict between congressional investigations and the Bill of Rights has increased in recent years because of decisions on the Speech or Debate Clause. The Constitution provides that members of Congress "shall not be questioned in any other Place" for any speech or debate. The purpose is not to benefit members (protecting them against prosecution) "but to support the rights of the people, by enabling their representatives to execute the functions of their office without fear of prosecutions, civil or criminal."[24] How much may Congress do, under the shield of this clause, to undermine individual liberties?

Committee investigations are subject to the Fourth Amendment's prohibition on unreasonable searches and seizures. Where there has been unlawful search and seizure to obtain information, the Speech or Debate Clause does not automatically protect a member or employee of Congress from suit. The courts, however, are reluctant to use the Fourth Amendment as a curb on committee investigations.[25]

The Speech or Debate Clause may erode First Amendment

---

[23]NAACP v. Alabama, 357 U.S. 449 (1958). See also Gibson v. Florida Legislative Investigation Committee, 372 U.S. 539 (1963).

[24]Chief Justice Parsons of Massachusetts, quoted approvingly in Kilbourn v. Thompson, 103 U.S. 168, 203 (1881).

[25]Nelson v. United States, 208 F.2d 505 (D.C. Cir. 1953), *cert. denied*, 346 U.S. 827 (1953); Dombrowski v. Eastland, 387 U.S. 82 (1967); McSurely v. McClellan, 521 F.2d 1024, 1037 (D.C. Cir. 1975). In McSurely v. McClellan, 553 F.2d 1277 (D.C. Cir. 1976), decided on rehearing *en banc*, an appellate court held that a congressional investigation that violates a federal court order may be subject to prosecution under Fourth Amendment grounds.

rights. In 1975 the Supreme Court upheld an investigation by a Senate subcommittee that threatened an organization's freedom of the press and its right of association. The majority opinion concluded that the actions of the subcommittee, the individual senators, and the chief counsel were protected by the Speech or Debate Clause "and are therefore immune from judicial interference." The "balancing test," even though it easily tilts in the government's favor, did not even come into play. Whenever the court is faced with a situation where an activity by Congress is within its "legitimate legislative sphere, balancing plays no part."[26] This holding surpasses even the *Barenblatt* doctrine.

Justice Douglas, dissenting, insisted that the powers of Congress may not be used to deprive people of their constitutional rights. Three members of the court (Justices Marshall, Brennan, and Stewart) concurred in the judgment of the court but parted company from its sweeping interpretation of the Speech or Debate Clause. That provision, they said, protected *legislators* and their *aides* from suit. It did not immunize all congressional action (such as by committees and subcommittees) from judicial review. Individuals subpoenaed by a committee should not be compelled to shed their constitutional right to withhold certain types of information. If by so acting they are cited for contempt, justice dictates that they have access to the courts to defend themselves.[27]

IMPEACHMENT

The investigative power in its most solemn form is called into action during the impeachment process. The Constitution provides

[26]Eastland v. United States Servicemen's Fund, 421 U.S. 491, 501, 510 (n. 16) (1975). See also Doe v. McMillan, 412 U.S. 306, 314 (1973) and Gravel v. United States, 408 U.S. 606 (1972).

[27]Eastland, at 513, 515. For an earlier decision on the Speech or Debate Clause as supportive of a far-reaching legislative investigation power, see Tenney v. Brandhove, 341 U.S. 367 (1951). An analysis of the Speech or Debate Clause by Robert J. Reinstein and Harvey A. Silverglate, is "Legislative Privilege and the Separation of Powers," 86 *Harv. L. Rev.* 1113 (1973).

that the president, vice-president and all civil officers of the United States shall be removed from office on "Impeachment for, and Conviction of, Treason, Bribery, or other high Crimes and Misdemeanors." The House impeaches by a majority vote; a two-thirds vote of the Senate is needed for conviction.

An unresolved issue concerns the grounds for removal. Treason does not present much of a problem; it is defined in Article III, Section 3 of the Constitution. Bribery, while not defined in the Constitution, is generally understood to mean the giving, offering, or taking of rewards as payment for favors. But what of "other high Crimes and Misdemeanors"? Does impeachment apply only to actions indictable in the courts (statutory offenses) or does it extend to abuses of office and "political crimes" against the government? A separate issue is whether courts may review an impeachment and conviction by Congress. On all such questions the authorities differ.

"What, then, is an impeachable offense?" asked the then Minority Leader Gerald Ford in 1970, during the attempted impeachment of Justice Douglas. The only "honest answer," he said, "is that an impeachable offense is whatever a majority of the House of Representatives considers it to be at a given moment in history; conviction results from whatever offense or offenses two-thirds of the other body considers to be sufficiently serious to require the removal of the accused from office."[28] This kind of open-ended definition parallels the vague grounds that James Madison so quickly and successfully opposed at the Philadelphia convention.

Madison did not disagree on the need for an impeachment provision. He believed it was indispensable that there be some way to defend the community against the "incapacity, negligence or perfidy of the chief Magistrate." The president might "pervert his administration into a scheme of peculation or oppression. He might betray his trust to foreign powers." But later in the convention, when George Mason moved to add "maladministration" as a basis for impeachment, because treason and bribery might be insufficient to reach other "great and dangerous offenses," Madison objected. He said that ill-defined and loose terms would be equivalent to hav-

[28]116 Cong. Rec. 11913 (1970).

ing the president serve at the pleasure of Congress. Mason withdrew the language and substituted "other high crimes & misdemeanors," which passed by a vote of eight to three.[29]

In subsequent years, during impeachment proceedings, it has
been characteristic for the counsel of the accused to contend that
the phrase "other high crimes and misdemeanors" refers only to an
indictable offense.[30] While it is correct that the framers rejected
vague grounds ("maladministration"), it would be an error in the
opposite direction to claim that they insisted on specific statutory
offenses. Alexander Hamilton, in Federalist 65, called the object of
impeachment

> those offenses which proceed from the misconduct of public
> men, or, in other words, from the abuse or violation of some
> public trust. They are of a nature which may with peculiar
> propriety be denominated POLITICAL, as they relate chiefly
> to injuries done immediately to the society itself.

Hamilton conceded in the same essay that there is danger that the
decision to impeach will be regulated "more by the comparative
strength of parties than by the real demonstrations of innocence or
guilt." The framers chose to live with the risk of unwarranted im-
peachments. The alternative, which they rejected, is to permit an
unfit person to remain in office, to the detriment of government
and the people, because the grounds are too narrowly drawn.

James Madison later reinforced the view that impeachment
covers abuses of office. In the First Congress he argued that the
removal power of the president would make him responsible for
the conduct of department heads "and subject him to impeachment
himself, if he suffers them to perpetrate with impunity high crimes
and misdemeanors against the United States, or neglects to superintend their conduct, so as to check their excesses."[31]

To insist on an indictable offense contradicts this record. Moreover, the emphasis on statutory crimes does not automatically

[29]Farrand, *Records*, II, 65–66, 550.

[30]For example, see the position of President Nixon's attorneys, "An
Analysis of the Constitutional Standards for Presidential Impeachment,"
Wkly Comp. Pres. Doc., X, 270–283 (Feb. 28, 1974).

[31]*Annals of Congress*, I, 372–373 (May 19, 1789).

yield the advantage claimed by supporters. Congress, by rewriting the criminal code, could subject presidents to impeachment for minor infractions. Even if unrevised, the criminal code contains actions of insufficient stature to merit impeachment. The indictable-offense theory presents other problems. The Constitution provides that a person convicted in an impeachment trial is still subject to indictment, trial, judgment, and punishment, according to law. If impeachment requires an indictable crime, that would amount to double jeopardy, prohibited by the Fifth Amendment. And if impeachment is conducted as a criminal prosecution, the individual should be entitled to Sixth Amendment privileges for a public trial by an impartial jury.[32] The impracticality of this position cannot be surmounted. Impeachment is a political, not a judicial, act. The purpose is to remove someone from office, not to punish for a crime. Impeachable conduct need not be criminal.[33]

Both Irving Brant and Raoul Berger, authors of two leading works on impeachment, draw on British precedents for their conclusions. Although the language in the United States Constitution is lifted from English history, care must be taken not to borrow too much. The English Parliament had far greater power to punish than its American counterpart; the American president has more independence and coequal status than the British prime minister; and the American system of separated branches differs fundamentally from the close executive-legislative linkage that exists in England. After the development of ministerial responsibility to Parliament, impeachment in England became an anachronism. It remains a necessary check in America.

Is there need for judicial review? The question turns in large part

---

[32]See Raoul Berger, *Impeachment* 79–84 (1973).

[33]This is also the conclusion reached by the staff of the House Committee on the Judiciary, in preparation for the impeachment of President Nixon. *Constitutional Grounds for Presidential Impeachment*, Report by the Staff of the Impeachment Inquiry, House Committee on the Judiciary, 93d Cong., 2d Sess. (Comm. Print Feb. 1974). Even Irving Brant, who repudiated Gerald Ford's position and insisted on a narrow definition of the grounds needed for impeachment, did not go so far as to insist on statutory offenses alone. He believed that a president or judge could be impeached for violating the oath of office (such as by gross and willful neglect of duty); Irving Brant, *Impeachment* 20–23, 67, 73 (1972).

on what constitutes an impeachable offense—statutory offenses or political abuses. If the latter, the court is an inappropriate forum. Raoul Berger, relying heavily on *Powell* v. *McCormack*,[34] concludes that the courts may review impeachment and conviction. But *Powell* involved clear criteria for the qualifications of members of Congress: age, citizenship, and resident of the state from which he is chosen. The standards for impeachable activity are not spelled out in the Constitution with the same precision.[35]

It is possible to conceive of circumstances where courts might play a role. There could be blatant procedural irregularities, such as providing inadequate time for the accused to prepare a defense or denying the accused an opportunity to cross-examine. Treason is defined in the Constitution; Congress cannot apply the term loosely. Some of the grounds for impeachment might be of a frivolous nature. For example, Article X against Andrew Johnson charged that he attempted to disgrace Congress by making and delivering "with a loud voice certain intemperate, inflammatory, and scandalous harangues . . . amid the cries, jeers, and laughter of the multitudes." Such thin-skinned reactions from Congress obviously fall short of describing an impeachable offense. Also, Article VII charged him with violating the Tenure of Office Act of 1867, which I believe (but a majority of Congress did not) was itself an unconstitutional limitation on the president's control over his secretary of war.

If Congress decides that an officeholder has committed "high crimes and misdemeanors," even if unindictable in the courts, and builds a record to demonstrate that the individual acted in a manner harmful to the political system and must be removed, there is no recourse to the judiciary. Institutionally it does not make sense to believe that the courts, after someone is driven from government and a successor chosen, will order the disgraced person to resume office.

EXECUTIVE PRIVILEGE

The claim of an executive privilege sets the stage for a confrontation between two "absolutes": the power of Congress to investigate

[34]Powell v. McCormack, 395 U.S. 486 (1969).
[35]Berger, *Impeachment* 103–121 (1973).

and the power of a president to withhold information. Although these prerogatives are often cast in unqualified and unconditional terms, there are normally opportunities to negotiate a settlement that is satisfactory to both branches. If the two branches cannot agree, the matter may find its way into the courts. The political and legal controversies over the past two centuries are so numerous that it is possible to identify broad areas where control is exclusive and where it is shared.

Access by Congress

The House of Representatives has the "sole Power of Impeachment." It cannot discharge that constitutional responsibility unless it has full access to the materials needed for an investigation. When President Washington refused to share with the House certain papers regarding the Jay Treaty, he did so because the House is constitutionally excluded from the treaty-making process. Had the House sought the papers as part of an impeachment, Washington suggested, the information would have been made available. As it was, the papers did not relate to any responsibility of the House, "except that of an impeachment, which the resolution has not expressed."[36] The power of impeachment, said President Polk, gives to the House of Representatives

> the right to investigate the conduct of all public officers under the Government. This is cheerfully admitted. In such a case the safety of the Republic would be the supreme law, and the power of the House in the pursuit of this object would penetrate into the most secret recesses of the Executive Departments. It could command the attendance of any and every agent of the Government, and compel them to produce all papers, public or private, official or unofficial, and to testify on oath to all facts within their knowlege.[37]

Even short of impeachment, executive privilege is inappropriate when there are charges of administrative malfeasance. President Jackson, a jealous defender of executive prerogatives, told Congress that if it could "point to any case where there is the slightest

[36]Richardson, *Messages and Papers*, I, 187 (March 30, 1796).
[37]*Id.* at V, 2284 (April 20, 1846).

reason to suspect corruption or abuse of trust, no obstacle which I can remove shall be interposed to prevent the fullest scrutiny by all legal means. The offices of all the departments will be opened to you, and every proper facility furnished for this purpose."[38] In the Watkins case, in 1957, the Supreme Court noted that the power of Congress to conduct investigations "comprehends probes into departments of the Federal Government to expose corruption, inefficiency or waste."[39]

Several barriers stand in the way of full disclosure to Congress. The Supreme Court noted in 1959 that Congress "cannot inquire into matters which are within the exclusive province of one of the other branches of the Government."[40] Were Congress to seek information concerning a pardon, the president could decline on the ground that the matter is solely executive in nature and of no concern to Congress (unless it required Congress to fund an amnesty program). The president need not disclose to anyone in Congress the details of a treaty being negotiated. He may do so to enlist the support of legislators, but the invitation is voluntary on his part. He does so for political, not constitutional, reasons. Nor is the president under any obligation to share with members of Congress the plans of tactical military operations.[41]

Similarly, until the president submits to the Senate the name of a nominee, Congress has no grounds for gaining access to the applicant's file. Requests for personnel and medical files might also be regarded by the president as an unwarranted intrusion into personal privacy.[42] The removal power over executive officials is strongly attached to the president's office. Grover Cleveland once

[38]*Cong. Debates*, 24th Cong., 2d Sess., Vol. 13, Pt. 2, Appendix, at 202, but see entire discussion at 188–225.

[39]Watkins v. United States, 354 U.S. 178, 187 (1957).

[40]Barenblatt v. United States, 360 U.S. 109, 112 (1959).

[41]Legislation adopted in 1974 requires the president to report to designated committees of Congress concerning covert military operations by the Central Intelligence Agency; 88 Stat. 1804, sec. 32.

[42]Such files are specifically exempted under the Freedom of Information Act (Exemption 6); 5 U.S.C. 552 (1970). This exemption limits the public, not Congress, but subsequent discussion in this chapter shows that this distinction does not always survive in practice.

withheld from the Senate various papers and documents that pertained to a suspended official. The power to remove, he said, was solely an executive prerogative and could not be shared or compromised with the Senate.[43]

Investigatory files in the executive branch also enjoy a protected status. Whereas the judicial process calls for strict rules of evidence and procedural safeguards to protect the accused, looser standards prevail during congressional investigations. The president may therefore feel an obligation to protect an individual against the disclosure of allegations and hearsay. It is possible to extend this argument to the protection of security files for federal employees (except for confirmation purposes).[44] The Freedom of Information (FOI) Act specifically exempts "investigatory files compiled for law enforcement purposes except to the extent available by law to a party other than an agency" (Exemption 7). When amended in 1974, the FOI Act tightened this exemption to read:

> investigatory records compiled for law enforcement purposes, but only to the extent that the production of such records would (A) interfere with enforcement proceedings, (B) deprive a person of a right to a fair trial or an impartial adjudication, (C) constitute an unwarranted invasion of personal privacy, (D) disclose the identity of a confidential source and, in the case of a record compiled by a criminal law enforcement authority in the course of criminal investigation, or by an agency conducting a lawful national security intelligence investigation, confidential information furnished only by the confidential source, (E) disclose investigative techniques and procedures, or (F) endanger the life or physical safety of law enforcement personnel; . . .[45]

Congressional investigations into matters pending in the courts have unique hurdles to overcome. The Senate Watergate Committee failed in its attempt to obtain certain documents and tapes

[43]Grover Cleveland, *The Independence of the Executive* 48–82 (1913).

[44]See 40 Ops. Att'y Gen. 45 (1941) and Archibald Cox, "Executive Privilege," 122 *U. Pa. L. Rev.* 1383, 1427 (1974).

[45]88 Stat. 1563–1564, sec. 2(b).

directly from President Nixon. Stymied in its effort, the committee appealed to the judiciary, only to be told by a district court that it lacked jurisdiction. Congress passed a special statute to confer jurisdiction, but this time the lower courts held that the release of material to the committee created undue risk of pretrial publicity in the pending Watergate prosecutions.[46]

This decision raises the question of whether information can be shared with Congress without its eventually leaking to the public. For example, Congressman John E. Moss sought information on a company's reserve estimates for all of its natural gas leases and contracts. Such information is protected by Exemption 4 of the Freedom of Information Act ("trade secrets and commercial or financial information obtained from a person and privileged or confidential"). However, Moss requested the information not as a member of the public but in his capacity as subcommittee chairman. Another argument used to withhold the information from him relied on language in the Federal Trade Commission Act, which empowers the commission to release information "except trade secrets and the names of customers." The company maintained that the restriction also applied to Congress, implying that what was shared with Congress would soon find its way into the public domain. Two courts refused to conclude that the transfer of information from the FTC to the subcommittee would lead "inexorably to either public dissemination" or disclosure to the company's competitors. Judges presume that congressional committees will exercise their powers responsibly.[47]

Common sense imposes limits on Congress. Senator William Fulbright once remarked that Congress could not inquire into the president's personal habits: "what he has for breakfast . . . is none of our business. Nor is what his personal relations are with members of his family and others." When a witness commented that the president's first draft of a message was none of Congress's business,

---

[46]Senate Select Com. on Pres. Campaign Activities v. Nixon, 366 F.Supp. 51 (D.D.C. 1973); 87 Stat. 736 (1973); and Senate Select Com. on Pres. Campaign Activities v. Nixon, 370 F.Supp. 521 (D.D.C 1974), *aff'd*, 498 F.2d 725 (D.C. Cir. 1974).

[47]Ashland Oil, Inc. v. F.T.C., 409 F.Supp. 297, 308 (D.D.C. 1976). This decision was affirmed, in its essentials, by Ashland Oil v. FTC, No. 76-1174 (with 76-1304) (D.C. Cir. Sept. 20, 1976).

Fulbright replied: "Sure. What did he say to Mr. Kissinger this morning before breakfast? I think that is out."[48]

Access by the Courts

The withholding of information gives ground when evidence is needed for criminal prosecution. When government prosecutors attempt to withhold from the judiciary sensitive materials needed for a trial (statements by witnesses for the government, an informer's identity, and the like), the courts offer the prosecutors a choice: either produce the information or drop the charges.[49] Congress passed legislation to empower federal judges to inspect sensitive materials *in camera* (in the privacy of their chambers). If the government decides not to comply with this procedure the courts may strike from the record the testimony of the goverment's witness or else declare a mistrial.[50]

A brief for President Nixon, during his impeachment process, acknowledged that executive privilege "cannot be claimed to shield executive officers from prosecution for crime." But Nixon believed that the president, not the courts, should determine whether information fell beyond the scope of the privilege. The brief concluded that the "public interest in a conviction, important though it is, must yield to the public interest in preserving the confidentiality of the President's office."[51] In a subsequent brief, Nixon maintained that the only constitutional recourse against a president in matters of executive privilege "is by impeachment and through the electoral process."[52]

In its unanimous decision in *United States* v. *Nixon* (1974), the

---

[48]*Transmittal of Executive Agreements to Congress*, hearings before the Senate Committee on Foreign Relations, 92d Cong., 1st Sess. 31, 33 (1971).

[49]Roviaro v. United States, 353 U.S. 53 (1957) and Jencks v. United States, 353 U.S. 657 (1957).

[50]71 Stat. 595 (1957). See also Alderman v. United States, 394 U.S. 165, 181 (1969) and Giordano v. United States, 394 U.S. 310 (1969).

[51]*Wkly Comp. Pres. Doc.*, IX, 968-969 (Aug. 7, 1973). The brief also stated that "Executive privilege does not vanish because the grand jury is looking into charges of criminal conduct." *Id.* at 967.

[52]*Id.* at X, 662 (June 21, 1974).

Supreme Court required Nixon to produce certain Watergate tape recordings and documents relating to his conversations with aides. A federal grand jury had returned an indictment charging seven men—employed either by the White House or by the Committee for the Re-Election of the President—with a number of offenses, including conspiracy to defraud the United States and to obstruct justice. To permit an absolute, unqualified executive privilege would have prevented the judiciary from carrying out its duties under the Constitution. The adversary nature of the American judicial system requires access to information in order to establish guilt or innocence. "The ends of criminal justice," said the court, "would be defeated if judgments were to be founded on a partial or speculative presentation of the facts." The integrity of the judicial system depends on the compulsory process of producing evidence needed by the prosecution or defense.[53]

A prosecutor had to persuade the trial court that the materials sought were relevant, admissible as evidence, and specific. Once this had been done, the trial judge could inspect the requested materials *in camera*, determining which portions were required for the trial. Of central importance was the conclusion that the courts, not the president, would decide the scope of executive privilege. Also significant was the first recognition by the court that executive privilege has its source in the Constitution. The president's privilege regarding communications with his aides is "fundamental to the operation of government and inextricably rooted in the separation of powers under the Constitution."[54] The question of what would happen when evidence is needed for *civil* litigation was left for another day.[55]

In this particular instance the president's general privilege of confidentiality in communications did not prevail against the needs of criminal justice. The presumptive confidentiality of presidential communications was narrowed again in 1977, when the Supreme

[53]United States v. Nixon, 418 U.S. 683, 709 (1974). President Nixon also lost two lower court tests: In re Subpoena to Nixon, 360 F. Supp. 1 (D.D.C 1973) and Nixon v. Sirica, 487 F. 2d 700 (D.C. Cir. 1973).

[54]United States v. Nixon, 418 U.S. 683, 708 (1974).

[55]*Id.* at 712 (n. 19).

Court (dividing seven to two) upheld a statute that gave custody of Nixon's public papers and tapes to Congress and the head of the General Services Administration. Since the statute applied only to Nixon, singling him out for special treatment, he contended that the act violated the Bill of Attainder Clause. But the court concluded that Nixon, because of his resignation, his acceptance of a pardon for offenses committed while in office, and the judgment of Congress that he was an unreliable custodian of his papers, constituted "a legitimate class of one."[56]

National Security Secrets

Even more privileged than executive confidentiality in communications, according to the Court in *Nixon* (1974), is the president's "need to protect military, diplomatic or sensitive national security secrets."[57] This is consistent with previous decisions that show great deference toward presidential responsibilities in military and diplomatic matters. In 1948 the Supreme Court said that it would be

> intolerable that courts, without the relevant information, should review and perhaps nullify actions of the Executive taken on information properly held secret. Nor can courts sit *in camera* in order to be taken into executive confidences. But even if courts could require full disclosure, the very nature of executive decisions as to foreign policy is political, not judicial.[58]

What happens when "secret" information is needed for a trial? In *Reynolds* v. *United States* (1952), three women tried to recover damages as widows of civilians killed in the crash of an air force plane. To support their claim they requested certain documents from the air force. A lower court announced that the government's

---

[56]Nixon v. Administrator of General Services, 45 U.S. L. W. 4917, 4930 (June 28, 1977).

[57]United States v. Nixon, 418 U.S. 683, 706.

[58]C. & S. Air Lines v. Waterman Corp., 333 U.S. 103, 111 (1948).

claim of privilege—withholding evidence required for a pending lawsuit—involved a justiciable question, "traditionally within the competence of the courts." The Supreme Court reversed the judgment by a six to three vote. While the court noted that judicial control over the evidence of a case cannot be "abdicated to the caprice of executive officers," it also held that the judiciary "should not jeopardize the security which the privilege is meant to protect by insisting upon an examination of the evidence, even by the judge alone, in chambers." To add weight to its judgment the court noted that "this is a time of vigorous preparation for national defense."[59] In essence, then, the court did indeed abdicate its role to executive officers. If courts are unwilling to examine national security evidence *in camera*, they cannot know whether administration officials are acting capriciously.

Since the early 1950s the courts have been drawn into several disputes involving secret information. The concept of "national security," used on occasion as an umbrella term to justify any number of executive actions, brings into play many competing sections of the Constitution. The Nixon administration, for example, attempted to have the courts enjoin two newspapers from publishing the Pentagon Papers. The Supreme Court held against the administration. The word "security," said Justice Black, "is a broad, vague generality whose contours should not be invoked to abrogate the fundamental law embodied in the First Amendment. The guarding of military and diplomatic secrets at the expense of informed representative government provides no real security for our Republic."[60] This decision has limited application to executive

[59]United States v. Reynolds, 345 U.S. 1, 9–10 (1952). For lower court case see Reynolds v. United States, 192 F.2d 987, 997 (3d Cir. 1951).

[60]New York Times Co. v. United States, 403 U.S. 713, 719 (1971). This was modified by United States v. Marchetti, 466 F.2d 1309 (4th Cir. 1972), *cert. denied*, 409 U.S. 1063 (1972), which required an author to submit to the Central Intelligence Agency (CIA)—prior to publication—any writing relating to the agency. The CIA could excise from the manuscript any passage that contained undisclosed classified information. In part the decision was based on the president's constitutional responsibility in foreign affairs and national security to prevent disclosure of classified materials (executive privilege), but the court also cited statutory grounds for agen-

privilege. The Pentagon Papers were leaked to the press. The question was therefore one of prior restraint on the press—a First Amendment test that an administration would find difficult to meet. Most instances of executive privilege involve documents over which the administration has retained control. Access to this material is regulated in part by the Freedom of Information (FOI) Act; the responsibility for enforcing the act is falling increasingly on the courts. As written in 1966, the FOI Act directed agencies to make information available to the public, subject to nine exemptions. The first consisted of matters "specifically required by Executive order to be kept secret in the interest of the national defense or foreign policy." The exemptions were supposed to limit access to information by the *public*, not Congress; the act explicitly states that the exemptions do not constitute authority "to withhold information from Congress."[61]

Nevertheless, the FOI act has been used to withhold information from individual members of Congress. In 1971 thirty-three members of the House of Representatives attempted to obtain documents prepared for President Nixon concerning an underground nuclear test scheduled for Amchitka Island, Alaska. The Supreme Court in the Mink case (1973) refused to examine the documents *in camera* to sift out "non-secret components" for their release.[62] Executive privilege was not at issue, since the information had been withheld on statutory grounds (Exemption 1 of the FOI Act). The court's interpretation prompted Congress to rewrite the Freedom of Information Act in 1974. Congress required that material withheld under Exemption 1 be "properly classified" pursuant to an executive order. This provision, coupled with a clarification of court review, overrode the holding of the court in the Mink case. Federal courts are now authorized to examine executive records in judges'

---

cy censorship (delegated power). For an illustration of how a court examines sensitive CIA documents, see *Knopf v. Colby*, 509 F.2d 1362 (4th Cir. 1975), *cert. denied*, 421 U.S. 992 (1975).

[61]Originally enacted in 1966 (80 Stat. 250), codified the following year with some changes (81 Stat. 54), and amended in 1974 (88 Stat. 1561). It is codified at 5 U.S.C. 552.

[62]*EPA v. Mink*, 410 U.S. 73 (1973).

chambers as part of a determination of the nine categories of exemptions under FOI.[63] This authority brings the courts a long way in terms of attitude, procedures, and capability in passing judgment on national-security withholdings. The new doctrine contrasts sharply with the rulings in *C. & S. Air Lines* (1948) and *Reynolds* (1952).

While it may be proper for the courts on some occasions to defer to the president on national security grounds, the same attitude should not be taken by Congress. Unlike the courts, Congress has explicit responsibilities under the Constitution to declare war, provide for the common defense, raise and support armies, and provide and maintain a navy. Legislative expertise exists in the Armed Services Committees, the defense appropriations subcommittees, the Budget committees, and a number of other subcommittees of the House and Senate. Deference by the courts, therefore, need not mean deference by Congress. In *C. & S. Air Lines*, the Supreme Court declined to settle an issue on the ground that foreign policy decisions "are wholly confided by our Constitution to the political departments of the government, Executive *and Legislative.*"[64]

This joint responsibility is illustrated by a recent example. Congressman John Moss, through his subcommittee, issued a subpoena to obtain from the American Telephone & Telegraph Company information on "national security" wiretaps by the administration. A district court, after balancing the investigative power of Congress against the president's executive privilege in foreign affairs, announced in 1976 that "if a final determination as to the need to maintain the secrecy of this material, or as to what constitutes an acceptable risk of disclosure, must be made, it should be made by the constituent branch of government to which the primary role in these areas is entrusted. In the areas of national security and foreign policy, that role is given to the Executive." An appellate court remanded this decision five months later. The election of Jimmy Carter had created new possibilities for resolving the matter out of

[63]88 Stat. 1562, sec. 4 (B). See H. Rept. No. 1380, 93d Cong., 2d Sess. 8–9, 11–12 (1974).

[64]C. & S. Air Lines v. Waterman Corp., 333 U.S. 103, 111 (1948). Emphasis supplied.

court. The appellate court returned the case to the lower court with the recommendation that Congress and the executive branch attempt to negotiate a settlement: "A compromise worked out between the branches is most likely to meet their essential needs and the country's constitutional balance."[65] Another interesting tug of war between the branches, with Congress the eventual victor, concerned Arab boycott reports compiled by the Commerce Department. Secretary Rogers Morton, who refused to comply with a committee subpoena, and faced contempt proceedings as a result, bowed to the will of Congress and released the material.[66]

The scope of executive privilege remains in a state of tension, and properly so, because of three competing demands: the integrity of the judicial process requires evidence; the executive branch needs a measure of confidentiality in its deliberations; and Congress depends on information to carry out its responsibilities. If the three branches of government are coequal in status, and have a right to preserve their independence and influence, it would be contrary to the Constitution for one branch to subordinate its interests to another. Accommodations by all parties are essential. The Supreme Court may claim to be the final arbiter in disputes involving executive privilege, but it can exercise that role only selectively and discreetly. It cannot (except at severe cost) referee every collision between Congress and the president.

[65]United States v. American Tel. & Tel. Co., 551 F.2d 384, 394 (D.C. Cir. 1976). See United States v. American Tel. & Tel. Co., 419 F.Supp. 454, 461 (D.D.C. 1976). After the two branches remained deadlocked and the issues had been further clarified, Judge Leventhal in 1977 concluded that he could responsibly intervene to guide the parties toward an acceptable accommodation; United States v. AT&T, No. 76-1712, (D.C. Cir. Oct. 20, 1977).

[66]*Contempt Proceedings Against Secretary of Commerce, Rogers C. B. Morton*, hearings before the House Committee on Interstate and Foreign Commerce, 94th Cong., 1st Sess. (1975) and 121 Cong. Rec. H12727 (daily ed. Dec. 16, 1975).

7

The Power of the Purse

Based primarily on its power to appropriate funds and its unique status as a representative body, Congress with good reason calls itself the "First Branch of Government." The power of the purse, James Madison noted in Federalist 58, represents the "most complete and effectual weapon with which any constitution can arm the immediate representatives of the people, for obtaining a redress of every grievance, and for carrying into effect every just and salutary measure." Article I, Section 9 of the Constitution places this weapon squarely in the hands of Congress: "No Money shall be drawn from the Treasury, but in Consequence of Appropriations made by Law." Madison, using pithier language in Federalist 48, said that "the legislative department alone has access to the pockets of the people."

The appropriations power, while broad, is restricted by other provisions in the Constitution. Congress cannot lawfully use its funding power to establish a religion, diminish the compensation of members of the federal judiciary, or take other actions specifically proscribed by the Constitution. In *United States* v. *Lovett* (1946), the Supreme Court declared invalid a section of an appropriations act that forbade the payment of federal salaries to three named "subversives." The section fell because it represented a bill of attainder prohibited by Article III, Section 3 of the Constitution. When a proviso in an appropriations act collides with the president's power to pardon and attempts to prescribe to the judiciary the effect of the pardon, the proviso cannot stand.[1] In 1977 Con-

---

[1]United States v. Klein, 13 Wall. 128 (1872) and Hart v. United States, 118 U.S. 62 (1886).

gress raised a constitutional issue by including in two appropriations bills a proviso that denied funds to President Carter to implement his pardon order.[2] By the time the provisos became law, some portions had no practical effect, but Carter objected to one feature (regarding entry of aliens) as an unconstitutional interference with his pardon order, a bill of attainder, and a denial of due process.[3]

In recent years the courts have had to decide whether Congress can, through the appropriations power, deny public funds to indigent women seeking an abortion. In 1976 a district court struck down the following language included in an appropriations act: "None of the funds contained in this Act shall be used to perform abortions except where the life of the mother would be endangered if the fetus were carried to term."[4] The following year the Supreme Court sustained the withholding of public funds from women electing to have an abortion, but the decisions did not directly concern the language in the appropriations act. However, on the basis of its decisions in 1977, the Supreme Court vacated the district court judgment of 1976 and returned it for further consideration in light of its own holdings.[5]

The Constitution prohibits the appropriation of funds to raise and support armies for a term of more than two years. Yet Congress, supported by opinions of the attorney general, has been able to provide funds to the Defense Department for longer periods—even providing "no-year" funds for defense procurement and research and development (making funds available until expended). This practice came to an end in 1970 when Congress appropriated on a two-year basis for research and development and three years for procurement (except five years for shipbuilding). Congress changed for policy, not constitutional, reasons.[6]

The legal justification for appropriating to the Defense Depart-

[2]P.L. 95-26, 91 Stat. 114, sec. 306 and P.L. 95-86, 91 Stat. 444, sec. 706.
[3]*Wkly Comp. Pres. Doc.*, XIII, 1164 (Aug. 3, 1977).
[4]McRae v. Mathews, 421 F.Supp. 533 (E.D. N.Y. 1976).
[5]Order of June 29, 1977, 45 U.S.L.W. 3849 (1977), based on Maher v. Roe, 45 U.S.L.W. 4787 (June 20, 1977) and Beal v. Doe, 45 U.S.L.W. 4781 (June 20, 1977).
[6]Louis Fisher, *Presidential Spending Power* 127–130 (1975).

ment for more than a two-year term relies on the following distinction: "raising and supporting" (subject to the two-year limit) and "equipping" (which is not). The drafts of the Constitution offer some support for this interpretation. The verb "equip" was initially applied to the navy, as in "raise armies, ⟨& equip Fleets.⟩"; "raising a military Land Force—and of equiping a Navy—"; or "raise Armies; to build and equip Fleets." When the draft was completed, the Constitution used "raise and support" for the army and "provide and maintain" for the navy. The two-year limit applied to armies, not navies. The framers, primarily concerned about a standing army, were less concerned that funds might remain available over a period of years for the construction of vessels. Taking this reasoning a step further, it can be argued that the two-year limit does not apply to a construction item that takes years to produce, even if for the army, air force, or marine corps.[7]

The topics discussed thus far in this chapter have been of recurrent interest throughout America's constitutional development, flaring up at times to present major controversies. But of more permanent concern, and forming the heart of this chapter, are two issues that have remained unresolved since 1789: (1) the establishment of budget priorities, as decided by Congress and the president; and (2) reliance on confidential and secret funds. The following is a backdrop to place in perspective the question of budget priorities.

The task of allocating funds to federal programs is governed by the Budget and Accounting Act of 1921. This statute attempted to pull together the scattered parts of a process that had become fragmented and uncoordinated over the years. Neither branch, prior to the act, could be said to have exercised financial control. The legislation remained faithful to constitutional principles by making the president responsible for budget estimates and giving Congress final control over appropriated levels. The two branches were supposed to work in tandem, each carrying out distinct and specific duties.

This assignment of functions has begun to unravel in recent

[7]Farrand, *Records,* II, 143, 158, 168, 182. See 25 Ops. Att'y Gen. 105 (1904) and 40 Ops. Att'y Gen. 55 (1948).

years. The lines of responsibility established by law and the Constitution are becoming blurred by actions on the part of both branches. Congress has passed a number of statutes that restrict the president's ability to put together a budget he can defend. No longer is he responsible for some of the budget estimates he submits to Congress; he is forbidden by law to alter them. On the other hand, when administrations resort to impoundment they frustrate Congress's ability to increase presidential estimates.

PRESIDENTIAL RESPONSIBILITY FOR ESTIMATES

The president formulates budget estimates and submits them to Congress in accordance with the Budget and Accounting Act. While this is the statutory source, the authority for submitting such estimates can also be found in the Constitution, which says that the president "shall from time to time give to the Congress Information on the State of the Union, and recommend to their Consideration such Measures as he shall judge necessary and expedient." So the president did not have to await statutory authority to submit a budget. Indeed, President Taft submitted a budget in 1912 despite opposition from Congress.

The dispute about Taft's budget originated in 1910, when Congress appropriated $100,000 to finance a study into more efficient and economical ways of conducting the public business. Taft used the money to set up a five-member Commission on Economy and Efficiency. In June 1912 he released the commission's report, which called for a national budget initiated by the president and for which the president would be held responsible. In that same month Taft ordered departmental heads to prepare two sets of estimates: one for the customary "Book of Estimates" (a loosely organized report consisting of unrelated bureau estimates) and one for the national budget recommended by the commission. Congress tried to stop Taft by passing legislation that directed executive officials to prepare estimates only in the customary manner.[8]

[8] 37 Stat. 415.

Taft, treating the statute as unconstitutional, reiterated to departmental heads his determination to have two sets of estimates:

> Under the constitution the President is intrusted with the executive power and is responsible for the acts of heads of departments and their subordinates as his agents, and he can use them to assist him in his constitutional duties, one of which is to recommend measures to Congress and to advise it as [to] the existing conditions and their betterment. . . . If the President is to assume a responsibility for either the manner in which business of the government is transacted or results obtained, it is evident that he cannot be limited by Congress to such information as that branch may think suffficient for his purposes. In my opinion, *it is entirely competent for the President to submit a budget*, and Congress can not forbid or prevent it.[9]

Taft went ahead with his plan to prepare and submit a model budget, but Congress took no action on it. The financial implications of World War I—especially the huge national debt that had to be managed by the Treasury Department—provided the principal force behind passage of the Budget and Accounting Act of 1921.[10]

The Budget and Accounting Act

A central purpose of the 1921 act was to place responsibility on the president. The House Select Committee on the Budget criticized the existing process on a number of grounds. Budget estimates submitted to Congress represented "only the desires" of the individual departments, establishments, and bureaus. Their requests were not subjected to a "superior revision with a view to bringing them into harmony with each other, to eliminating duplication of organization or activities, or of making them, as a whole, conform to the needs of the Nation as represented by the condition of the Treasury

[9]Frederick A. Cleveland, "The Federal Budget," *Proceedings of the Academy of Political Science*, III, 167–168 (1912–13), emphasis in original.

[10]Taft's model budget appears at 49 Cong. Rec. 3985 (1913). For evolution of the executive budget from 1789 to 1921, see Louis Fisher, *Presidential Spending Power* 9–35 (1975).

and prospective revenues." No one was responsible. Budget estimates were "a patchwork and not a structure." A great deal of the time of congressional committees was taken up "in exploding the visionary schemes of bureau chiefs for which no administration would be willing to stand responsible." The committee concluded that definite responsibility had to be placed upon the president to subject agency estimates to scrutiny, revision, and correlation.[11]

The 1921 act contained two exceptions to this principle of presidential responsibility. First, he was to set forth in his budget all estimates necessary "in his judgment" except those of the legislative branch and the Supreme Court. In a spirit of comity and mutual respect among coequal branches, these estimates are included in the budget without revision. Secondly, the act prohibited agency officials from submitting appropriations requests directly to Congress, or submitting recommendations as to how revenue needs should be met, "unless at the request of either House of Congress." For the most part, then, Congress authorized a newly created Budget Bureau to "assemble, correlate, revise, reduce, or increase the estimates of the several departments or establishments."[12]

This structure of presidential responsibility, after eroding slowly over time, appears to be on the verge of a more rapid disintegration. Budgets not subject to presidential review include not only those of the legislative branch and the judiciary, but also those of the Comptroller of the Currency, the Federal Deposit Insurance Corporation, the Milk Market Orders Assessment Fund, the Farm Credit Administration, the International Trade Commission, the Federal Reserve System Board of Governors, and a number of privately owned, government-sponsored enterprises.[13] Additional inroads have been made by Congress to circumvent the president and the Office of Management and Budget (OMB).

Bypassing the President

Senator Lee Metcalf introduced legislation (S. 448) in 1971 to provide that the appropriations requests for certain regulatory agencies be transmitted directly to Congress. Such estimates and re-

[11]H. Rept. No. 14, 67th Cong., 1st Sess. 4–5 (1921).
[12]42 Stat. 20, sections 201(a), 206, and 207.
[13]OMB Circular No. A-11, §11.1 (June 29, 1977).

quests, reflecting the judgment of the agency concerned, were not to be changed at the direction of any other agency of the executive branch. The bill covered seven agencies: the Civil Aeronautics Board, the Federal Communications Commission, the Federal Maritime Commission, the Federal Power Commission, the Federal Trade Commission, the Interstate Commerce Commission, and the Securities and Exchange Commission.

Deputy OMB Director Caspar Weinberger, testifying against the bill, hoped that it would be rejected "speedily and decisively." The effect, he said, would be to remove the seven agencies from the "normal budget controls and unified overall approach to budgeting that has been a vital part of the Government for over 50 years." Having just left his former position as federal trade commissioner, he was in a favorable position to argue that any regulatory agency head who did his homework properly, had fortitude, and believed in his budget estimates could expect considerable success in negotiating with OMB.[14]

Metcalf's bill was not reported from committee. During the Ninety-third Congress he introduced S. 704, which repeated the requirement for submission of budget estimates directly to Congress. As reported from committee in 1974, however, the bill was modified to provide that the estimates would be sent *concurrently* to OMB and to Congress. The president could alter the commissions' requests but would have to include in the budget the commissions' original requests as well as his proposals. The Senate did not act on the reported bill.[15]

Congress has enacted other types of proposals to weaken OMB control. The Consumer Products Safety Commission, created in 1972, is required to submit its budget concurrently to OMB and to Congress. In signing the bill, President Nixon said that the provision was "unfortunate and should not be regarded as precedent for future legislation."[16] His prediction was wide of the mark. Congress

[14]*Regulatory Agency Budgets* (Part 2), hearings before the Senate Government Operations Committee, 92d Cong., 2d Sess. 296–399 (1972).

[15]S. Rept. No. 1319, 93d Cong., 2d Sess. 21–22 (1974).

[16]86 Stat. 1229, sec. 27 (k) (1) and *Public Papers of the Presidents, 1972,* at 1050. For the confused legal status of CPSC see *Deferral and Recission of Appropriations, 1975–1976* (Part 3), hearings before the House Committee on Appropriations, 94th Cong., 1st Sess (1975).

adopted the same type of feature in 1973 for the National Railroad Passenger Corporation; in 1974 for the U. S. Railway Association, the Federal Election Commission, the Commodity Futures Trading Commission, and the Privacy Protection Study Commission; in 1975 for the National Transportation Safety Board; and in 1976 for the Interstate Commerce Commission.[17]

Far more serious from the standpoint of presidential control and the principles of the Budget and Accounting Act is the Trade Act of 1974. It provides that the estimated expenditures and proposed appropriations for the United States International Trade Commission (formerly the Tariff Commission) shall be included in the president's budget "without revision." Budget watchers on Capitol Hill (including the author) learned of the provision months after enactment. President Ford had made no mention of the provision when he signed the bill.[18]

Another innovation, tucked away in a statute with little fanfare in 1974, related to the Postal Service. For several years President Nixon had recommended about $200 million less each year than the Postal Service requested for third-class mail. Congress responded by changing the procedure for the budget. The requests of the Postal Service for "public service costs" (rural delivery) and "foregone revenue" (subsidies for third-class mail) had to be included by the president "with his recommendation but without revision, in the budget transmitted to Congress under section 11 of title 31."[19]

President Ford placed the Postal Service's request, without revision, in the appendix to the fiscal 1976 budget. Side by side he stated his own recommendations. So far so good. But in the regular budget document he included only his own recommendations, not those of the Postal Service. OMB officials contended that this budget presentation satisfied the requirements of the 1974 legislation. The history of this legislation strongly suggests, however, that Congress wanted the Postal Service's estimates placed in the presi-

[17]In order of listing: 87 Stat. 553, sec. 601(b) (1); 87 Stat. 992, sec. 202 (g)(2), 88 Stat. 1283, sec. 311(d)(1), 88 Stat. 1390-1391, sec. 101(9)(A), and 88 Stat. 1906, sec. 5(a)(5)(A); 88 Stat. 2170, sec. 304(b)(7); 90 Stat. 60, sec. 311.

[18]88 Stat. 2011, sec. 175(a)(1) and *Wkly Comp. Pres. Doc.*, XI, 10–11 (1975).

[19]88 Stat. 288, sec. 3.

dent's regular budget, not merely in the appendix. When the bill was pending, OMB Director Roy Ash complained that the feature would have the effect of "restricting the President's presentation of the Postal Service's budget. We believe that such a provision is contrary to the sound provisions embodied by Congress in the Budget and Accounting Act."[20]

It is understandable that OMB hedged a bit by limiting its compliance to the appendix. The 1974 legislation regarding the Postal Service raised profound and troublesome questions about the nature of a president's budget. If the budget is to set forth information in such form and detail "as the President may determine" (31 U.S.C. 11), can Congress require him to include unrevised agency estimates? The concept of a budget, at least since 1921, is synonymous with a president's recommendations. Take away executive judgment and the idea of a budget disappears.

Another diminution of presidential responsibility concerns the Legal Services Corporation. Legal services to the poor initially were administered by the Office of Economic Opportunity and later by the Community Services Administration. Because the program was threatened by impoundments and dismantlings during the Nixon administration, Congress created a Legal Services Corporation in 1974. Although it is created by statute and funded each year by an appropriation, the corporation is described as "private" and not part of the federal government. (What does that do to the notion of three branches?) As to its budget, nothing in the statute is to be construed "as limiting the authority of the Office of Management and Budget to review and submit comments upon the Corporation's annual budget request at the time it is transmitted to the Congress."[21]

The phrase "review and submit comments," in the eyes of the corporation, meant that OMB could not alter its budget request.

---

[20]H. Rept. No. 1084, 93d Cong., 2d Sess. 23 (1974). The intent of Congress can be found at 120 Cong. Rec. S7613 (daily ed. May 9, 1974) (remarks of Senator McGee); *id.* at H5263 (June 19, 1974) (remarks of Congressman Gross); and *id.* at H5256 (remarks of Congressmen Wright, Gross, and Derwinski).

[21]88 Stat. 380, sec. 1005(e)(2). For private status and independence from the government see sections 1003(a) and 1005(e)(1).

The corporation pointed to other statutes that specifically authorized OMB to "review and *revise.*" And since the corporation was not part of the federal government, agency officials argued that they should not be subject to OMB's apportionment process (the allocation of funds by quarters, or other periods, in order to prevent deficiencies). The corporation also maintained that its funds should not be deferred or rescinded pursuant to the Impoundment Control Act of 1974. President Ford asked Congress in 1976 to rescind $45 million for the Legal Services Corporation.[22] Congress did not support the request, however, and the money was eventually released. In 1977 the House of Representatives defeated an amendment to subject the corporation's budget request to presidential approval.[23]

Through these legislative initiatives, Congress has begun to cut into the integrity and responsibility of the president's budget. Thus far the programs have been of modest size and located on the fringe of the executive branch: regulatory agencies, private corporations, and the like. But small erosions on the periphery have a way of spreading to the center and this trend is disturbing. Congress should not prevent the president from articulating his own budget. Congress took the initiatives during an extraordinary period of heavy-handed activity by President Nixon and OMB. Because of arbitrary impoundments (almost all of which the federal courts struck down), Congress found itself handicapped in trying to revise the estimates submitted by the president.

CONGRESSIONAL REVISION OF ESTIMATES

The Budget and Accounting Act provided for an "executive budget" only in the sense that the president initiated the budget and took responsibility for it. The act allowed members of Congress full freedom, either in committee or on the floor, to decrease or in-

[22]S. Doc. No. 243, 94th Cong., 2d Sess. (1976) and S. Doc. No. 11, 95th Cong., 1st Sess. (1977). OMB contends that rescissions for the Legal Services Corporation may be submitted prior to the start of a fiscal year (October 1), but not after.

[23]123 Cong. Rec. H6545-6547 (daily ed. June 27, 1977).

crease his estimates. Increases have caused the most friction between the branches.

The Prerogative to Add

When John J. Fitzgerald, chairman of the House Appropriations Committee, met with the New York constitutional convention in 1915, he expressed support for a procedure in Congress that would make it as difficult as possible for legislators to increase the amounts proposed by the president. He believed that Congress should be prohibited from appropriating any money "unless it had been requested by the head of the department, unless by a two-thirds vote, or unless it was to pay a claim against the government or for its own expenses."[24]

Charles Wallace Collins, whose studies on budget reform provided part of the momentum for the 1921 act, was of a similar mind. In 1916 he published an article that argued for a form of parliamentary government. "Our institutions," he said, "being more nearly akin to those of England, it is to the English budget system that we more naturally look for the purpose of illustration." He noted that Parliament had long ago yielded the initiative in financial legislation to the cabinet. The budget in England was ordinarily ratified as introduced. A prime factor of the national budget system in America, according to Collins's view, would be

> the relinquishing of the initiative in financial legislation to the executive by the Congress. . . . The President would possess the functions of a Prime Minister in relation to public finance. He would take the responsibility for the prepartion of the budget. Complementary to this the Congress would yield its power of amendment by way of increasing any item in the budget, and also its power to introduce any bill making a charge upon the Treasury, without the consent of the executive.[25]

---

[24]"Budget Systems," *Municipal Research*, No. 62 (June 1915), at 312, 322, 327, 340. See also William Franklin Willoughby, *The Problem of a National Budget* 146–149 (1918).

[25]Charles Wallace Collins, "Constitutional Aspects of a National Budget System," 25 *Yale L. J.* 376 (1916).

Other changes were necessary to complete Collins's scenario. He would have granted members of the cabinet a seat in the House and a voice (but not a vote) in all legislative proceedings involving the budget. The committee system of making appropriations "would cease." Since the budget bill represented an administrative measure, Congress "should relinquish its power to add any new item, to increase any item, or to consider any measure which would impose a burden upon the Treasury unless such a measure had the sanction of the executive."[26]

In 1918 Representative Medill McCormick, strongly influenced by Collins, introduced a number of bills and resolutions calling for budget reform. He proposed a House budget committee to replace the committees on Ways and Means and Appropriations; it would have power to reduce presidential estimates but not to add to them, unless requested by the secretary of the treasury upon the authority of the president or unless the committee could muster a two-thirds majority. Members of the House would not be able to add to the budget bill when it reached the floor, except to restore what the president had originally requested.[27]

William McAdoo, Wilson's first secretary of the treasury, supported a system to prohibit Congress from increasing the president's requests: "let us be honest with ourselves and honest with the American people. A budget which does not cover the initiation or increase of appropriations by Congress will be a semblance of the real thing."[28] When Secretary of the Treasury Carter Glass submitted budget estimates in 1919, he said that the budget "as thus prepared for the President and on his responsibility should not, as such, be increased by the Congress."[29] David Houston, the next secretary of the treasury, asked Congress in 1920 not to add to the president's budget unless recommended by the secretary of the treasury or approved by a two-thirds vote.[30]

[26]*Id.* at 382–383.

[27]H. Doc. No. 1006, 65th Cong., 2d Sess. (1918).

[28]*Annual Report of the Secretary of the Treasury*, 1918–19, at 121 (from his testimony of Oct. 4, 1919 to the House Select Committee on the Budget).

[29]*Id.* at 117.

[30]David Houston, *Eight Years with Wilson's Cabinet*, II, 88 (1926).

This version of an executive budget was discarded by the 1921 Budget and Accounting Act. The budget was executive only in the sense that the president was responsible for the estimates submitted. It was legislative in the sense that Congress had full power to increase or reduce his estimates. Increases could be made in committee or on the floor, and in either place by simple majority vote. The act did not contemplate in any fashion the surrender of congressional power. It did not make Congresss subordinate to the president's plan. In reporting the bill, the House Select Committee on the Budget explained in straightforward language:

> It will doubtless be claimed by some that this is an Executive budget and that the duty of making appropriations is a legislative rather than Executive prerogative. The plan outlined does provide for an Executive initiation of the budget, but the President's responsibility ends when he has prepared the budget and transmitted it to Congress. To that extent, and to that extent alone, does the plan provide for an Executive budget, but the proposed law does not change in the slightest degree the duty of Congress to make the minutest examination of the budget and to adopt the budget only to the extent that it is found to be economical. If the estimates contained in the President's budget are too large, it will be the duty of Congress to reduce them. If in the opinion of Congress the estimates of expenditures are not sufficient, it will be within the power of Congress to increase them. The bill does not in the slightest degree give the Executive any greater power than he now has over the consideration of appropriations by Congress.[31]

Although Congress formally retained the power to increase budget estimates, the House Appropriations Committee, through a process of self-denial, adopted a strategy that favored decreases. This policy created a tug of war between the two houses.

Intercameral Strategies for Reductions

Legislative independence from the president's budget could have been asserted through either increases or decreases. But decreases,

[31]H. Rept. No. 14, 67th Cong., 1st Séss. 6-7 (1921).

by reducing resources and keeping them scarce, magnified the allocative power of the House Appropriations Committee. The effectiveness of the appropriations subcommittees would be measured (in the eyes of House Appropriations) by how much they could cut the president's budget.[32] Aware of this philosphy, executive agencies padded their budgets to prepare for cuts.

Contests between the House and the Senate also tilted congressional action toward decreases. House Appropriations would reduce an agency's budget below what the committee considered reasonable on the expectation that the Senate would restore some of the funds. The House could then condemn the Senate as profligate and irresponsible in money matters. Said one group of representatives: "In the past 10 years the Senate conferees have been able to retain $22 billion out of the $32 billion in increases which the Senate added to House appropriations—a two-to-one ratio in favor of the body consistently advocating larger appropriations, increased spending and corresponding deficits."[33] But many of the House "cuts" represented an elaborate institutional game. One veteran Senate Republican recalled:

> Over in the House it's a great thing to economize. They cut out a lot of things because they know very well that when the bill comes over here, we will restore the money. I know—I was in the House. I used to vote to cut all these funds and then come over here and ask my Senators to be sure that the money got back in. We get plenty of that around here.[34]

Impoundment

After Congress completes the appropriations process, further reductions occur when presidents impound funds. Harry Truman, Dwight Eisenhower, and John Kennedy impounded funds that

[32]Richard F. Fenno, Jr., *Congressmen in Committees* 48 (1973). See also Fenno's *The Power of the Purse* 102–108 (1966).

[33]*Cong. Q. Wkly Rept.*, July 20, 1962, at 1226, 1238, cited by Jeffrey L. Pressman, *House vs. Senate: Conflict in the Appropriations Process* 85 (1966).

[34]Fenno, *Power of the Purse*, at 632.

Congress had added to their defense budgets. Impoundment also affected funds that Congress added to domestic programs. In signing an agriculture appropriations bill in 1966, President Johnson objected to the $312.5 million that Congress had added to his budget request. Rather than veto the bill, he simply reduced expenditures for certain items "in an attempt to avert expending more in the coming year than provided in the budget."[35]

On an entirely different order were the impoundments carried out by the Nixon administration. They set a precedent in terms of magnitude, severity, and belligerence. The message from the White House came across without equivocation: congressional add-ons to the president's budget were irresponsible and wholly lacking in merit. Programs were either cut back to the president's request or, in some cases, terminated and dismantled.[36]

Some of the Nixon impoundments were justified on the ground that the president's budget contained requests to rescind (cancel) certain funds. Since the president wanted to rescind the funds, it was reasoned that he should not spend the money until Congress had an opportunity to consider his request. In three rescission cases the federal courts found the administration's rationale totally inadequate. A president's budget was merely a recommendation, the courts observed. The budget had no special standing. What deserved implementation was not a president's budget but a public law.[37] This principle, which the Nixon administration had ignored in its eagerness to alter federal programs, was reiterated many times by federal courts.

In a decision involving the Office of Economic Opportunity (OEO), a district court announced that it was not permissible for the Nixon administration to begin dismembering OEO simply because the president decided to omit funds for the agency in his

[35]*Public Papers of the Presidents, 1966,* II, 981. For defense impoundments see Louis Fisher, *Presidential Spending Power* 161–165 (1975).

[36]Fisher, *Presidential Spending Power,* 175–201.

[37]National Association of Collegiate Veterans v. Ottina, Civ. Action No. 349-73 (D.D.C. 1973); Minnesota Chippewa Tribe v. Carlucci, Civ. Action No. 628-73 (D.D.C. 1973); National Association of State Universities and Land Grant Colleges v. Weinberger, Civ. Action No. 1014-73 (D.D.C. 1973).

budget. The president's budget was "nothing more than a proposal to the Congress for the Congress to act upon as it may please."[38] Regarding subsidized housing funds, another federal court stated that the administration could not "refuse to execute laws passed by Congress but with which the Executive presently disagrees."[39] And in yet another decision, affecting mental health funds, a federal judge noted that the president "does not have complete discretion to pick and choose between programs when some are made mandatory by conscious, deliberate congressional action."[40]

In response to the massive impoundments by the Nixon administration, Congress passed legislation in 1974 to limit the president's power. Precisely what the Impoundment Control Act intended is impossible to say. Like many legislative measures, it is a hybrid, representing bits and pieces of previous House and Senate bills plus some imaginative innovations by conferees. There is enough ambiguity in the act to allow the executive ample room for interpretation.

The 1974 Impoundment Control Act requires special messages from the president whenever he proposes to rescind or defer appropriations. To rescind funds, both houses must complete action on a bill or joint resolution within forty-five days of continuous session. In the case of a deferral, it remains in effect unless one house passes a resolution of disapproval. For rescissions, then, the burden is on the president to obtain the approval of both houses within a specified period of days. For deferrals the burden is on one house to veto the president's proposal.[41]

Buried within the mass of special messages from President Ford is a general theme: the administration used the deferral-rescission procedure to single out congressional add-ons for delay or cancella-

[38]Local 2677, the American Federation of Government Employees v. Phillips, 358 F.Supp. 60, 73 (D.D.C. 1973).
[39]Commonwealth of Pennsylvania v. Lynn, 362 F.Supp. 1363, 1372 (D.D.C. 1973), footnote omitted; reversed by Commonwealth of Pennsylvania v. Lynn, 501 F.2d 848 (D.C. Cir. 1974).
[40]National Council of Community Mental Health Centers v. Weinberger, 361 F.Supp. 897, 902 (D.D.C. 1973).
[41]P.L. 93-344, 88 Stat. 332, Title X.

tion. Time after time the administration decided to adhere to the president's budget rather than the higher amounts voted by Congress. Senator Ted Stevens, a Republican from Alaska, told a departmental witness that "wherever there are congressional add-ons, there are automatic rescissions, just like the automatic impoundments. We have gone through it before. Everything that was added on by the Congress was impounded. Now almost everything that is added by the Congress is rescinded. You just have a new mechanism for delay."[42]

This overall pattern did not have high visibility. Members of Congress, while acting on specific deferrals and rescissions, rarely comprehended the larger strategy pursued by the administration. During his two and a half years in office, President Ford sent to Congress a total of 480 impoundment actions—330 deferrals and 150 rescissions. The total picture was lost among the details.

Congressional understanding would be helped by eliminating reports on routine impoundments, such as the placing of funds in reserve for contingencies and savings (Antideficiency Act impoundments) or pursuant to specific statutory authority (other than the Impoundment Control Act). Congress could then focus on "policy impoundments" that have the effect of furthering administration priorities at the expense of those enacted by Congress. If the presidsent were required to list the add-on amount next to his proposed rescission or deferral, that would provide an early warning signal to Congress and give the administration some pause before discriminating against congressional initiatives. To be even-handed, policy impoundments ought to take into account events (*after* passage of an appropriations bill) that cast doubt on the need to spend funds. Such events should discredit not merely congressional add-ons but the president's original budget requests as well.[43]

Also in dispute are some interpretations of the Impoundment

[42]*Budget Rescissions and Deferrals, 1975* (Part 1), hearings before the Senate Committee on Appropriations, 94th Cong., 1st Sess. 283 (1975).

[43]For a more detailed analysis of the Impoundment Control Act and the operation of the Budget Committees and the Congressional Budget Office, see Louis Fisher, "Congressional Budget Reform: The First Two Years," 14 *Harv. J. Legis.* 413 (1977).

Control Act by the General Accounting Office (GAO). First there is the question of whether the act constitutes new authority to impound. Although Congress passed the act to curb presidential action, ambiguities in the legislation, particularly those adopted during conference committee deliberation, permit the ironic conclusion that the act did indeed constitute new authority to withhold funds. GAO arrived at that judgment in 1975, suggesting that Congress "may want to re-examine the act and clarify its intent through further legislative action." Also controversial is a GAO decision in 1977 which held that "a lump-sum appropriation for programs A, B, and C used to carry out only program C would not necessarily indicate the existence of impoundments regarding programs A and B. So long as all budgetary resources were used for program C, no impoundment would occur even though activities A and B remained unfunded."[44] This interpretation allows an administration to move funds around within an appropriation even to the extent of obliterating programs, which is contrary to the motivation behind the passage of the Impoundment Control Act.

Several important issues remain unresolved. Should the executive branch intrude on the ability of Congress to increase appropriations? Should the legislative branch interfere with the president's formulation of estimates? Each branch, as the record amply demonstrates, can encroach on another. The fundamental issue is not one of power and short-run tactics. More crucial are the long-range implications for each branch and the effectiveness of national policy. Each branch would do well to step back and examine the principles established in the Constitution and reiterated in the Budget and Accounting Act of 1921. Congress should not be in the business of undercutting presidential responsibility. As for the president, after he exhausts his veto power he should recognize that a public law not to his liking is a public law nonetheless. At present the overlap between the two branches leads to duplication, confusion, and a loss of accountability.

[44]S. Doc. No. 18, 94th Cong., 1st Sess. 14 (1975); 123 Cong. Rec. S10597 (daily ed. June 24, 1977).

SECRET SPENDING

The framers placed in the Constitution this safeguard for financial accountability: "A regular Statement and Account of the Receipts and Expenditures of all public Money shall be published from time to time." It is surprising that this provision, so essential to democratic budgeting, did not appear in the draft of the Constitution until the final few days. The manner in which it was added clouds its meaning.

The Statement and Account Clause

On September 14, 1787, George Mason proposed that "an Account of the public expenditures should be annually published." Gouverneur Morris objected that publication would be "impossible in many cases."[45] Morris, proexecutive in outlook, probably believed in some element of secrecy and confidentiality. During his service with the Continental Congress he chided those who assumed that legislative committees could manage the people's business. The burden fell on the committee chairman, who at that time performed the role of executive. As Morris recalled: "Necessity, preserving the democratical forms, assumed the monarchical substance of business"—that is, the chairman did the work of the committee. At the Philadelphia convention he favored executive power, regarding the president as the "guardian of the people, even of the lower classes, ag[ain]st. Legislative tyranny." He warned that Congress would "continually seek to aggrandize & perpetuate themselves."[46] This kind of attitude does not make for open government.

Rufus King found fault with Mason's proposal: "the term expenditures went to every minute shilling. This would be impracticable. Cong[res]s. might indeed make a monthly publication, but it would be in such general Statements as would afford no satisfactory information." Unlike Morris, King appears to be concerned about detail and frequency of publication rather than the need for secrecy.

[45]Farrand, *Records*, II, 618.

[46]*Id.* at 52-54. See also *Diary and Letters of Gouverneur Morris* (Anne Cary Morris ed.), I, 12.

James Madison proposed to delete "annually" from the motion and insert "from time to time." The purpose was to give Congress discretion over the timing of the publication instead of insisting on an arbitrary schedule that might be ignored altogether. Several statements at this point suggest the need for secrecy. James Wilson, supporting Madison, said "Many operations of finance cannot be properly published at certain times," while Thomas Fitzsimons insisted that it was "absolutely impossible to publish expenditures in the full extent of the term." The convention accepted Madison's amendment without a dissenting vote. Mason's proposal, as rewritten, included an accounting for receipts as well as expenditures, and applied the requirement for publication to "all public Money."[47]

This clause was discussed at the Virginia ratifying convention in 1788. Mason said that the phrase "from time to time" had been added because "there might be some matters which might require secrecy." This explanation indicates that Congress could delay the publication of sensitive material. Mason then presented this confusing elaboration:

> In matters relative to military operations, and foreign negotiations, secrecy was necessary sometimes. But he did not conceive that the receipts and expenditures of the public money ought ever to be concealed. The people, he affirmed, had a right to know the expenditures of their money.[48]

This position is consistent only if Mason assumed that the cost of secret operations, after some period of time, would be made public.

The Growth of Secret Funding

With such a fragmentary and cryptic record, it would be hasty to conclude that the framers insisted on the publication of every expenditure by the federal government. The men who assembled at Philadelphia had just been through a decade of secret operations in the war against Great Britain. In Federalist 64, drawing on his own experiences, John Jay justified secrecy in the diplomatic area: "It

[47]Farrand, *Records*, II, 619.
[48]*Id.* at III, 326.

seldom happens in the negotiation of treaties, of whichever nature, but that perfect *secrecy* and immediate *dispatch* are sometimes requisite. There are cases where the most useful intelligence may be obtained, if the persons possessing it can be relieved from apprehension of discovery." Expenditures made public, then, could not reveal the parties involved.

This special need for diplomacy was soon recognized by statute. In 1790 Congress provided the president with a $40,000 account to be used for foreign intercourse. It was left to his judgment to decide the extent to which the expenditures should be made public. Three years later Congress specified that the president could make a certificate of the amount of expenditures in foreign intercourse "he may think it advisable not to specify." A certificate (simply a statement that funds have been spent, but providing no details) is regarded as a sufficient voucher for the sums expended.[49]

Confidential funds in diplomatic affairs became the source of a dispute between President Polk and Congress. The House of Representatives, in an effort to embarrass Daniel Webster, passed a resolution in 1848 requiring the president to deliver certain State Department records from the period of March 4, 1841, to May 9, 1843. This interval dovetailed nicely with Webster's tenure as secretary of state. Part of the information requested dealt with confidential funds in foreign intercourse. Polk refused to give the House the information on funding, pointing out that Congress, by statute, had given the president total discretion over the degree to which such funds should be made public. While it was his practice to settle all expenditures for contingent expenses of foreign intercourse by regular vouchers, he declined to surrender the certificates made by his predecessor.[50]

[49]1 Stat. 129 (1790) and 1 Stat. 300 (1793).

[50]Richardson, *Messages and Papers*, V, 2281–2286. Secret spending by President Lincoln, for the purpose of paying a spy during the Civil War, was upheld by the Supreme Court in Totten, Administrator v. United States, 92 U.S. (2 Otto.) 105 (1875). In 1974 a district court stated that *Totten* "is inapplicable to criminal actions and has been modified by a century of legal experience, which teaches that the courts have broad authority to inquire into national security matters so long as proper safeguards are applied to avoid unwarranted disclosures"; United States v. Ehrlichman, 376 F.Supp. 29, 32 (note 1) (D.D.C. 1974).

On another occasion, in 1811, Congress passed a secret statute that gave President Madison $100,000 to take temporary possession of territory south of Georgia. The law was not published until 1818.[51] The only recurrent exception to the Statement and Account Clause throughout the nineteenth century was the president's contingency account in foreign intercourse. By 1899 the account reached the annual amount of $63,000.

The next exception occurred in 1916, just before the United States entered World War I. Congress authorized the secretary of the navy to make a certificate of expenses for "obtaining information from abroad and at home." Congress added a third exception in 1935 by giving the Federal Bureau of Investigation a confidential fund of $20,000 (later raised to $70,000).[52] This is an impressive record. From 1789 to 1935—a period of 146 years (or more than three-quarters of our history as a national government)—Congress departed from the Statement and Account Clause only on rare occasions and for relatively small amounts of money.

The record changed dramatically with the onset of World War II, which has had a profound and lasting effect on democratic budgeting. Millions of dollars were given to the president on a confidential basis in order to expedite war production. The atomic bomb, costing billions of dollars, was developed and produced with secret funds. Congress authorized a confidential fund for the newly created Atomic Energy Commission. In quick succession Congress established confidential funds for the White House, the Defense Department, the District of Columbia, the National Aeronautics and Space Administration, the Bureau of Narcotics and Dangerous Drugs, the Secret Service, the Coast Guard, the Bureau of Customs, the National Science Foundation, the Immigration and Naturalization Service, and others. To provide greater control over these funds, Congress is presently considering legislation to require specific authorization for all unvouchered expenditures, make the amount and nature of the confidential funds visible in appropriations bills, provide for annual reports, and permit the GAO to

[51]3 Stat. 471–472. See David Hunter Miller, *Secret Statutes of the United States* (1918).

[52]39 Stat. 557 (1916), codified at 31 U.S.C. 108 (1970); 49 Stat. 78 (1935), codified at 28 U.S.C. 537 (1970).

carry out a limited audit to ensure that funds are actually expended for purposes authorized by law.[53]

The Intelligence Community

Overshadowing other confidential funds, both in dollar amounts and character of operation, are those spent on the U.S. intelligence community. The Central Intelligence Act of 1949 provided several extraordinary features of financial independence. The director of the Central Intelligence Agency (CIA) may spend funds on a confidential basis, using certificates rather than vouchers. More important, the CIA does not receive a direct appropriation from Congress. Funds are initially appropriated to the Defense Department. OMB, after being advised of the CIA budget by the Appropriations Committee, approves the transfer of that amount from the Defense Department to the CIA. The act of 1949 authorized the CIA to transfer to and receive from other government agencies "such sums as may be approved" by OMB for the performance of any "functions or activities" authorized by the National Security Act of 1947.[54]

Precisely what Congress anticipated by "functions or activities" has long been at issue. Covert operations in Laos and Chile, secret funding of Radio Free Europe and Radio Liberty, and subsidies to religious organizations, student groups, and labor unions have all sparked intense controversies about the proper scope of CIA activities. But of direct interest in this chapter is the tension between the Statement and Account Clause and the method used to fund the CIA. One citizen decided to take the matter to the courts.

William B. Richardson, a resident of Greensburg, Pennsylvania, asked the federal courts to declare the Central Intelligence Act in

[53]Louis Fisher, "Confidential Funding: A Study of Unvouchered Accounts," prepared for the House Committee on the Budget, 95th Cong., 1st Sess. (Comm. Print March 1977).

[54]For CIA statutory authority for funding, see 50 U.S.C. 403 (1970). The relationship between Congress, CIA, and OMB is discussed in a letter from OMB Director Roy Ash to Senator William Proxmire, April 29, 1974, reprinted at 120 Cong. Rec. S9603-9604 (daily ed. June 4, 1974). Further discussion on CIA funding appears in Louis Fisher, *Presidential Spending Power* 214–223 (1975).

violation of the Statement and Account Clause. A series of rulings from 1969 to 1974 ended with the Supreme Court's decision that Richardson lacked standing to maintain his suit. But he picked up some notable support along the way. An appellate court, in 1972, emphasized the importance of the clause in these terms:

> A responsible and intelligent taxpayer and citizen, of course, wants to know how his tax money is being spent. Without this information he cannot intelligently follow the actions of the Congress or of the Executive. Nor can he properly fulfill his obligation as a member of the electorate. The Framers of the Constitution deemed fiscal information essential if the electorate was to exercise any control over its representatives and meet their new responsibilities as citizens of the Republic.[55]

And Justice Douglas, one of three members to dissent from the Supreme Court's decision, rejected the proposition that Congress, by statute, is at liberty to suspend a constitutional provision. The claim that Congress had the power to read the Statement and Account Clause out of the Constitution was to him "astounding."[56]

Pressure gradually mounted in Congress to publish an aggregate figure for the entire intelligence community (a budget of perhaps $6 to $8 billion, of which CIA represents some 10 to 15 percent). Past CIA Directors William E. Colby and James R. Schlesinger, as well as Director Stansfield Turner (appointed in 1977), agreed that publication of the aggregate figure would not jeopardize national security. What makes them uneasy is the political demand for further details and the possibility that trends and "bumps" in the budget totals from year to year may communicate useful information to America's enemies. But as Colby noted on one occasion, the

[55]Richardson v. United States, 465 F. 2d 844, 853 (3d Cir. 1972), footnote omitted.

[56]United States v. Richardson, 418 U.S. 166, 200–201 (1974). In 1977 a federal court decided that Congressman Michael J. Harrington lacked standing to bring suit against the use of public funds for illegal CIA activities; Harrington v. Bush, 553 F.2d 190 (D.C. Cir. 1977). In 1976 a federal court held that the Freedom of Information Act exempted disclosure of the CIA budget; Halperin v. Colby, Civ. Action No. 75-676 (D.D.C. June 4, 1976).

American constitutional system probably requires publication of more information on the CIA budget than might be convenient from the agency's point of view.[57] In 1976 the House Select Committee on Intelligence (the Pike Committee), at the end of its tumultuous existence, recommended "that there be disclosure of the total single sum budgeted for each agency involved in intelligence, or if such an item is a part or portion of the budget of another agency or department that it can be separately identified as a single item."[58] Less ambitious was the conclusion of the Senate study committee on intelligence activities (the Church Committee) to publish the aggregate figure for the intelligence community. In voting eight to three for this recommendation, the committee highlighted one of the major objections of secret budgeting: "most Members of Congress and the public are deceived about the appropriations and expenditures of other government agencies whose budgets are inflated to conceal funds for the intelligence community."[59] Sums were not only concealed, but also distorted the totals of other appropriations accounts.

President Ford intervened in 1976 to urge the Senate committee to reconsider its decision. He believed that the "net effect of such a disclosure could adversely affect our foreign intelligence efforts and therefore would not be in the public interest." CIA Director George Bush wrote to the Senate Appropriations Committee, agreeing with the president's position.[60] Also during that time, the Senate was in the process of creating a new committee (the Senate Select Committee on Intelligence) which would have jurisdiction over the authorization of intelligence activities. A specific responsibility placed

[57]*Nomination of William E. Colby,* hearings before the Senate Committee on Armed Services, 93d Cong., 1st Sess. 17, 181 (1973); *Nomination of James R. Schlesinger, To Be Secretary of Defense,* hearing before the Senate Committee on Armed Services, 93d Cong., 1st Sess. 67–68 (1973); *Nomination of Admiral Stansfield Turner,* hearings before the Senate Select Committee on Intelligence, 95th Cong., 1st Sess. 83–84 (1977).

[58]H. Rept. No. 833, 94th Cong., 2d Sess. 3 (1976).

[59]S. Rept. No. 755, 94th Cong., 2d Sess. 384 (1976).

[60]*Whether Disclosure of Funds Authorized for Intelligence Activities is in the Public Interest,* hearings before the Senate Select Committee on Intelligence, 95th Cong., 1st Sess. 391–394 (1977).

upon this new committee was to study whether disclosure of budgetary figures would be in the public interest. The Senate deferred action while awaiting the committee's recommendation.

In 1977 the Select Committee voted nine to eight in favor of disclosing for fiscal 1978 the aggregate amount of funds appropriated for national foreign intelligence activities. CIA Director Turner had testified that neither he nor President Carter objected to the publication of this figure.[61] Congress took no further action during 1977, but was expected to face the issue the following year after convening for the second session of the Ninety-fifth Congress.

---

[61]S. Rept. No. 274, 95th Cong., 1st. Sess. (1977).

8

Treaties and Executive Agreements

American public interest in international agreements has been meager and spasmodic. Geographical isolation, an abundance of natural resources, and a native distrust of "entangling alliances" are some of the inhibiting factors. Occasionally an emotional issue such as the Jay Treaty or the Versailles Treaty will command public attention, but for more prosaic subjects it has been difficult to sustain interest even among those who are motivated.

This general record of apathy is undergoing important changes. The United States now depends heavily on foreign trade, finds itself vulnerable to oil embargoes and other interruptions of essential supplies, experiences price effects from so-called exogenous variables and sees its currency fluctuating widely because of international pressures. Consequently we seek cooperation on matters that can be resolved only by regional and worldwide compacts. As executive agreements are relied on more frequently as a substitute for the treaty process, creating charges on the Treasury, both houses of Congress are called upon to scrutinize them with greater care. These events are forcing the House of Representatives to participate on a more equal basis with the Senate.

TREATIES

It is commonplace today to assign to the president the leading role in foreign policy and international affairs. But quite late in the deliberations at the Philadelphia convention the delegates entrusted the predominant voice to the Senate. As late as August 6 the constitutional draft gave the Senate exclusive power to make treaties and appoint ambassadors. Opposition surfaced, however. By early September the convention decided that the president should make treaties "by and with the advice and consent of the Senate," and should nominate "and by and with the advice and consent of the Senate . . . appoint Ambassadors . . ."[1] Treaties require two-thirds support of the senators present.

Does Senate "advice" on treaties apply only to the final product, as fashioned by the president and his assistants, or to the intermediate stages of negotiation as well? Contemporary judgment generally excludes the Senate from any participation in treaty negotiation. The process of drafting and negotiating a treaty is widely regarded as a "presidential monopoly."[2] And yet this conclusion is contradicted by the Philadelphia debates, precedents established by the Washington administration, and the practices and understandings developed thereafter.

Negotiation

The Constitution does not divide treaty making into two distinct and sequential stages: negotiation by the president and approval by the Senate. The president "makes" treaties, by and with the advice and consent of the Senate. The constitutional language for treaties differs significantly from that used for appointments. For the latter the president "shall nominate, and by and with the Advice and Consent of the Senate, shall appoint Ambassadors . . ." Here the president's authority to nominate is set apart solely as an executive responsibility. This differs from the language for treaties: The president "shall have Power, by and with the Advice and Consent of

[1]Farrand, *Records*, II, 155, 169, 183, 297–298, 392–394, 495.

[2]*The Constitution of the United States of America: Analysis and Interpretation*, S. Doc. No. 92-82, at 481 (1973); Edward S. Corwin, *The President* 211–212 (1957 ed.); United States v. Curtiss-Wright Corp., 299 U.S. 304, 319 (1936). Also see statement by the legal adviser for the State Department in *Congressional Oversight of Executive Agreements—1975*, hearings before the Senate Committee on the Judiciary, 94th Cong., 1st Sess. 38 (1975).

the Senate, to make Treaties . . ." In this operation the two branches are inextricably linked.

When Washington first communicated with the Senate regarding the appropriate procedure for treaties, he stated that oral communications with the Senate "seem indispensably necessary; because in these a variety of matters are contained, all of which not only require consideration, but some of them may undergo much discussion; to do which by written communications would be tedious without being satisfactory."[3] This policy suggests an active role for the Senate, not a mere Yea or Nay to what a president submits.

A subsequent communication from Washington underscores the partnership status of the Senate on treaty making: "In the appointment to offices, the agency of the Senate is purely executive, and they may be summoned to the President. In treaties, the agency is perhaps as much of a legislative nature and the business may possibly be referred to their deliberations in their legislative chamber." Repeatedly he expressed his intention to send "propositions" to the Senate, again implying that the Senate would be invited to make changes and offer recommendations to treaty drafts.[4] Hamilton, in Federalist 75, had observed that the power of making treaties "will be found to partake more of the legislative than of the executive character, though it does not seem strictly to fall within the definition of either of them."

Washington met with senators on August 22, 1789, to secure their advice and consent to an Indian treaty. The meeting was conducted at an awkward time, putting all parties under considerable strain. The Senate had just rejected Washington's nomination of Benjamin Fishbourn to be naval officer in Georgia. The legislators felt uncomfortable in Washington's presence and disliked having to rely solely on information provided by the secretary of war, who was present. Conditions in the room—with noisy carriages traveling by—made it difficult to hear what was said. Under these circumstances the senators decided that they would not commit themselves to any positions that day. Washington, annoyed by the

---

[3]*Writings of Washington* (Fitzpatrick ed.), XXX, 373.
[4]*Id.* at 378.

inconvenience, returned two days later and obtained the Senate's consent.[5] He did not repeat the experiment.

It is a misreading of this episode to conclude that henceforth the Senate was excluded from any role in the negotiation process. Washington continued to seek its advice, but through written communications rather than personal appearances. Far from being a "presidential monopoly," the negotiation of treaties has often been shared with the Senate in order to secure legislative understanding and support.[6]

Woodrow Wilson held a different view. As a scholar he urged the president not to consult with the Senate and treat it as an equal partner. Instead, he recommended that negotiations be pursued independently. After these unilateral executive actions, legislative compliance would be compelled by getting the country "into such scrapes, so pledged in the view of the world to certain courses of action, that the Senate hesitates to bring about the appearance of dishonor which would follow its refusal to ratify the rash promises or to support the indiscreet threats of the Department of State."[7] This mousetrap theory of the treaty power had disastrous consequences on Wilson's record in office as well as international events after World War I. One of his gravest miscalculations was the decision to exclude the Senate from the negotiation of the Versailles Treaty.

A healthier model of Senate-presidential cooperation is supplied by the North Atlantic Treaty. It was foreshadowed by Senate Resolution 239, passed in 1948, calling for "regional and other collective

---

[5]William Maclay, *Sketches of Debate in the First Senate of the United States* 122–126 (1880).

[6]Many examples are cited by George H. Haynes, *The Senate of the United States*, II, 576–602 (1938).

[7]Woodrow Wilson, *Congressional Government* 233–234 (1885). Similar views appear in his *Constitutional Government in the United States* 77–78 (1908). His constitutional analysis is effectively refuted by Forrest R. Black, "The United States Senate and the Treaty Power," 4 *Rocky Mt. L. Rev.* 1 (1931) and Richard E. Webb, "Treaty-Making and the President's Obligation to Seek the Advice and Consent of the Senate with Special Reference to the Vietnam Peace Negotiations," 31 *Ohio State L. Rev.* 490 (1970).

arrangements for individual and collective self-defense." The Senate developed the resolution in close collaboration with the State Department. Between the time of its passage and ratification of the treaty, ranking members of the Senate Foreign Relations Committee consulted with the State Department. The committee as a whole helped formulate the terms of the treaty. Dean Acheson, although he entertained inflated notions of executive prerogatives during his tenure as secretary of state, stated in 1971 that the treaty process is formally divided into negotiation and ratification stages but "anybody with any sense would consult with certainly some of the members of the ratifying body before he got himself out on the very end of a limb from which he could be sawed off." He recalled that during the negotiations of the North Atlantic Treaty, Senators Thomas Connally and Arthur Vandenburg "were with me all the time," while Senator Walter George actually wrote one of the provisions of the treaty.[8] The substantial overlap between domestic and foreign matters in contemporary times creates the need to include congressional leaders in the negotiation of international agreements and to establish machinery to permit more effective integration of congressional interests.[9]

Efforts to protect the president's responsibility for negotiating with foreign nations go back to the Logan Act of 1799. The previous year, after American negotiations with France had foundered, a Philadelphia physician by the name of George Logan set sail for Europe to try his hand at diplomacy. His trip provoked a resolution in Congress directed against private citizens who "usurp the Executive authority of this government, by commencing or carrying on any correspondence with the Governments of any foreign Prince or State . . ." The same Congress that passed the Alien and Sedition Acts gave birth to the Logan Act. It provides for fines and imprisonment to punish American citizens who carry on unauthor-

---

[8]*Executive Privilege: The Withholding of Information from the Executive*, hearing before the Senate Committee on the Judiciary, 92d Cong., 1st Sess. 262–264 (1971). See Richard H. Heindel *et al.*, "The North Atlantic Treaty in the United States Senate," 43 *Am. J. Int'l L.* 633 (1949).

[9]See Bayless Manning, "The Congress, the Executive and Intermestic Affairs: Three Proposals," 55 *Foreign Affairs* 306 (1977).

ized correspondence or intercourse with foreign governments for the purpose of influencing American policy.[10] Hundreds of individuals have defied this act, but only one was indicted and he was found not guilty. During the Vietnam War, pacifist leaders and American office seekers maintained frequent contact with North Vietnam and the peace delegations at Paris. The most recent dispute concerned former President Nixon's trip to China in 1976, at the time of the New Hampshire primary. Senator Barry Goldwater said that Nixon had violated the Logan Act and would do the United States a favor by remaining in China. Goldwater announced that the law was passed in recognition that the "unauthorized actions of private individuals have a potential of interfering with and disturbing the ability of the Executive to make and carry out foreign policy, and if it has application to any situation it must be this one."[11] Because the Logan Act is vague in meaning and serves as a restriction on First Amendment freedoms, it is of doubtful constitutionality.[12] The historical record certainly suggests that the sanctions are too harsh to be applied.

The Role of the House

In 1976 President Ford vetoed a bill that Congress had passed to implement United States obligations under a treaty. The bill contained a one-house veto which, he said, "would allow the House of Representatives to block adoption of what is essentially an amendment to a treaty, a responsibility which is reserved by the Constitution to the Senate."[13] The assumption here—that the House is ex-

[10]1 Stat. 613 (1799). The Resolution is cited in *Annals,* 5th Cong. 2489. See Charles Warren, *History of Laws Prohibiting Correspondence with a Foreign Government and Acceptance of a Commission,* S. Doc. No. 696, 64th Cong., 2d Sess. (1917).

[11]122 Cong. Rec. S2630 (daily ed. March 2, 1976); *Washington Post,* Feb. 26, 1976, at A7:1.

[12]Detlev F. Vagts, in "The Logan Act: Paper Tiger or Sleeping Giant?" 60 *Am. J. Int'l L.* 268 (1966), analyzes the act and concludes that it is probably unconstitutional.

[13]*Wkly Comp. Pres. Doc.,* XII, 1486 (Oct. 10, 1976). Substantially the same bill (substituting a two-house for a one-house veto) became law the following year; P.L. 95-75, 91 Stat. 308 (1977). See H. Rept. No. 447, 95th

cluded from treaty matters—has been contested in the past and even more so today.

Several delegates at the Philadelphia convention favored a check on treaties by both houses rather than by the Senate alone. They reasoned that treaties, accorded the status of law under the Constitution, should be approved by Congress as a whole. At one point it was suggested that "no Treaty shall be binding on the U.S. which is not ratified by a law." Madison wondered whether a distinction might not be made between different types of treaties, allowing the president and the Senate to make "Treaties eventual and of Alliance for limited terms—and requiring the concurrence of the whole Legislature in other Treaties." A later proposal, joining the House with the Senate in advising and consenting to treaties, was decisively beaten back with only one state in favor and ten opposed.[14] The Constitution adopted in September reserved the treaty-making power to the president and to the Senate, but the power to make laws and appropriate funds would soon propel the House into an active role in international agreements.

A major dispute regarding the authority of the House developed in 1796 when Washington notified it that the Jay Treaty had been ratified. Congressman Edward Livingston offered a resolution requesting the president to transmit to the House a copy of the instructions that had been given to the United States minister who negotiated the treaty, together with correspondence and other documents relating to the treaty. Five days later he modified the resolution to permit the president to withhold any papers which existing negotiations might render improper to be disclosed. Livingston maintained that the House possessed "a discretionary power of carrying the Treaty into effect, or refusing it their sanction."[15] Congressman Albert Gallatin of Pennsylvania was even more specific. He said that certain powers delegated to Congress by the Constitution, such as the authority to regulate trade, might clash with

---

Cong., 1st Sess. (1977). President Carter expressed "serious constitutional reservations" about the two-house veto provision; *Wkly Comp. Pres. Doc.*, XIII, 1128–1129 (July 28, 1977).

[14]Farrand, *Records*, II, 392–394, 538.

[15]*Annals of Congress*, 4th Cong., 1st Sess. 426–428.

the treaty-making powers. The House did not have to acquiesce in decisions agreed to by the president and the Senate. The legislative powers specifically delegated to Congress served as limitations on the treaty process; the general power of granting funds constituted yet another restraining force.[16]

After several weeks of debate the House supported Livingston's resolution by a margin of sixty-two to thirty-seven. Washington denied the request for papers and documents by citing a number of reasons, including the need for caution and secrecy in foreign negotiations as well as the exclusive role of the Senate to participate as a member of the legislative branch. Shortly thereafter Congressman Thomas Blount introduced a resolution (adopted fifty-four to thirty-seven), stating that the House of Representatives did not claim any agency in making treaties,

> but that when a Treaty stipulates regulations on any of the subjects submitted by the Constitution to the power of Congress, it must depend, for its execution, as to such stipulations, on a law or laws to be passed by Congress. And it is the Constitutional right and duty of the House of Representatives, in all such cases, to deliberate on the expediency or inexpediency of carrying such Treaty into effect, and to determine and act thereon, as, in their judgment, may be most conducive to the public good.[17]

Some of the issues of the Jay Treaty reappeared during debate on the Louisiana Purchase. The Jefferson administration, on the basis of a provisional appropriation of $2 million to be applied toward the purchase of New Orleans and the Floridas, entered into an agreement with France to buy the whole of Louisiana. Congressional support required not only the advice and consent of the Senate to the treaty, but also funds supplied by both houses. Accordingly, Jefferson sent copies of the ratified treaty to the House of

---

[16]*Id.* at 437, 466–474.

[17]*Id.* at 771–782. This language has been adopted on other occasions. such as one on April 20, 1871; *Hinds' Precedents*, II, §1523. See Ivan M. Stone, "The House of Representatives and the Treaty-Making Power," 17 *Ky. L. J.* 217 (1929).

Representatives and to the Senate, explaining: "You will observe that some important conditions can not be carried into execution but with the aid of the Legislature, and that time presses a decision on them without delay."[18] The House debated at length a resolution requesting from Jefferson certain papers and documents relating to the treaty. Some portions of the resolution were adopted, others rejected. The resolution as a whole went down to defeat, fifty-nine to fifty-seven. The House subsequently joined with the Senate in passing legislation to enable Jefferson to take possession of the Louisiana Territory.[19]

On other occasions the House has opposed treaties that required appropriations, two examples being the Gadsden purchase treaty with Mexico in 1853 and the Alaskan purchase treaty with Russia in 1867. The need to have support from both houses for certain treaties was recognized in a reciprocity treaty with the Hawaiian Islands in 1876. A proviso made the treaty dependent on legislative consent by both houses.[20]

The Constitution empowers Congress to "regulate Commerce with foreign Nations, and among the several States, and with the Indian Tribes . . ." For nearly a century Congress treated the tribes as independent nations, subject to the treaty-making power of the president and the Senate. The Civil War changed the government's policy to one of assimilation and citizenship. During this time the Office of Indian Affairs came under heavy fire for corruption and maladministration. In response to those developments the House of Representatives began to voice strong opposition to its exclusion from Indian affairs. When the Senate inserted funds in a bill to fulfill treaties it had ratified with the Indians, the House refused to go along. The session expired in 1869 without an appropriation for the Indian Office. Congress reached a compromise the following session, but the dispute between the two houses persisted. Finally, an act approved in 1871 contained the following clause: *"Provided,*

[18]Richardson, *Messages and Papers*, I, 350–351 (Oct. 21, 1803).

[19]*Annals of Congress*, 8th Cong., 1st Sess. 385–419; 2 Stat. 245, 247 (1803).

[20]Chalfant Robinson, "The Treaty-Making Power of the House of Representatives," 12 *Yale Rev.* 191 (1903).

That hereafter no Indian nation or tribe within the territory of the United States shall be acknowledged or recognized as an independent nation, tribe, or power with whom the United States may contract by treaty . . ."[21]

In 1880 the House declared that the negotiation of a commercial treaty, fixing the rates of duty to be imposed on foreign imports, would be "an infraction of the Constitution and an invasion of one of the highest prerogatives of the House of Representatives."[22] The commerce power was again at issue a few years later. A commercial treaty with Mexico in 1883 contained a clause making its validity dependent on action by both houses. The House Ways and Means Committee interpreted the language to mean that the House had a right to a voice in treaties affecting revenue. Although additional conventions were entered into, to extend the time available for congressional approval, the House did not support the treaty and it did not take effect.[23] The prerogatives of the House in matters of foreign commerce, tariffs, and revenues have been protected by the use of statutes for the authorization of reciprocal trade agreements.[24]

Legislation sometimes serves as a direct substitute for treaties. When the Senate failed to ratify a treaty for the annexation of Texas, President Tyler advised the House of Representatives: "The power of Congress is, however, fully competent in some other form of proceeding to accomplish everything that a formal ratification of the treaty could have accomplished . . ."[25] He laid before the House the rejected treaty, together with all the correspondence and documents that had previously been made available to the Senate. Instead of having to obtain a two-thirds vote from the Senate, the annexation of Texas was consummated by simple majority votes from

[21]16 Stat. 566. See U.S. Department of the Interior, *Federal Indian Law* 138–214 (1958).

[22]*Hinds' Precedents*, II, §1524.

[23]24 Stat. 975 (1883), 25 Stat. 1370 (1885), 24 Stat. 1018 (1886), and *Hinds' Precedents*, II, §§1526-1528.

[24]For the development of reciprocal trade legislation see Louis Fisher, *President and Congress* 133–155 (1972).

[25]Richardson, *Messages and Papers*, V, 2176 (June 10, 1844).

both houses.[26] Hawaii was annexed in 1898 by the same method, after Senate opposition prevented action on a treaty. The St. Lawrence Seaway plan, rejected by the Senate in 1934 in treaty form, passed Congress in 1954 as a regular bill.

During World War II proposals were put forth to give the House equal treaty-making powers with the Senate. In part this development reflected criticism of the Senate's performance over the past half century.[27] Members of the House also challenged the traditional arguments offered in support of the Senate's treaty prerogative. In Federalist 64, Jay had claimed that decisions on treaties should be placed in the hands of the Senate, whose members were chosen by the "select assemblies" of State legislatures and would therefore possess greater expertise than Members of the House. The force of this argument was diluted after the Seventeenth Amendment subjected senators to popular election. Jay also argued that the small size of the Senate permitted greater secrecy and dispatch than could be expected of the House. But by 1944 the Senate had grown in size from twenty-six members to ninety-six, or larger than the original House membership of sixty-five. On the basis of these changes in the political system, the House in 1945 adopted by a vote of 288 to 88 a resolution to amend the Constitution to provide for treaty ratification by a majority of both houses. Not surprisingly, the Senate took no action on the measure.[28]

But the issue persists. Most recently the House asserted its role in the treaty power with regard to the Panama Canal and Spain. Ever since Theodore Roosevelt "took Panama" in 1903, the United States has been under pressure to compensate other nations for the venture. In 1922 the Thompson-Urrutia Treaty gave Colombia (previous owner of Panama) special canal rights and a cash grant of $25 million as penance for Roosevelt's use of force.[29] The American presence in the Canal Zone remained a problem, creating a riot in 1964 and leading to talks for a new treaty.

The House of Representatives watched these negotiations with

[26]9 Stat. 1 (1845).

[27]H. Rept. No. 2061, 78th Cong., 2d Sess. 4–5 (1944).

[28]91 Cong. Rec. 4326–4368 (1945).

[29]Robert K. Murray, *The Harding Era* 340–341 (1969).

growing apprehension. The prospect of surrendering control of the canal raised questions of military needs and national security. But the constitutional interest of the House was twofold: appropriations and the cession of United States property. Article IV, Section 3, Clause 2 of the Constitution states: "The Congress shall have Power to dispose of and make all needful Rules and Regulations respecting the Territory or other Property belonging to the United States . . ." In 1975, on a floor vote of 246 to 164, the House adopted an amendment to prohibit the use of any funds "for the purpose of negotiating the surrender or relinquishment of any U.S. rights in the Panama Canal Zone." Here was an effort not only to exert control over a completed treaty but to influence negotiations as well. In fact, opponents of the amendment contended that it would make further negotiation impossible. As softened by the conference committee and enacted into law, the language read: "It is the sense of the Congress that any new Panama Canal treaty or agreement must protect the vital interests of the United States in the Canal Zone and in the operation, maintenance, property and defense of the Panama Canal."[30] Advocates of House prerogatives continued to insist that a treaty with Panama, providing for the transfer of American property or payment of money to Panama, could not be accomplished by the treaty process alone: "such treaty provisions would require implementation by both Houses of Congress."[31]

The second dispute, over the Spanish Bases Treaty of 1976, began as an executive-legislative conflict. The Senate successfully argued that an agreement with Spain over military bases should be accomplished not by executive agreement, as in the past, but by treaty. Having conceded this point to Congress, the administration ran into other difficulties. Members of both houses objected to language in the treaty that appeared to make mandatory the appropriation of funds over a five-year period. In addition, the adminis-

[30]P.L. 94-121, 89 Stat. 617, sec. 104. See debate at 121 Cong. Rec. H6226–6236 (daily ed. June 26, 1975).

[31]122 Cong. Rec. H6177 (daily ed. June 18, 1976). In 1977 four senators filed suit with the Supreme Court, asking it to rule that the president has no power to act on the Canal Zone without authorization from both houses; 123 Cong. Rec. S17132 (daily ed. Oct. 13, 1977).

tration maintained that the treaty constituted an *authorization* to have funds appropriated. This threatened the jurisdiction of the Senate Committee on Foreign Relations and the House Committee on International Relations. Responding to both issues, the Senate Resolution of Advice and Consent contained a declaration that the sums referred to in the Spanish treaty "shall be made available for obligation through the normal procedures of the Congress, including the process of prior authorization and annual appropriations . . ." Congress adopted legislation in 1976 to authorize the appropriation of funds needed to implement the treaty.[32]

EXECUTIVE AGREEMENTS

The precise boundary between treaties and executive agreements has never been defined to anyone's satisfaction. Of course treaties require the advice and consent of the Senate, while executive agreements do not. As a second distinction, treaties (unlike executive agreements) may supersede prior conflicting statutes.[33] Otherwise, there is considerable discretion on the part of administration officials to make international compacts by either treaty or executive agreement. Among the more controversial executive agreements are the destroyers-bases deal with Great Britain in 1940, the Yalta and Potsdam agreements in 1945, the Vietnam peace agreement of 1973, the Sinai agreements of 1975, and recent military base agreements with Spain, Diego Garcia, and Bahrain.

Sources of Authority

During the early years of the Republic, executive agreements were carried out under statutory authority. For example, legislation in 1792 authorized the postmaster general to make arrangements with foreign postmasters for the receipt and delivery of letters and

---

[32]P.L. 94-329, 90 Stat. 765, sec. 507, and P.L. 94-537, 90 Stat. 2498.

[33]United States v. Schooner Peggy, 5 U.S. (1 Cr.) 103 (1801); memorandum by Monroe Leigh, legal adviser to the State Department, Oct. 8, 1975, reprinted at 121 Cong. Rec. S20104 (daily ed. Nov. 14, 1975).

packets.[34] Executive officials entered into reciprocal trade agreements on the basis of statutory authority. While such agreements lacked what the Supreme Court in 1912 called the "dignity" of a treaty since they did not require Senate approval, they are nonetheless valid international compacts.[35] Treaties, too, become a source of authority for executive agreements.

The executive branch also claims four sources of constitutional authority under which the president may enter into executive agreements: (1) his duty as chief executive to represent the nation in foreign affairs; (2) his authority to receive ambassadors and other public mininsters; (3) his authority as commander in chief; and (4) his duty to "take care that the laws be faithfully executed."[36] These powers are so open-ended that Congress may find its own sphere of action constricted because of ambitious executive interpretations. Particularly nebulous are the first, second, and fourth constitutional sources. A more solid case can be made for the commander-in-chief authority, for surely a president may enter into an armistice or cease-fire agreement with a foreign power (subject to Senate action on a peace treaty at a later date). Other reasonable actions by the president as commander in chief include agreements to protect troops, control occupied areas, and carry out military training.

Few would deny that the president has constitutional authority to recognize foreign governments. However, such determinations may involve the settlement of claims that affect other provisions of the Constitution. Recognition of Soviet Russia by President Roosevelt led to the "Litvinov Assignment" in 1933 and subsequent property claims in the courts. In *United States* v. *Belmont* (1937) the Supreme Court unanimously upheld the assignment as a valid international compact.[37] Five years later, in *United States* v. *Pink* (also involving Roosevelt's recognition of the Soviet Union), Justice

[34]1 Stat. 239 (1792).

[35]Altman & Co. v. United States, 224 U.S. 583, 600–601 (1912). For an opinion by Acting Attorney General McGranery in 1946, upholding the legality of an executive agreement made pursuant to a joint resolution, see 40 Ops. Att'y Gen. 469.

[36]11 FAM [Foreign Affairs Manual] 721.2(b)(3) (Oct. 25, 1974).

[37]United States v. Belmont, 301 U.S. 324 (1937).

Douglas declared that the powers of the president in the conduct of foreign affairs "included the power, without consent of the Senate, to determine the public policy of the United States with respect to the Russian nationalization decrees." To Douglas, the president had authority to do more than simply determine which government to recognize. Presidential authority included the power to determine the policy to go with recognition. Objections to the policy or the recognition were to be "addressed to the political department and not to the courts." And yet the judiciary could not sidestep the subject so deftly. Suppose that an executive agreement, affecting private claims, interfered with such constitutional privileges as the due process and just compensation clauses of the Fifth Amendment?[38]

Inevitably the courts were drawn back into the dispute. The executive agreement in the Belmont and Pink cases represented the exercise of an implied presidential power: recognition of foreign governments. It also involved a federal question: the balancing of interests between the national government and legislation adopted by a state government. The circumstances were unique and narrowly drawn. But the president is not free to enter into executive agreements that violate constitutional provisions. As the State Department admits, an agreement cannot be "inconsistent with legislation enacted by Congress in the exercise of its constitutional authority."[39] This principle was given substance by the Capps decision of 1953, which struck down an executive agreement because it contravened an existing commercial statute with Canada. Imports from a foreign country represented foreign commerce "subject to regulation, so far as this country is concerned, by Congress alone."[40]

The timing of these decisions on executive agreements should not be overlooked. *Capps*, as a restriction on executive authority, was handed down less than a year after the Youngstown case declared

[38]United States v. Pink, 315 U.S. 203, 229 (1942). See Note, "United States v. Pink—A Reappraisal," 48 *Colum. L. Rev.* 890 (1948).

[39]11 FAM 721.2(b)(3) (1974).

[40]United States v. Guy W. Capps. Inc. 204 F.2d 655, 660 (4th Cir. 1953), *aff'd on other grounds*, 348 U.S. 296 (1955).

invalid President Truman's seizure of the steel mills. *Belmont*, a ringing affirmation of executive agreements, was decided just five months after Justice Sutherland in the Curtiss-Wright case lent his enthusiastic support to presidential prerogatives in external affairs. The issue in *Capps* arose because of a conflicting statute. Naturally, the opportunity for presidential action widens when specific legislation in foreign commerce does not exist. The Nixon administration entered into so-called Voluntary Restraint Arrangements (VRA) with European and Japanese steel companies as a means of protecting domestic suppliers. Consumers Union took the issue to court, contending that the import quotas encroached upon Congress's authority over foreign trade and violated the Sherman Antitrust Act. In 1973 a district court declined to issue an injunction, as requested by Consumers Union, but urged the administration and the foreign steel companies to reexamine their actions as a possible violation of the Sherman Antitrust Act.[41] The following year an appellate court, dividing two to one, held that while the president could not impose mandatory import quotas without legislative authority, nothing in the Constitution or existing legislation foreclosed voluntary arrangements. The issue of the Sherman Act was vacated after the plaintiffs requested it be dismissed. A lengthy dissent by Judge Leventhal viewed the president's action as a transgression on congressional authority over foreign commerce. Far from being "voluntary," the arrangments on steel were negotiated bilateral understandings that could be enforced by sanctions imposed by the president.[42]

Other court decisions have limited the reach of executive agreements. *Seery* v. *United States* (1955) involved an executive agreement in which the United States agreed to pay Austria a flat sum to settle all obligations incurred by United States armed forces. A naturalized American citizen brought suit to recover damages to her home in Austria, which had been used by American troops as

[41]Consumers Union of U.S., Inc. v. Rogers, 352 F.Supp. 1319 (D.D.C. 1973).

[42]Consumers Union of U.S., Inc. v. Kissinger, 506 F.2d 136 (D.C. Cir. 1974), *cert. denied*, 421 U.S. 1004 (1975). See Michael H. Salisbury, "Presidential Authority in Foreign Trade: Voluntary Steel Import Quotas From a Constitutional Perspective," 15 *Va. J. Int'l L.* 179 (1974).

an officers' club. The United States Court of Claims held that the woman was entitled to compensation under the Fifth Amendment: "we think that there can be no doubt that an executive agreement, not being a transaction which is even mentioned in the Constitution, cannot impair Constitutional rights."[43] And in *Reid* v. *Covert* (1957) the Supreme Court declared invalid an executive agreement that permitted American military courts in Great Britain to rely on trial by court martial for offenses committed by American military personnel or their dependents. The plaintiff fought successfully for the constitutional right to a trial by jury. The court declared that an executive agreement with a foreign nation could not confer power "on the Congress, or on any other branch of Government, which is free from the restraints of the Constitution."[44]

Reporting

Prior to 1950, executive agreements were published in the U.S. Statutes at Large. Since that time they have been printed in *Treaties and Other International Agreements*.[45] A number of sensitive agreements, however, were never made known to Congress or to the public. During a Senate hearing in 1972, a State Department official was asked: "Now, you do have some executive agreements in force that are not listed in this publication, do you not?" He replied: "A very small percentage, classified."[46]

The extent of secret executive agreements was carefully documented by the Symington Subcommittee (of the Senate Foreign Relations Committee) during its hearings in 1969 and 1970. Field

[43]Seery v. United States, 127 F.Supp. 601, 606 (Ct. Cl. 1955).

[44]Reid v. Covert, 354 U.S. 1, 16 (1957). The treaty power is also subject to the restraints found in the Constitution: "It would not be contended that it extends so far as to authorize what the Constitution forbids, or a change in the character of the government or in that of one of the States, or a cession of any portion of the territory of the latter, without its consent"; Geofroy v. Riggs, 133 U.S. 258, 269 (1890).

[45]64 Stat. 979 (1950).

[46]*Congressional Oversight of Executive Agreements*, hearing before the Senate Committee on the Judiciary, 92d Cong., 2d Sess. 284 (1972).

trips by committee staff uncovered a number of significant agreements that United States administrations had made covertly with South Korea, Thailand, Laos, Ethiopia, and Spain, among others. Congress passed legislation in 1972 to keep itself informed about such agreements. The statute (known as the Case Act) requires the secretary of state to transmit to Congress within sixty days the text of "any international agreement, other than a treaty," to which the United States is a party. If the president decides that publication of an agreement would be prejudicial to national security he may transmit it to the Senate Committee on Foreign Relations and the House Committee on International Relations under an injunction of secrecy removable only by the president.[47]

Over the next few years several senators protested that the Nixon and Ford administrations had failed to comply with the Case Act. Senator James Abourezk testified that the "administration has admitted to both Senator Case and myself that there are some agreements they do not submit at all under the Case Act."[48] A GAO study in 1976 disclosed that a number of agreements (delicately called "arrangements" by the executive branch) had never been submitted to Congress or even to the Office of Treaty Affairs in the State Department.[49] A Senate study in 1977 discovered that 39 percent of the executive agreements entered into the previous year were submitted after the sixty-day period (171 out of 440). Thirty-five of those were submitted a *year* late.[50]

To improve administrative compliance with the Case Act, Congress passed legislation in 1977 requiring any department or agency of the United States government that enters into any international agreement on behalf of the United States to transmit to the Department of State the text of the agreement not later than twenty days after its signing.[51]

---

[47]86 Stat. 619 (1972), 1 U.S.C. 112b.

[48]*Early Warning System in Sinai*, hearing before the Senate Committee on Foreign Relations, 94th Cong., 1st Sess. 6 (1975).

[49]"U.S. Agreements with the Republic of Korea," ID-76-20 (Feb. 20, 1976).

[50]123 Cong. Rec. S8353 (daily ed. May 23, 1977).

[51]P.L. 95-45, 91 Stat. 224, sec. 5.

Congressional Control

Reporting after the fact is inadequate protection for Congress. Legislators want to be advised of significant agreements while they are in the process of being negotiated. The State Department's policy for executive agreements is contained in "Circular 175." Language adopted in 1955 (at the height of the Bricker Amendment drive to curb treaties and executive agreements) called for consultation with congressional leaders and committees whenever there was any "serious question" whether an international agreement required adoption as a treaty, a joint resolution, or executive agreement. Such consultation would be carried out "whenever circumstances permit." The language was changed in 1974, in the face of renewed congressional criticism, by deleting the word "serious." The 1974 version also added the following guideline for choosing between a treaty and an executive agreement: "The extent to which the agreement involves commitments or risks affecting the nation as a whole." The legal adviser to the State Department, speaking in 1972, commented that, "I think nobody questions that agreements which involve a basic political commitment, such as an undertaking to come to the defense of another country if it is attacked, should be cast in the form of a treaty in the constitutional sense."[52]

Three years later the State Department advised a Senate committee that if the president were to make an agreement to establish a military base, Congress might disapprove the involvement and deny any funds for constructing the facility. The administration witness added: "I have no doubt that Congress has the clear power to withhold funds, and I see no constitutional objection to their doing so, and in fact I think that is the principal safeguard for Congress' role in this difficult area."[53] Theoretically this is possible, but

[52]*Congressional Oversight, supra* note 46, at 256. For Circular 175 Procedure, the versions of Dec. 13, 1955 and June 6, 1969 are reprinted in those hearings at 289–306, while an amended version of Oct. 25, 1974 appears in *Congressional Oversight of Executive Agreements—1975,* hearings before the Senate Committee on the Judiciary, 94th Cong., 1st Sess. 279–301 (1975).

[53]*Congressional Oversight—1975, supra* note 52, at 223.

Congress finds it difficult to exercise its power of the purse if doing so means diplomatic embarrassment and humiliation to a president.

Instead of being politically trapped by executive initiatives, Congress needs an opportunity to pass judgment at an earlier stage, when more options are open. Legislation has been introduced to permit Congress to disapprove executive agreements during a waiting period. The emphasis behind this legislation is not so much the desire to veto executive agreements as to compel the executive branch to consult earlier with Congress to avoid a veto. A Senate bill, passed in 1974, provided that executive agreements would go into effect unless Congress passed a concurrent resolution of disapproval within sixty days.[54] The House did not act on the measure. It did not have much application anyway. Section 5 of the bill excluded from its reach "any executive agreement entered into by the President pursuant to a provision of the Constitution or prior authority given the President by treaty or law." Remove these categories and there is little left except agreements entered into subject to subsequent statutory approval. Different legislation was introduced in 1975 to allow for legislative disapproval simply by Senate resolution.[55] This bill was meant to preserve the Senate's prerogative in treaty making, but there is little likelihood that the House will count itself out of a role in executive agreements.

The State Department has opposed these legislative efforts. It estimates that more than 95 percent of executive agreements ("probably as high as 97 or 98 percent") are pursuant to congressional approval or implementation, or entered into in implementation of treaties.[56] This estimate indicates that the area of congressional concern is a minuscule 2 to 5 percent, but in fact it is considerably larger. An administration may enter into controversial agreements on the basis of highly questionable interpretations of statutes and

[54]S. Rept. No. 93-1286; 120 Cong. Rec. S19867 (daily ed. Nov. 21, 1974).

[55]121 Cong. Rec. S4467 (daily ed. March 20, 1975).

[56]*Transmittal of Executive Agreements to Congress*, hearings before the Senate Committee on Foreign Relations, 92d Cong., 1st Sess. 59 (1971).

treaties. Attorney General Jackson upheld the destroyers-bases deal of 1940 partly on statutory authority.[57] The Nixon administration, after entering into an executive agreement with Portugal in 1971 concerning the use of military facilities, contended that the agreement was made pursuant to Article 3 of the North Atlantic Treaty.[58] Subsequently the Senate passed a resolution insisting that the agreement should have been submitted as a treaty.[59]

Also included within the State Department's 95 to 98 percent category are executive agreements requiring congressional implementation. While in theory it is true that specific amounts for military and economic assistance are subject to congressional action, the general size of a financial commitment might be morally and politically fixed. This situation prevailed in 1975 when the Ford administration entered into the Sinai agreements, promising several billions of dollars in military and economic assistance to Israel and Egypt. The only agreement submitted to Congress for legislative action was an "early warning system" in the Sinai: 200 American civilian observers who would operate electronic equipment to monitor Israeli and Egyptian military activities.

The administration claimed that the two sets of agreements were legally distinct and that legislative support for the 200 technicians (at an annual cost of some $10 million) would not constitute an endorsement of the aid package. But hearings by Congress indicated that the two agreements were joined by a number of significant strands.[60] Congress added Section 5 to the Sinai agreements, stating that the authority for the technicians "does not signify approval of the Congress of any other agreement, understanding, or commitment made by the executive branch."[61] This was so much whistling

---

[57]39 Ops. Att'y Gen. 484, 488–493 (1940).

[58]*Executive Agreements with Portugal and Bahrain*, hearings before the Senate Committee on Foreign Relations, 92d Cong., 2d Sess. 7–8, 35–39 (1972).

[59]S. Rept. No. 92–632, 118 Cong. Rec. 6866–6870 (1972).

[60]*Middle East Agreements and the Early Warning System in Sinai*, hearings before the House Committee on International Relations, 94th Cong., 1st Sess. (1975); *Early Warning System in Sinai*, hearings before the Senate Committee on Foreign Relations, 94th Cong., 1st Sess. (1975).

[61]P.L. 94-110, 89 Stat. 572 (1975).

in the dark. The political process and momentum compelled Congress to appropriate essentially what the administration requested. Congress is faced with a difficult situation. It would like to acknowledge that the president has some reservoir of constitutional power to enter into executive agreements, but at the same time limit his ability to commit the nation militarily and financially. A bill introduced in the House in 1975 was specifically aimed at national commitments regarding the introduction, basing, or deployment of armed forces on foreign territory, as well as any military training, equipment, or financial or material resources provided to a foreign country. Such commitments would be subject to a sixty-day waiting period, during which time Congress could disapprove the commitments by passing a concurrent resolution.[62] The following year the Senate Foreign Relations Committee held hearings on legislation to require that any international agreement, involving a "significant political, military, or economic commitment" to a foreign country, be submitted to the Senate as a treaty for its advice and consent.[63]

The problem with both bills is their inability to define what is "significant" and worthy of legislative attention. Also implicit in the behavior of Congress in 1977 is the decision that legislation might not be necessary when the legislative and executive branches are under the control of the same political party. This attitude jars with the record of the twentieth century. It also puts Congress back in the position of making personal, instead of institutional, judgments.

---

[62]H.R. 4438: 121 Cong. Rec. H1451-1452 (daily ed. March 6, 1975) and *Congressional Review of International Agreements*, hearings before the House Committee on International Relations, 94th Cong., 2d Sess. (1976).

[63]*Treaty Powers Resolution*, hearings before the Senate Committee on Foreign Relations, 94th Cong., 2d Sess. (1976).

9

The War Power

Members of Congress can point to specific language in the Constitution for their authority to declare war and provide armed forces. More difficult to locate are the legal sources for presidential authority. Largely because of custom and events, presidents have been able to make war before Congress has had a chance to act. The history of the past two centuries is one of balancing and reconciling the two acivities: war declaring by Congress, war making by the president.

For constitutional as well as practical reasons, the two activities are supposed to work in concert. The president commands the troops but only Congress can provide them. Congress declares war but depends on the president to execute it. An associate of President Cleveland was once present when a delegation from Congress arrived at the White House with this announcement: "We have about decided to declare war against Spain over the Cuban question. Conditions are intolerable." Cleveland responded in blunt terms: "There will be no war with Spain over Cuba while I am President." A member of Congress protested that the Constitution gave Congress the right to declare war, but Cleveland countered that the Constitution also made him commander in chief. "I will not mobilize the army," he told the legislators. "I happen to know that we can buy the Island of Cuba from Spain for $100,000,000, and a war will cost vastly more than that and will entail another long list of pensioners. It would be an outrage to declare war."[1]

We can speculate on what would happen if Congress declared war with an unwilling president in office. Much more to the point,

[1]Robert McElroy, *Grover Cleveland*, II, 249–250 (1923).

214

however, is the fact that Congres rarely declares war. Although the war power has ben exercised hundreds of times by American presidents, only five wars have been declared and in only one (the War of 1812) did legislators actually debate the merits of entering into hostilities. In all other cases members simply recognized that a state of war did in fact exist.

COMMANDER IN CHIEF

The Constitution provides that the president "shall be Commander in Chief of the Army and Navy of the United States, and of the Militia of the several States, when called into the actual Service of the United States . . ." Scholars have long disagreed about whether this merely confers a title (commander in chief) or implies additional powers for the president. Justice Jackson underscored the elusive nature of this power by remarking that the commander-in-chief clause implies "something more than an empty title. But just what authority goes with the name has plagued presidential advisers who would not waive or narrow it by nonassertion yet cannot say where it begins or ends."[2]

To some scholars the commander-in-chief clause should be construed narrowly. Raoul Berger writes: "How narrowly the function was conceived may be gathered from the fact that in appointing George Washington Commander-in-Chief, the Continental Congress made sure . . . that he was to be 'its creature . . . in every respect.'" Instructions drafted by John Adams, R. H. Lee, and Edward Rutledge told Washington that he was "punctually to observe and follow such orders and directions . . . as you shall receive from this or a future Congress."[3] Citing these precedents is of little value for at least two reasons. First, they ignore the extensive delegations that the Continental Congress soon found necessary. For example, an order to General Washington in 1775 stated that

> whereas all particulars cannot be foreseen, nor positive instructions for such emergencies so before hand given but that

[2]Youngstown Co. v. Sawyer, 343 U.S. 579, 641 (1952).
[3]Raoul Berger, *Executive Privilege* 62 (1974).

many things must be left to your prudent and discreet management, as occurrences may arise upon the place, or from time to time may fall out, you are therefore upon all such accidents or any occasions that may happen, to use your best circumspection . . ."[4]

Second, the precedents are from the wrong period. The office of president of 1787 was created as a separate and independent branch, not as a mere agent of Congress (its status under the Continental Congress).

The need to trust in executive judgment and discretion, rather than the specific instuctions drafted for Washington at the start of the Revolutionary War, more accurately represents the understanding of the framers. At the Philadelphia convention they recognized an implied power of the president to "repel sudden attacks." When it was proposed that Congress be empowered to "make war," Charles Pinckney objected that legislative proceedings "were too slow" for the safety of the country in an emergency. He anticipated that Congress would meet but once a year. Madison and Elbridge Gerry moved to insert "declare" for "make," thereby "leaving to the Executive the power to repel sudden attacks." Their motion carried.[5]

Alexander Hamilton appeared to offer a modest definition of commander in chief powers. In Federalist 69 he said that the office "would amount to nothing more than the supreme command and direction of the military and naval forces, as first general and admiral of the Confederacy . . ." But as Washington's military aide during the war, surely Hamilton knew quite well that "command and direction" are more than clerical tasks. They can determine the scope and duration of war. As the Supreme Court noted in 1850, the president as commander in chief "is authorized to direct the movements of the naval and military forces placed by law at his

[4]*Journals of the Continental Congress*, II, 101 (1905). See W. Taylor Reveley, III, "Constitutional Allocation of the War Powers Between the President and Congress: 1787–1788," 15 *Va. J. Int'l L.* 73, 91–93 (1974).

[5]Farrand, *Records*, II, 318–319.

command, and to employ them in the manner he may deem most effectual to harass and conquer and subdue the enemy."[6]

Powers Put to Use

Presidential invoking of the commander-in-chief power has frequently been controversial. A celebrated example was Lincoln's conduct during the Civil War. In his message to Congress in 1861, he claimed that the "war power" was his for the purpose of suppressing the rebellion. No choice was left, he said, "but to call out the war power of the Government and so to resist force employed for its destruction by force for its preservation." With "deepest regret" he found the duty of employing the "war power in defense of the Government forced upon him."[7] It was under the "war power" (actually a fusion of legislative and executive powers) that Lincoln took his extraordinary actions to preserve the Union. Congress supported his initiatives, as did a sharply divided Supreme Court in *The Prize Cases*.[8]

Another controversial use of presidential power was Franklin Roosevelt's during World War II. More than 100,000 Japanese (about two-thirds of them natural-born United States citizens) were herded into "relocation centers" after Roosevelt issued an executive order, based in part on "the authority vested in me as President of the United States, and Commander in Chief of the Army and Navy . . ."[9] Bitter oposition came from members of the Supreme Court. Justice Murphy, concurring in *Hirabayashi* (1943), said that the initial curfew action against the Japanese Americans "bears a melancholy resemblance to the treatment accorded to the members of the Jewish race in Germany and in other parts of Europe." In

[6]Fleming v. Page, 50 U.S. (9 How.) 602, 614 (1850). Also see the dissenting opinion by Chief Justice Chase—joined by Justices Wayne, Swayne, and Miller— in Ex parte Milligan, 4 Wall. 2 (1866).

[7]Richardson, Messages and Papers, VII, 3224–3225, 3232 (July 4, 1861).

[8]Congressional sanction was given in 12 Stat. 284, 326 (1861). The Prize Cases, 2 Black 635 (1863). See also Edward S. Corwin, *The President* 228–234, 448–453 (1957).

[9]E.O. 9066, 7 Fed. Reg. 1407 (1942).

spite of such misgivings, a unanimous court nonetheless supported the curfew.[10] *Korematsu* (1944), splitting the court six to three, upheld the exclusion of Japanese Americans and their relocation to detention camps. Murphy, one of the dissenters, protested that the exclusion order resulted from an erroneous assumption of "racial guilt" found in the commanding general's report, which referred to all individuals of Japanese descent as "subversives" belonging to "an enemy race" and whose "racial strains are undiluted." Jackson, also dissenting, concluded that "here is an attempt to make an otherwise innocent act a crime merely because this prisoner is the son of parents as to whom he had no choice, and belongs to a race from which there is no way to resign."[11]

A third controversial invoking of the commander-in-chief power was when President Truman seized the steel mills in 1952, in the wake of a labor-management dispute, as part of his efforts to prosecute the Korean War. He did so on the basis of authority vested in him as president "by the Constitution and laws of the United States, and as President of the United States and Commander-in-Chief of the armed forces of the United States." The Supreme Court struck down this use of power in a six-to-three decision, but there were as many views as there were justices. Each of the six representing the majority wrote separate opinions. Justice Jackson divided the commander-in-chief power along an outward-inward axis: "I should indulge the widest latitude of interpretation to sustain his exclusive function to command the instruments of national force, at least when turned against the outside world for the security of our society. But, when it is turned inward, not because of rebellion but because of a lawful economic struggle between industry and labor, it should have no such indulgence . . ."[12] This outward-inward distinction would be revived two decades later in cases in-

---

[10]Hirabayashi v. United States, 320 U.S. 81 (1943).

[11]Korematsu v. United States, 323 U.S. 214 (1944). See Nanette Dembitz, "Racial Discrimination and the Military Judgment: The Supreme Court's Korematsu and Endo Decisions," 45 *Colum. L. Rev.* 175 (1945) and Eugene V. Rostow, "The Japanese American Cases—A Disaster," 54 *Yale L. J.* 489 (1945).

[12]Youngstown Co. v. Sawyer, 343 U.S. 579, 645 (1952).

volving electronic surveillance for national-security purposes (pp. 222–226).

"Defensive War"

Throughout the nineteenth century the concept of defensive war was limited mainly to protective actions along the borders of the United States. Naval wars against the Barbary pirates and France stretched those boundaries, but such actions were infrequent. Nevertheless, these conflicts favored presidential power. Hostilities could exist in either a perfect state of war (formally marked by a declaration from Congress) or an imperfect state of war (more confined and limited in its nature and extent).[13]

President Polk invited war in 1846 by sending troops into disputed territory along the Texas-Mexican border. Two years later the House of Representatives censured him for "unnecessarily and unconstitutionally" starting a war.[14] President McKinley defended intervention in Cuba in 1898 by describing the conflict as "right at our door."[15] These were isolated events, however. Only after World War II did the idea of defensive war take a quantum jump, both conceptually and in practice. American bases were dispersed around the globe. Military commitments became imbedded in various defense pacts and treaties, often with little visibility to Congress or the public. No longer did the administration confine the notion of "repelling sudden attacks" to military actions on our continental boundaries. The legal adviser to the State Depatment offered this scenario in 1966:

> Under the Constitution, the President, in addition to being Chief Executive, is Commander in Chief of the Army and Navy. He holds the prime responsibility for the conduct of United States foreign relations. These duties carry very broad powers, including the power to deploy American forces abroad and commit them to military operations when the

[13]Bas v. Tingy, 4 U.S. (4 Dall.) 36 (1800) and Talbot v. Seeman, 1 Cr. 1 (1801).
[14]Cong. Globe, 30th Cong., 1st Sess. 95 (1848).
[15]Richardson, *Messages and Papers*, XIII, 6289 (April 11, 1898).

President deems such action necessary to maintain the security and defense of the United States. . . .

In 1787 the world was a far larger place, and the framers probably had in mind attacks upon the United States. In the 20th century, the world has grown much smaller. An attack on a country far from our shores can impinge directly on the nation's security.[16]

This idea of a shrinking globe has been part of the conceptual shift behind the enlargement of presidential power. We apply the concept to travel and communication with neutral effect, but constitutionally it shrinks not merely the globe but congressional power as well. In 1962, after the discovery of missile sites in Cuba, President Kennedy announced that the Western Hemisphere ("as far north as Hudson Bay, Canada, and as far south as Lima, Peru") was in danger. The launching of any nuclear missile from Cuba, against any nation in the Western Hemisphere, would be regarded by the administration as "an attack by the Soviet Union on the United States, requiring a full retaliatory response upon the Soviet Union."[17] When President Johnson requested the Tonkin Gulf Resolution two years later, he argued that a threat in Southeast Asia "is a threat to all, and a threat to us."[18] Often these "defensive actions" are intertwined with explanations that the president must act to protect American lives and property (pp. 226–231).

Delegated Emergency Powers

Once the nation is engaged in war, the reservoir of presidential power fills rapidly as Congress delegates vast new duties and responsibilities to the executive branch. It is characteristic of this legislation to offer little in the way of guidelines for administrative action, and yet the courts regularly uphold the statutes.[19] Further-

---

[16]*Dep't of State Bull.*, LIV, 484 (1966).

[17]*Public Papers of the Presidents, 1962*, at 485.

[18]*Public Papers of the Presidents, 1963–1964*, at II, 931.

[19]For example, United States v. Bethlehem Steel, 315 U.S. 289 (1942); Bowles v. Willingham, 321 U.S. 503 (1944); Yakus v. United States, 321 U.S. 414 (1944); and Lichter v. United States, 344 U.S. 742 (1947).

more, these delegations remain in the hands of the president long after hostilities have ended, long after American troops have returned home. Here too the courts defer to the chief executive in determining when a state of war is over.[20]

Other statutes contain latent or dormant authority for the president, ready to spring to life whenever he issues a proclamation declaring the nation to be in a state of emergency. It came as a surprise to many members of Congress to learn in 1971 that the United States had been in a state of declared national emergency ever since March 9, 1933, when President Roosevelt proclaimed an emergency at the time of the banking crisis. Also still in effect were national emergencies proclaimed by President Truman on December 16, 1950 (after China's entry into the Korean War) and by President Nixon on March 23, 1970, and August 15, 1971.

These discoveries prompted the Senate to establish a special committee to study the possibility of terminating the states of declared national emergency. A committee report in 1973 disclosed that the four proclamations mentioned above had brought to life 470 provisions of federal law. Each statute extended to the president some facet of control over the lives of American citizens. Among other things, he could seize property, organize and control the means of production, institute martial law, control all transportation and communication, and restrict travel.[21]

In 1976 Congress passed the National Emergencies Act to restrict the use of presidential emergency powers. Its general thrust is to terminate emergency authorities two years from the date when the act became law (September 14, 1976). In future national emergencies the president has to publish the declaration in the Federal Register. Congress may terminate the national emergency by passing a concurrent resolution. To prevent emergencies from lingering for decades without congressional attention or action, the 1976

---

[20]For example, United States v. Anderson, 9 Wall. 56 (1870); The Protector, 12 Wall. 700 (1872); Stewart v. Kahn, 11 Wall. 493 (1870); Hijo v. United States, 194 U.S. 315 (1904); Hamilton v. Kentucky Distilleries, 251 U.S. 146 (1919); Commercial Trust v. Miller, 262 U.S. 51 (1923); Chastleton Corp. v. Sinclair, 264 U.S. 533 (1924); and Woods v Miller, 333 U.S. 138 (1948).

[21]S. Rept. No. 549, 93d Cong., 1st Sess. iii (1973).

legislation includes an action-forcing mechanism. No later than six months after a national emergency is declared by the president, and at least every six months thereafter while the emergency continues, each house of Congress has to meet to consider a vote on a concurrent resolution to determine whether the emergency should be terminated.[22]

The National Emergencies Act exempted certain provisions of law, including Section 5(b) of the Trading With the Enemy Act, originally enacted in 1917. Over the years this provision had been the basis for controlling domestic as well as international financial transactions. Its reach went far beyond trading with the enemy, and it became a source of presidential authority in peacetime as well as wartime. For example, it was under Section 5(b) that President Roosevelt declared a national emergency in 1933 and announced a bank holiday to prevent hoarding of gold. Presidents Johnson and Nixon also invoked this clause to justify other controversial actions.

Legislation in 1977, as passed by Congress, limits the use of the Trading With the Enemy Act to time of war *as declared by Congress.* A second set of powers, more restricted than those available during time of war, would be given to the president upon his declaration of a national emergency in time of peace. The legislation subjects these powers to the procedural restrictions of the National Emergencies Act (including an opportunity for Congress to terminate the emergency by passing a concurrent resolution).[23]

Another issue of constitutional dimensions concerns wiretapping and electronic surveillance by executive officials without a warrant. How does this practice square with the Fourth Amendment's

[22]P.L. 94-412, 90 Stat. 1255 (1976). See *The National Emergencies Act (Public Law 94-412), Source Book: Legislative History, Texts, and Other Documents,* Senate Committee on Government Operations and Senate Special Committee on National Emergencies and Delegated Emergency Powers, 94th Cong., 2d Sess. (Comm. Print Nov. 1976).

[23]H. Rept. No. 459, 95th Cong., 1st Sess. (1977) and 123 Cong. Rec. H6868-6872 (daily ed. July 12, 1977). See *Trading With the Enemy: Legislative and Executive Documents Concerning Regulation of International Transactions in Time of Declared National Emergency,* prepared by the House Committee on International Relations, 94th Cong., 2d Sess. (Comm. Print Nov. 1976). Enacted as P.L. 95-223 (Dec. 28, 1977).

requirement that a judicial warrant be obtained, upon probable cause, prior to a search and seizure? Various administrations, beginning in the 1920s but especially from the time of Franklin D. Roosevelt forward, have resorted to wiretapping for the purpose of controlling domestic crime and protecting national security. Differing interpretations by all three branches have compounded and confounded the problem.

Section 605 of the Communications Act of 1934 made it a crime to intercept wire or radio communications.[24] This restriction was reinforced by Supreme Court decisions in 1937 and 1939, holding that the statute applied to federal agents and prohibited information obtained by wiretapping from being introduced as trial evidence.[25] In 1940 President Roosevelt, in a directive to his attorney general, maintained that the decisions did not apply to "grave matters involving the defense of the nation."[26] Subsequent actions by presidents, courts, and Congress left unclear whether the president possessed inherent power to authorize wiretapping and electronic surveillance when needed for national security.[27]

Title III of the Omnibus Crime Control Act of 1968 authorized the use of wiretaps in cases of domestic crimes, but only after the issuance of a judicial warrant based on probable cause. The act did not attempt to cover "national security" wiretaps. Nothing in the 1968 legislation, or in Section 605 of the Communications Act of 1934, was meant to limit the

> constitutional power of the President to take such measures as he deems necessary to protect the Nation against actual or potential attack or other hostile acts of a foreign power, to obtain foreign intelligence information deemed essential to the security of the United States, or to protect national security information against foreign intelligence activities.[28]

[24]48 Stat. 1103 (1934), 47 U.S.C. 605 (1970).

[25]Nardone v. United States, 302 U.S. 379 (1937) and Nardone v. United States, 308 U.S. 338 (1939).

[26]Reprinted in Zweibon v. Mitchell, 516 F.2d 594, 673–674 (D.C. Cir. 1975).

[27]See *Warrantless Wiretapping and Electronic Surveillance*, report by the Senate Committees on Foreign Relations and the Judiciary, 94th Cong., 1st Sess. (Comm. Print Feb. 1975).

[28]82 Stat. 214, 18 U.S.C. 2511(3) (1970).

In short, for more than a quarter of a century, presidents had authorized warrantless surveillance without specific guidelines from Congress or the courts. No one could say with certainty whether the authority was delegated (by implication) or inherent in the president's office.

Of major significance in defining the president's power is the 1972 Supreme Court's holding in *United States* v. *United States District Court* (also known as *Keith*). The Nixon administration had approved wiretaps to gather intelligence information deemed necessary to protect the nation from attempts by *domestic organizations* "to attack and subvert the existing structure of the Government." The actions were taken in the name of the president's inherent power to protect national security. The court, voting eight to zero, held that Fourth Amendment freedoms cannot be guaranteed if domestic security surveillances are conducted solely at the discretion of the executive branch. For such surveillance to be constitutional, a warrant issued by the judiciary is essential. The court regarded the case before it as purely a domestic matter, for no evidence existed that the organization was involved, directly or indirectly, with a foreign power. The court offered no guidance with regard to the president's surveillance power over "the activities of foreign powers, within or without this country."[29]

One week after the court had limited domestic surveillance, however, it refused to decide whether the army's surveillance of domestic activities constituted a chilling effect on First Amendment rights. Divided five to four, the court held that the issue as presented was not a justiciable controversy. It declined to act as a continuing monitor over the wisdom and soundness of executive action, stating that "such a role is appropriate for the Congress acting through its committees and the 'power of the purse'; it is not the role of the judiciary, absent actual present or immediately threatened injury resulting from that unlawful governmental action."[30] It should be noted that some lower courts held that the president did have inherent authority, over and above the Warrant Clause of the Fourth

[29]United States v. United States District Court, 407 U.S. 297, 308 (1972).
[30]Laird v. Tatum, 408 U.S. 1, 15 (1972).

Amendment, to order warrantless wiretaps for the purpose of gathering foreign intelligence.[31]

Before long the federal courts faced a hybrid case that did not fit either the domestic sector (governed by *Keith*) or foreign affairs. The Jewish Defense League (JDL), originally founded to protect Jews in New York neighborhoods, expanded its interests to include the treatment of Soviet Jews and Soviet emigration policies. Tactics of the group ranged from peaceful picketing of the Soviet mission at the United Nations to vandalizing Soviet offices in New York and Washington and bombing Soviet airline offices in New York City. The Nixon administration claimed that the JDL, although a domestic organization, threatened the president's conduct of foreign relations. The Justice Department began wiretapping telephone lines, without a warrant, at the JDL's New York office.

In *Zweibon* v. *Mitchell* (1975), a circuit court held that the wiretap on the JDL violated the Fourth Amendment. The court did not accept the general justification of dispensing with warrants in foreign security surveillance. A majority held that warrants were necessary, at least in cases where a domestic organization was neither an agent nor a collaborator of a foreign power.[32] The court also concluded that the executive practice of conducting national security surveillance without a warrant had been supported by statutory interpretations, not by claims of inherent presidential power.

Throughout this litigation on national security wiretaps the courts were telegraphing Congress for assistance. The intent of the Communications Act of 1934 had been the subject of much speculation, as was Title III of the Omnibus Crime Control Act of 1968.

[31]United States v. Butenko, 494 F. 2d 593 (3d Cir. 1974), *cert. denied, sub. nom.* Ivanov v. United States, 419 U.S. 881 (1974); United States v. Brown, 484 F.2d 418 (5th Cir. 1973); and United States v. Hoffman, 334 F.Supp. 504 (D.D.C. 1971). See also United States v. Clay, 430 F.2d 165 (5th Cir. 1970). In United States v. Ehrlichman, 376 F.Supp. 29 (D.D.C. 1974) a federal district court held illegal a warrantless break-in of a psychiatrist's office—an action justified by the defendants on the grounds of national security.

[32]Zweibon v. Mitchell, 516 F.2d 594, 614 (D.C. Cir. 1975), *cert. denied,* 425 U.S. 944 (1976). See Note, "The Fourth Amendment and Judicial Review of Foreign Intelligence Wiretapping: *Zweibon* v. *Mitchell,*" 45 *G.W. L. Rev.* 55 (1976).

Two roads lay open: either define by statute the scope of executive action as a delegated power, or else recognize that the power to wiretap without a warrant derives from Article II of the Constitution.

Legislation has been introduced to place statutory restrictions on executive action. The basic thrust is to require a judicial warrant, based on the "probable cause" standard, before a president can engage in electronic surveillance for purposes of obtaining foreign intelligence information. A limited number of federal judges appointed by the chief justice would review applications submitted by federal agents for electronic surveillance within the United States. Consistent with *Zweibon*, the legislation would limit surveillance to foreign powers or agents of foreign powers working as members of that power's intelligence network. The general outlines of this legislation have found support from both the Ford and Carter administrations.[33]

LIFE AND PROPERTY ACTIONS

Presidents, with neither statutory authority nor a declaration of war, have used force abroad on many occasions, ostensibly to protect life and porperty. They have justified their actions on the basis of executive responsibilities they find inherent in the Constitution. Expeditions of this nature number around two hundred although if the total were to include actions that merely represent a show of force (such as deploying a battleship off a coast), it would be larger.[34]

[33]For example, see comments of executive and legislative leaders at *Wkly Comp. Pres. Doc.*, XIII, 749–754 (May 18, 1977) and 123 Cong. Rec. S7856–7866 (daily ed. May 18, 1977); but see also criticism of legislation by Congressman Drinan, 123 Cong. Rec. H5420–5424 (daily ed. June 3, 1977).

[34]J. Terry Emerson, "War Powers Legislation," 74 *W. Va. L. Rev.* 53 (1972) and his "Constitutional Authority of the President to Use Armed Forces in Defense of American Lives, Liberty, and Property," reprinted at 121 Cong. Rec. S7526 (daily ed. May 6, 1975). For further details see James Grafton Rogers, *World Policing and the Constitution* (1945);

The constitutionality of this presidential activity was reviewed by a circuit court in 1860. In 1854 an American vessel had been dispatched to Greytown (now San Juan del Norte), Nicaragua, after an affront to an American diplomat and some property losses suffered by an American firm. When the commander of the ship decided that local authorities had failed to make appropriate amends, he bombarded the town and sent troops ashore to wreak further vengeance. A resident sued for damages to his property. The court, in *Durand* v. *Hollins*, came to the commander's defense:

> as it respects the interposition of the Executive abroad, for the protection of the lives or property of the citizen, the duty must, of necessity, rest in the discretion of the President. Acts of lawless violence, or of threatened violence to the citizen or his property, cannot be anticipated and provided for; and the protection, to be effectual or of any avail, may, not unfrequently, require the most prompt and decided action.[35]

Bland legalese cannot hide the ferocity of the Greytown bombing. A more measured and deliberate policy was promised by legislation in 1868, directing the president to demand from a foreign government the reason for depriving any American citizen of liberty. If it appeared wrongful and in violation of the rights of American citizenship, the president was to demand the citizen's release. If the foreign government delayed or refused, the president could use such means, "not amounting to acts of war," as he thought necessary and proper to obtain the release.[36]

This statute did not put an end to heavy-handed American actions abroad. Theodore Roosevelt, William Howard Taft, and

---

Background Information on the Use of United States Armed Forces in Foreign Countries, prepared for the House Committee on Foreign Affairs, 91st Cong., 2d Sess. 50–57 (Comm. Print 1970); and R. Ernest Dupuy and William H. Baumer, *The Little Wars of the United States* (1968). Show-of-force actions were reported in the *Washington Post*, Jan. 3, 1977, at A1:4.

[35]Durand v. Hollins, 4 Blatch. 451, 454 (1860). A description of the bombing appears in Milton Offutt, "The Protection of Citizens Abroad by the Armed Forces of the United States," *Johns Hopkins Univ. Studies in Hist. and Pol. Sci.*, Series XLIV, No. 4, at 32–34 (1928).

[36]15 Stat. 223 (1868); 22 U.S.C. 1732 (1970).

other presidents resorted to force not simply for the purpose of protecting American lives and property but to pursue foreign policy objectives. Woodrow Wilson, taking the Greytown bombardment as an acceptable precedent, ordered American forces to occupy Veracruz in 1914. In a message delivered to a joint session of Congress, he stressed the need for immediate action, offering this legal analysis:

> No doubt I could do what is necessary in the circumstances to enforce respect for our Government without recourse to the congress, and yet not exceed my constitutional powers as President; but I do not wish to act in a matter possibly of so grave consequence except in close conference and co-operation with both the Senate and the House.[37]

The House acted with alacrity to authorize the use of armed force, but when senators had the audacity to pause for one day to think about what they were doing, Wilson went ahead and ordered landing operations by the marines. The following day—two days after his request—Congress passed a joint resolution justifying the president's use of force. This episode, which began with a trivial incident involving U.S. seamen in Tampico, escalated in the bombardment of Veracruz, American occupation for seven months, and the downfall of the Mexican president, Victoriano Huerto. The following year Wilson intervened in Haiti to secure a more acceptable government there, while confiding to his secretary of state that "we have not the legal authority to do what we apparently ought to do . . ."[38] American troops were to remain in Haiti until 1934.

Recent decades have lengthened the list of life-and-property actions. President Eisenhower sent troops into Lebanon in 1958 "to protect American lives and by their presence there to encourage the Lebanese government in defense of Lebanese sovereignty and integrity."[39] President Johnson intervened in the Dominican Republic in 1965 to prevent what he feared would be a communist takeover,

[37]Richardson, *Messages and Papers*, XVI, 7936.

[38]Arthur S. Link, *Wilson, The Struggle for Neutrality* 536 (1960). For the joint resolution of support for Veracruz action, see 38 Stat. 770 (1914). A vivid account is given by Robert E. Quirk in *An Affair of Honor: Woodrow Wilson and the Occupation of Veracruz* (1962).

[39]*Public Papers of the Presidents, 1958*, at 549.

though he later explained that "99 percent of our reason for going in there was to try to provide protection for these American lives and for the lives of other nationals."[40] President Nixon justified his invasion of Cambodia in 1970 on the ground that enemy actions "clearly endanger the lives of Americans who are in Vietnam now and would constitute an unacceptable risk to those who will be there after withdrawal of another 150,000"[41] When the Nixon administration provided support for the South Vietnamese invasion of Laos the following year, the State Department said that the action would "protect American lives."[42] President Ford, as will be described later, used troops for evacuations from Southeast Asia and for the rescue of the *Mayaguez* vessel.

Contemporary use of force cannot be justified on the basis of gunboat diplomacy and forays into Mexico or the Caribbean a half century ago. Ratification of the United Nations Charter imposes restrictions on member states that can be ignored only at substantial political cost. Article 2, Paragraph 4 states that all members "shall refrain in their international relations from the threat or use of force against the territorial integrity or political independence of any state, or in any other manner inconsistent with the purposes of the United Nations." There are only two exceptions: the right of individual or collective self-defense against an armed attack (Article 51) and collective action taken by the United Nations to deal with serious disturbances of the peace. Even the Nixon administration, after its intervention in Cambodia in 1970, acknowledged that whatever the practices prior to 1945, adoption of the UN Charter "changed the situation by imposing new and important limitations on the use of armed force."[43] A body of international legal norms has developed since 1945 that constrain the actions of sovereign nations.

Early drafts of the War Powers Resolution of 1973 (to be dis-

[40]*Public Papers of the Presidents, 1965,* II, at 616.

[41]*Wkly Comp. Pres. Doc.,* VI, 597 (1970).

[42]*New York Times,* Feb. 9, 1971, at 17:6. For a discussion of the constitutional limits when force is used to protect troops, see 65 *Am. J. Int'l L.* 34–35, 79–80 (1971).

[43]Statement by John R. Stevenson, Legal Adviser to the Department of State, May 29, 1970, reprinted at 64 *Am J. Int'l L.* 933, 940 (1970).

cussed later in this chapter) recognized the responsibility of the president to protect life and property. A bill introduced by Senator Jacob Javits in 1971 would have allowed the president to use armed force "to protect the lives and property, as may be required, of United States nationals abroad." Javits later deleted the words "and property" for fear that they might be interpreted in a nineteenth century sense of protecting American business investments abroad.[44] The rest of the language disappeared in the House-Senate compromise that became law.

This lack of legislative authority, together with other statutory restrictions on the use of force in Southeast Asia, created an awkward and confusing situation in 1975. President Ford asked Congress to clarify the statutory restrictions so that he could evacuate American citizens and foreign nationals from South Vietnam and Cambodia. He gave Congress nine days to act.[45] Instead of trying to act while a presidential timer ticked away, party leaders in Congress should have issued a statement saying that the president had enough authority for the evacuations, provided he used a minimum of force. Ford had already announced that the War Powers Resolution, as he interpreted it, gave the president "certain limited authority to protect American lives. And to that extent, I will use that law."[46] Why then ask Congress for legislative authority? The issue was complicated by the need to rescue foreign nationals as well, but it was politically unreasonable and unrealistic to expect Congress to legislate on such an explosive issue in nine days.

Members agonized for weeks, trying to discover the right language that would give Ford the authority he wanted without leading to military reinvolvement in Southeast Asia. Legislators were whipsawed by conflicting feelings. On the one hand they wanted to relate all military operations to the procedures of the War Powers Resolution. On the other hand they were apprehensive that any legislation, no matter how meticulously drafted, would become an-

---

[44]*War Powers Resolution*, hearings before the Senate Committee on Foreign Relations, 92d Cong., 1st Sess. 35–36, 95–96, 128 (1971).

[45]*Wkly Comp. Pres. Doc.*, XI, 363 (April 10, 1975).

[46]*Id.* at 329 (April 3, 1975).

achronous and ambiguous due to the rapidly changing situation in Southeast Asia.

While Congress anguished over the wording of the legislation, Ford went ahead with the evacuations from Cambodia and South Vietnam. In each case he based his action on the president's "executive power" under the Constitution and on his authority as commander in chief.[47] He took these actions before Congress could deliver the "clarifying authority." But even though the evacuations were over, some members of Congress argued that the legislation should be passed. They reasoned that the president had conducted the evacuations within the limitations of the legislation under consideration (although Ford cited only constitutional sources in his reports); Congress should therefore enact the legislation to establish its authority and legalize the president's action. For such legislators the integrity of the War Powers Resolution was at stake. Others, however, believed that the bill was moot because of the evacuations. Passage of the legislation would merely lift the restrictions that barred reintroduction of troops into Southeast Asia. The House, capping three weeks of legislative frenzy, voted down the conference report. This was an ignominious finale to an ill-conceived legislative exercise.[48]

Following these evacuations and Ford's rescue of the *Mayaguez* crew, Senator Thomas Eagleton introduced legislation explicitly recognizing the president's right to protect lives (but not property). It stipulated various conditions limiting this grant of power: the citizens to be rescued would have to be involuntarily held with the express or tacit consent of the foreign government; there would have to be a direct and imminent threat to their lives; the foreign government either could not or would not protect the individuals; and the evacuations would have to take place as expeditiously as possible and with a minimum of force.[49] Eagleton's proposal, along with other amendments to the War Powers Resolution, has not been acted upon by Congress.

[47]H. Doc. Nos. 105 and 124, 94th Cong., 1st Sess. (1975).

[48]121 Cong. Rec. H3540-3551 (daily ed. May 1, 1975).

[49]*Id.* at S8825-8828 (daily ed. May 21, 1975).

THE WAR POWERS RESOLUTION OF 1973

Because of continuing controversy about the war power, especially as exercised by Lyndon Johnson and Richard Nixon, Congress passed the War Powers Resolution of 1973. Gerald Ford, after leaving the presidency, claimed that the War Powers Resolution "seeks by simple legislation to codify the military powers of the President, spelling out exactly what he can and cannot do, and how, and under what circumstances, to defend the United States and its citizens from international danger."[50] This is a good description of what the Senate tried to do, but not of the version of the resolution that became public law. A review of House and Senate actions serves to clarify this point.

Legislative History

In 1970 the House of Representatives conceded a measure of war prerogatives to the President. A war powers resolution, passed by a vote of 289 to 39, recognized that the president "in certain extraordinary and emergency circumstances has the authority to defend the United States and its citizens without specific prior authorization by the Congress." Instead of trying to define the precise conditions under which presidents may act, the House relied on procedural safeguards. The president would be required, "whenever feasible," to consult with Congress before sending American forces into armed conflict. He was also to report the circumstances necessitating the action; the constitutional, legislative, and treaty provisions authorizing the action, together with his reasons for not seeking specific prior congressional authorization; and the estimated scope of activities.[51] The Senate did not act on the measure.

Both houses later passed war powers resolutions that went be-

[50]Address to the University of Kentucky, April 11, 1977, reprinted at 123 Cong. Rec. S6174–6177 (daily ed. April 21, 1977). Quoted remark appears at S6175, col. 3.

[51]116 Cong. Rec. 37398–37408 (1970). Passed again the next year under suspension of the rules (requiring two-thirds support), 117 Cong. Rec. 28870–28878 (1971).

yond mere reporting requirements. The House of Representat es, following its earlier example, did not try to define or codify presidential war powers. It directed the president "in every possible instance" to consult with Congress before sending forces into hostilities or situations where hostilities might be imminent. If unable to do so, he was to report to Congress within seventy-two hours, setting forth the circumstances and details of his action. Unless Congress declared war within 120 days, or specifically authorized the use of force, the president had to terminate the commitment and remove the troops. Congress could also direct disengagement at any time during the 120-day period by passing a concurrent resolution.[52]

The Senate attempted to spell out the conditions under which presidents could take unilateral action. Armed force could be used in three situations: (1) to repel an armed attack upon the United States, its territories and possessions, retaliate in the event of such an attack, and forestall the direct and imminent threat of such an attack; (2) to repel an armed attack against U.S. armed forces located outside the United States, its territories and possessions, and forestall the direct and imminent threat of such an attack; and (3) to rescue endangered American citizens and nationals in foreign countries or at sea. The first situation (except for the final clause) conforms to the understanding developed at the Philadelphia convention. The other situations reflect the changes that have occurred in the concept of defensive war and life-and-property actions.

The Senate bill required the president to cease military action unless Congress, within thirty days, specifically authorized the president to continue. A separate provision allowed him to sustain military operations beyond the thirty-day limit if he determined that "unavoidable military necessity respecting the safety" of the armed forces required their continued use for purposes of "bringing about a prompt disengagement."[53] This effort to codify presidential war powers carried a number of risks. Because of ambiguities in the language, legislation might widen presidential power instead of restricting it. Executive officials could interpret in broad fashion such

[52]119 Cong. Rec. 24653–24708 (1973).
[53]*Id.* at 25051–25120.

terms as "necessary and appropriate retaliatory actions," "imminent threat," and "endangered citizens."

The two houses presented a compromise measure to President Nixon. He vetoed the bill primarily because he regarded it as impractical and dangerous to fix in a statute the procedure by which president and Congress should share the war power. He also believed that the legislation encroached upon the president's constitutional responsibilities as commander in chief. He reminded Congress that the "only way in which the constitutional powers of a branch of the Government can be altered is by amending the Constitution—and any attempt to make such alterations by legislation alone is clearly without force."[54] Both houses mustered a two-thirds majority to override the veto: the House narrowly (284 to 135), the Senate by a more comfortable margin (75 to 18).[55]

Although the War Powers Resolution of 1973 overcame a veto, it has not survived doubts about its quality and effectiveness. Some of the congressional support for the resolution was based on party politics and symbolic value rather than on its contents. Consider the voting record of fifteen members of the House.[56] After voting against the House bill and the conference version, they inconsistently voted to override the veto. If they opposed the legislation because they considered it inadequate or unsound, why vote to make it public law?

This reversal occurred in part because of fear that a vote to sustain might lend credence to the views advanced in Nixon's veto message. Despite serious misgivings about the quality of the bill, some legislators concluded that congressional inaction could be interpreted as a concession to the constitutional claims of Nixon (and Johnson). Other legislators used the override to propel the House toward impeachment of Nixon. One of those who voted against the House resolution and the conference version but the in favor of overriding the veto—Democrat Bella Abzug of New York—ad-

[54]*Public Papers of the Presidents, 1973,* at 893.

[55]P.L. 93-148, 87 Stat. 555 (1973).

[56]Representatives Abzug, Drinan, Duncan, Flynt, Harsha, Hechler (W. Va.), Holtzman, Hungate, Landrum, Lott, Maraziti, Milford, Natcher, Stubblefield, and Whitten.

vised her colleagues that "This could be a turning point in the struggle to control an administration that has run amuck. It could accelerate the demand for the impeachment of the President."[57]

Another factor was that Democrats were anxious to override a Nixon veto. Eight times during the Ninety-third Congress he had vetoed legislation; eight times Congress came up short on the override. A number of members looked upon the War Powers Resolution as a vehicle to test congressional power.[58] This attitude was especially tempting in the wake of the Watergate scandals. The "Saturday Night Massacre," which sent Special Prosecutor Archibald Cox, Attorney General Elliot Richardson, and Deputy Attorney General William Ruckelshaus out of the government, occurred just four days before Nixon's veto of the War Powers Resolution.

Analysis of the Bill

The War Powers Resolution sets forth three main procedures: presidential consultation with Congress, presidential reports to Congress, and congressional termination of military action. The purpose of the resolution, according to Section 2(a), is "to insure that the collective judgment" of both branches will apply to the introduction of U.S. forces into hostilities. Yet an examination of other sections, together with executive interpretations and congressional behavior, supplies ample evidence that collective judgment is by no means assured.

The president is to consult with Congress "in every possible instance." This language obviously leaves considerable discretion to the president as to the form and timing of consultation. The Carter administration noted that the president's responsibilities under the sections involving consultation and reporting "have not been delegated, so that the final decision as to whether consultation is possible and as to the manner in which consultation be undertaken or reports submitted rests with the President."[59]

The authors of the resolution did not expect the president to con-

[57]119 Cong. Rec. H9661 (daily ed. Nov. 7, 1973).

[58]See Thomas F. Eagleton, *War and Presidential Power* 213–220 (1974).

[59]123 Cong. Rec. S11319 (daily ed. June 30, 1977).

sult with 535 legislators. But whom should he contact? The leadership? The chairmen and ranking members of designated committees? Selected advisers? And should they be merely briefed or does consultation mean a more active role for Congress? The legislative history makes clear that consultation goes beyond simply being informed of a decision. However, to participate on equal terms, legislators would need the same information made available to the president. Congressman Paul Findley, a House conferee on the resolution, remarked that legislators would have to drop everything during a crisis and remain with the National Security Council to "evaluate the facts as they are perceived and as they may change during this period of time."[60] Congress has yet to organize itself to play a consultative role.

The War Powers Resolution requires that the president, after introducing forces into hostilities, report to Congress within forty-eight hours. Precisely what conditions require a report is unclear from the legislation. If the report is delayed for any reason, so are the mechanisms for congressional control. For example, military action must terminate within sixty days after the report unless Congress (1) declares war or enacts a specific authorization, (2) extends by law the sixty-day period, or (3) is physically unable to meet as a result of an armed attack upon the United States. The president may extend the period by an additional thirty days if he determines that force is needed to protect and remove American troops. Congress has two means of control: either a decision not to support the president during the sixty- to ninety-day period, or passage of a concurrent resolution at any time to direct the president to remove forces engaged in hostilities.

Although the resolution states that nothing in it is intended to alter the constitutional authority of the Congress or the president, some members of Congress were concerned that the new procedure had the effect of broadening presidential power. William Green, a

[60]Findley: *War Powers: A Test of Compliance*, hearings before the House Committee on International Relations, 94th Cong., 1st Sess. 57 (1975). Intention of consultation appears in H. Rept. No. 287, 93d Cong., 1st Sess. 6–7 (1973). Congressman Zablocki stated that "it was not the intention of section 3 to expect the President to consult with all 535 members": *War Powers*, at 55.

Democrat from Pennsylvania, felt that it put a sixty- to ninety-day congressional "stamp of approval" on presidential actions.[61] Bob Eckhardt, a Texas Democrat, argued that for up to ninety days the Congress would provide the president with the "color of authority" to exercise a war-making power.[62]

Section 2(c) appears to restrict the president's exercise of his powers as commander in chief to three situations: a declaration of war, specific statutory authorization, or a national emergency created by an attack on the United States, its territories or possessions, or its armed forces. However, the conference report on the resolution explains that the sections on consultation, reporting, and congressional action are *not* dependent on the language of Section 2(c). The restrictive force of the section is divorced from the procedural steps that follow.[63] Consequently, the president may use his own judgment as to when and where to introduce forces into hostilities. He could so firmly commit the nation's forces and prestige during the ninety-day period that Congress would find it politically and militarily impossible to reverse the operation. What begins as marginal or contrived has the potential of deteriorating into a genuine emergency, compelling congressional support. As the sixty- to ninety-day deadline grew near, legislators would likely "rally 'round the flag" rather than independently debate the wisdom and merits of the president's decision.

Presidential power, nourished by this early support from Congress, could be extended in other ways. Once engaged in hostilities, the president might draw upon his constitutional authority to repel sudden attacks and protect American troops. It might not be possible for Congress to curb such activity by passing a concurrent resolution ordering him to disengage, or letting the ninety-day period expire without legislative support. The legal adviser to the State Department told a House committee in 1975 that if the president

[61]119 Cong. Rec. H9643 (daily ed. Nov. 7, 1973).

[62]*Id.* at H9648.

[63]H. Rept. No. 547, 93d Cong., 1st Sess. 8 (1973). Section 2(c) is carefully analyzed by William B. Spong, Jr., in "The War Powers Resolution Revisited: Historic Accomplishment or Surrender?" 16 *Wm. & Mary L. Rev.* 823, 837–841 (1975).

has the power to put men into combat "that power could not be taken away by concurrent resolution because the power is constitutional in nature."[64]

Since passage of the War Powers Resolution, the executive has stated its belief that the president's power goes beyond protecting American territory and armed forces. The Ford administration argued that there were six other situations in which the president has constitutional authority to introduce armed forces into hostilities: to rescue American citizens abroad; to rescue foreign nationals where such action directly facilitates the rescue of American citizens abroad; to protect U.S. embassies and legations abroad; to suppress civil insurrection; to implement and administer the terms of an armistice or cease-fire designed to terminate hostilities involving the United States; and to carry out the terms of security commitments contained in treaties. The statement from the Ford administration added: "We do not, however, believe that any such list can be a complete one."[65]

Several amendments have been introduced to perfect the War Powers Resolution. One relates to the failure of the resolution to recognize the president's right to rescue endangered citizens (pp. 226–231). Another relies on the appropriations power to fortify congressional control (pp. 241–246). A third has to do with the fact that the resolution places restrictions only on the president's power to dispatch armed *service personnel* into hostilities. Not covered are activities by civilian combatants and "paramilitary operations." An effort by Senator Eagleton to include such operations within the coverage of the War Powers Resolution was defeated in 1973. Two years later he introduced legislation to make the provisions of the resolution apply to civilian combatants, such as those employed by the CIA in Angola from 1975 to 1976.[66] Congress has yet to act on such legislation.

[64]*War Powers, supra* note 60, at 91.

[65]*Id.* at 90–91.

[66]121 Cong. Rec. S22254 (daily ed. Dec. 16, 1975). See also legislation introduced by Congressmen James Scheuer, 122 Cong. Rec. H189 (daily ed. Jan. 22, 1976).

The *Mayaguez* Capture

After the evacuations from Southeast Asia in April 1975, the War Powers Resolution was put to another test the following month. The U.S. merchant ship *Mayaguez*, traveling from Hong Kong to Sattahip, Thailand, was seized by Cambodians. Two days later the United States recovered the vessel and its crew, but only after President Ford had ordered air strikes against Cambodia and called upon marine ground forces. Weeks and months would pass before Congress had an adequate picture of what had taken place.

Nevertheless, on the very day of the recovery, members of Congress rushed forward with glowing words of praise. A spirit of jingoism filled the air. The episode became a "proud new chapter in our history." Members expressed pride in their country and in their president, exclaiming with youthful enthusiasm that it was "great to be an American."[67] A few members reserved judgment, which was sensible, for no one knew exactly what had happened or why. A legislator could have announced: "I am happy that the crew is back. Unfortunately, many lives were lost in the effort. It is still too early, the facts still too incomplete, for us to make judgment." Most members, however, felt compelled to outdo one another with words of commendation and jubilation.

As details of the capture trickled in, Ford's action looked less and less appealing. Approximately forty-one Americans lost their lives trying to rescue thirty-nine crewmen. The administration spent little effort in probing diplomatic avenues before resorting to force. The quality of military intelligence was not reassuring. The marines suffered heavy casualties during the assault on Koh Tang Island, under the erroneous impression that the crewmen were detained there. A punitive spirit seemed to infuse the operations. The United States bombed the Cambodian mainland *after* the crew had been released. A 15,000-pound bomb—the largest conventional bomb in America's arsenal—was dropped on a Cambodian island that measured just a few square miles.[68]

[67]See especially the Congressional Record of May 15, 1975.

[68]*War Powers, supra* note 60; *Seizure of the Mayaguez*, hearings before

Administration leaders suggested that this use of force contained valuable lessons regarding America's determination to meet its international commitments, but the application of this event to future contingencies is hard to envision. Anthony Lewis of *The New York Times* said that for "all the bluster and righteous talk of principle, it is impossible to imagine the United States behaving that way toward anyone other than a weak, ruined country of little yellow people who have frustrated us."[69] An editorial in the *Washington Post* noted with alarm that the use of force by the greatest power in the world against a small country could serve as such a tonic in the nation's capital: "That anyone could find the Mayaguez affair a valid or meaningful guide to the requirements of post-Vietnam foreign policy at other times and places defies common sense."[70]

As for compliance with the War Powers Resolution, there was little consultation with Congress. Representative Clement Zablocki, principal author of the House version of the War Powers Resolution, said that the administration's effort to consult with Congress was inadequate.[71] Senator Jacob Javits, a leading sponsor of the resolution, also criticized the administration's consultation record.[72] In subsequent hearings the House Committee on International Relations expressed frustration because it could not obtain information from administration officials who were at the center of the decision-making process.[73]

It is difficult to believe that one month after the costly disengagement from Southeast Asia, after the United States had finally

---

the House Committee on International Relations, 94th Cong., 1st Sess. (1975); and statement by Senator Javits, 121 Cong. Rec. S10338 (daily ed. June 11, 1975). See also Jordan J. Paust, "The Seizure and Recovery of the *Mayaguez*," 85 *Yale L. J.* 774 (1976).

[69]*New York Times*, May 20, 1975.

[70]*Washington Post*, May 16, 1975.

[71]*War Powers, supra* note 60, at vi, and also 81–82, 100.

[72]*Id.* at 61–75 and 121 Cong. Rec. S10339 (daily ed. June 11, 1975).

[73]*Seizure of the Mayaguez, supra* note 68, Part 2 at 137, 147–152, and Part 3 at 259–270. See Robert Zutz, "The Recapture of the S.S. Mayaguez: Failure of the Consultation Clause of the War Powers Resolution," 8 *N.Y.U. J. Int'l L. & Pol.* 457 (1976).

broken free from a lengthy and violent war that racked the country, there could be such a celebration of force. What happened to the "deliberative process" of Congress? The independent legislative capability? The promise of closer scrutiny of executive actions? Unless members take the time personally to analyze a president's decision, Congress cannot expect a coequal status or a share in "collective judgment." Instead, legislators will become prematurely associated with a policy they may later find unworthy of support.

The Purse and the Sword

Conflicts between Congress and the president over the war power are generally examined by the judiciary at a safe distance; it is intensely interested but in no mood to intervene. Deference has reached the point where courts treat the entire area of the "conduct of the foreign relations" as purely political, in no way subject to judicial inquiry or decision.[74] In 1950 the Supreme Court claimed that "it is not the function of the Judiciary to entertain private litigation—even by a citizen—which challenges the legality, the wisdom, or the propriety of the Commander-in-Chief in sending our armed forces abroad or to any particular region."[75]

What is proper deference by the courts in one case may be obsequiousness in another. Actions taken in the name of national security, whether by Congress or the president, can threaten individual freedoms protected elsewhere in the Constitution. As the Supreme Court noted in *Baker* v. *Carr*: "it is error to suppose that every case or controversy which touches foreign relations lies beyond judicial cognizance."[76]

During the Vietnam War the question arose in the federal courts whether Congress, because it appropriated funds for the Defense Department, had sanctioned the president's war policy. A State Department memorandum in 1966 argued that Congress had shown its support for the war policy of the Johnson administration by enacting the necessary appropriations. Defense appropriations con-

[74]Oetjen v. Central Leather Co., 246 U.S. 297, 302 (1918).
[75]Johnson v. Eisentrager, 339 U.S. 763, 789 (1950).
[76]Baker v. Carr, 369 U.S. 186, 211 (1962).

stituted "a clear congressional endorsement and approval of the acitons taken by the President."[77]

Judge Templar, in *Velvel* v. *Johnson* (1968), rejected the notion that Congress had been forced against its better judgment to appropriate money for military operations in Vietnam. Congress had the power—both political and constitutional—to terminate military action. The court could not "infer that courage is lacking among the members of Congress, should the majority of the elected representatives of the people conclude to take such action."[78] Nor could Judge Dooling, in *Orlando* v. *Laird* (1970), believe that defense appropriations had been "extorted by the exigencies created by presidential seizures of combat initiatives."[79]

Expert witnesses advised the courts that House and Senate rules prohibited major declarations of policy in appropriations bills. The parliamentary process limited substantive legislation to authorization bills. They also pointed out that some members had voted for military appropriations not because they endorsed the war policy but because they felt an obligation to support American soldiers already committed to battle. Initially the courts were unimpressed by this line of argument. As Judge Judd noted in *Berk* v. *Laird* (1970):

> That some members of Congress talked like doves before voting with the hawks is an inadequate basis for a charge that the President was violating the Constitution in doing what Congress by its words had told him he might do. . . . The entire course of legislation shows that Congress knew what it was doing, and that it intended to have American troops fight in Vietnam.[80]

Members of the judiciary began to backtrack from the proposi-

[77]*Dep't of State Bull.*, LIV, 487 (1966).

[78]Velvel v. Johnson, 287 F.Supp. 846, 853 (D. Kans. 1968).

[79]Orlando v. Laird, 317 F.Supp. 1013, 1018 (E.D. N.Y. 1970). See also Davi v. Laird, 318 F.Supp. 478, 481 (W.D. Va. 1970) and Orlando v. Laird, 443 F.2d 1039, 1042 (2d Cir. 1971).

[80]Berk v. Laird, 317 F.Supp. 715, 724, 728 (E.D. N.Y. 1970). The position of expert witnesses for the plaintiffs appears at 718 and 721. See also DaCosta v. Laird, 448 F.2d 1368, 1369 (2d Cir. 1971).

tion that Congress could indirectly endorse a war simply by appropriating funds. Circuit Judge Adams, in 1972, said that such a determination would require the interrogation of legislators regarding the intent behind their votes, followed by a synthesis of the various replies. He concluded that it would be impossible to gather and evaluate such information.[81] Judges Wyzanski and Bazelon, who had earlier accepted appropriations acts as identical with congressional consent, reversed their positions by 1973. They could now no longer be

> unmindful of what every schoolboy knows: that in voting to appropriate money or to draft men a Congressman is not necessarily approving of the continuation of a war no matter how specifically the appropriation or draft act refers to that war. A Congressman wholly opposed to the war's commencement and continuation might vote for the military appropriations and for the draft measures because he was unwilling to abandon without support men already fighting. An honorable, decent, compassionate act of aiding those already in peril is no proof of consent to the actions that placed and continued them in that dangerous posture. We should not construe votes cast in pity and piety as though they were votes freely given to express consent.[82]

A major appropriations battle occurred in 1973. President Nixon's basis for military operations in Vietnam seemed to have disappeared with the signing of a cease-fire agreement in Paris on January 27, 1973, and the withdrawal of all American troops by the end of March. The Tonkin Gulf Resolution had been repealed by Congress several years earlier. No longer could the president point to that as authority, or cite the need to protect American soldiers. Yet Nixon continued to maintain a massive bombing operation in Cambodia. When a supplemental appropriations bill reached the

[81]Atlee v. Laird, 347 F.Supp. 689, 706 (E.D. Pa. 1972).

[82]Mitchell v. Laird, 488 F.2d 611, 615 (D.C. Cir. 1973). Wyzanski's earlier position appears in Massachusetts v. Laird, 327 F.Supp. 378, 381 (D. Mass. 1971). For the ambivalent quality of defense appropriations, see Campen v. Nixon, 56 F.R.D. 404, 406 (N.D. Cal. 1972).

House floor in May, Clarence Long of Maryland offered an amendment to prohibit the use of any funds authorized by the bill to support directly or indirectly U.S. combat activities in, over, or from off the shores of Cambodia. The amendment was adopted, 224 to 172. The Senate passed an even stronger amendment, forbidding the use of any funds to support combat activities in Cambodia or Laos (a restriction covering not only the supplemental funds but funds made available by previous appropriations). The bill presented to Nixon included the Senate version.[83]

Nixon vetoed the bill, claiming that the "Cambodian rider" would destroy the chances for a negotiated settlement in Cambodia. He also warned that nine agencies, dependent upon funds in the bill, would soon exhaust their authority to pay the salaries and expenses of their employees. According to his line of reasoning, the wheels of government would grind to a halt if Congress persisted in presenting objectionable statutory language to the president. Congress failed to override.

The issue of the appropriations power was now firmly joined. Congress could argue that the restrictions in the supplemental bill represented an appropriate effort to limit the president's ability to wage war and to commit the nation to vast expenditures. If Nixon refused to acknowledge congressional preeminence in matters of the purse, legislators could have held *him* responsible for the paralysis of agency operations. In this raw, high-noon confrontation, Congress backed off. A revised bill delayed the cutoff of funds from June 30 to August 15, 1973, in effect allowing the president to bomb Cambodia for another forty-five days—which is what he did. But at least Congress, by agreeing to the compromise, succeeded in using its power of the purse to conclude military operations in Southeast Asia.

The "August 15 Compromise" aborted several cases that had been working their way through the federal courts. In a decision of July 25, 1973, a federal judge in New York held that Congress had not authorized the bombing in Cambodia. The fact that Congress could not muster a two-thirds majority to override the president's

[83]This paragraph, and the following three, are drawn from Louis Fisher, *Presidential Spending Power* 110–118 (1975).

veto should not, he said, be interpreted as an affirmative grant of authority. This decision was later reversed, in part because a circuit judge held that the August 15 date did indeed constitute congressional approval of the bombing.[84] In other decisions the courts accepted the compromise date as evidence that the two political branches were no longer in resolute conflict; therefore there was no need for the courts to referee.[85]

If the War Powers Resolution turns into a mere parchment barrier, rendered permeable because of ambiguities in the language, Congress may want to act directly through its legislative authority to control appropriations. The resolution already clarifies one point: defense appropriations do not, by themselves, endorse a military policy. Section 8(a) of the resolution states that the authority to introduce armed forces into hostilities, or into situations where circumstances indicate involvement, shall not be inferred from any provision of law—including any provision contained in any appropriations act—unless such provision specifically authorizes the introduction of troops.

More explicit would be a cutoff of funds, after the sixty- or ninety-day period expires, to prevent the president from resorting to unused balances available to him. Denial of funds could be tied to passage of a concurrent resolution at any time prior to the expiration date provided in the War Powers Resolution.[86] Executive officials would probably regard this as an encroachment upon presidential responsibilities, but Congress would be operating from a solid base of constitutional authority. Acting in this manner would give firm meaning to the hope once expressed by Jefferson: "We

[84]Holtzman v. Schlesinger, 361 F.Supp. 553, 563–565 (E.D. N.Y. 1973), stayed by the Supreme Court, 414 U.S. 1304, 1316, 1321, before being reversed, Holtzman v. Schlesinger, 484 F.2d 1307, 1313–1314 (2d Cir. 1973).

[85]Drinan v. Nixon, 364 F.Supp. 854, 860–861, 864 (D. Mass. 1973).

[86]Michael J. Glennon, "Strengthening the War Powers Resolution: The Case for Purse-Strings Restrictions," 60 *Minn. L. Rev.* 1, 32–33 (1975) and legislation by Congressman Solarz, 123 Cong. Rec. E4463 (daily ed. July 14, 1977). See also Garry Wooters, "The Appropriations Power as a Tool of Congressional Foreign Policy Making." 50 *B.U.L. Rev.* 34 (Special Issue 1970).

have already given in example one effectual check to the Dog of war by transferring the power of letting him loose from the Executive to the Legislative body, from those who are to spend to those who are to pay."[87]

[87]Thomas Jefferson, *Papers* (Boyd ed.), XV, 397.

10

Conclusions

The general drift of authority and responsibility to the president over the past two centuries is unmistakeable. This trend by itself should not be cause for alarm. More threatening is executive activity cut loose from legislative moorings and constitutional restrictions—presidential action no longer tethered by law. To remain consistent with the Constitution, executive authority and administrative discretion should be directed and channeled by legislative policy.

This may appear to be a static and formalistic model of the Constitution, for it is well known that the powers of the federal government are not neatly divided between the three branches. There is indeed an overlapping of functions and a sharing of responsibilities. But the fact that uncertainties bedevil our constitutional principles, ushering in a variety of interpretations, is no reason to embrace a policy of expediency and opportunism. We will never be able to define with any precision the meaning of executive and legislative, or show where one branch fades and begins to blend into another. Still, the general theory and practice of separated powers can be retained. No one doubts the difference between night and day, or between youth and old age, though we cannot say with certainty where one ends and the other begins.[1]

The inability to define by statute the actions a president may take—be they impoundment, military initiatives, executive privilege, or executive agreements—invites heavy reliance on the leg-

[1]See Erwin N. Griswold, "Drawing Lines," *Evaluating Governmental Performance: Changes and Challenges for GAO,* a Series of Lectures Delivered at the United States General Accounting Office, 1973–1975, at 110.

islative veto. The compromise, and a workable one, is to leave the arena for presidential operation somewhat nebulous but subject executive decisions to congressional review and disapproval.

In extraordinary situations the president may have to act promptly without clear constitutional or statutory support. Quick action is not a quality or purpose of a legislative assembly. Congress is essentially a deliberative body. Under extreme conditions it is better to let the president call upon his "prerogative" without claiming the slightest shred of legal support, perhaps even admitting that his action violates the law. The burden is then on him to justify his decision and rest his case before Congress and the public. Both would be free, after careful examination of the evidence and the circumstances, to render a verdict of exoneration or condemnation.

The precise jurisdictions and fields of operation for Congress and the president will always elude us. Fortunately, the political process has a self-correcting mechanism, although it comes late and after extensive cost. Ambiguities in the Constitution permit one branch to infringe upon another. Generally this encroachment consists of brief raids in and out of the neutral zone. But at some point, after passing beyond a threshold of common sense and prudence, aggressive actions become counterproductive. They trigger revolts, leading to the recapture of ground taken not only in the most recent assault but in earlier offenses as well. It is not true that "let one occupant of the presidency exercise an additional power, and the advantage thus acquired is never abandoned."[2] Consider what happened with impoundment, the pocket veto, reorganization authority, and executive privilege. Power distorted the judgment of the wielder. The moth circled too close to the flame.

Some students of the presidency believe that the problem of executive power can be brought under control by selecting with greater care the person to occupy the Oval Office. To use the classification of James David Barber, we are urged to elect an "active-positive": someone who is energetic at the job and derives enjoyment from the exercise of power.[3] Other political scientists, including Charles

---

[2]Norman J. Small, *Some Presidential Interpretations of the Presidency* 198 (1932).

[3]James David Barber, *The Presidential Character* (1972).

Hardin, prefer to cast a skeptical eye on whoever finds himself in the office of president.[4] Here I side with Hardin; not to dwell on the dark side of human nature or to encourage a climate of distrust and suspicion, but because it is an illusion to think that a president will have the technical competence, political instinct, and moral character that will permit us to rest easy while he wields power.

To call for "comity" and "consultation" is not enough. The record suggests that this too is an illusion. Representative Paul Findley remarked in 1976 that he had been in Congress for sixteen years, most of that time serving on the House Committee on International Relations. The chairman of that committee, Clement Zablocki, had been in Congress for twenty-eight years. Throughout this period—which spanned Democratic as well as Republican administrations—Zablocki tried to encourage consultation by the executive branch, but Findley was hard put to think of any cases in which consultation actually occurred in advance of an executive decision. It was out of this "rather dismal experience," Findley said, that many members of Congress decided to propose extraordinary remedies for executive agreements, the war power, and other conflicts with the executive branch.[5]

If Congress has strong misgivings about an issue, it should resolve the matter by relying on language in a public law, not by informal understandings with executive officials. In 1977 members of the House were worried about being inundated by reorganization plans sent down by President Carter. OMB Director Bert Lance assured the House Committee on Government Operations that the administration appreciated the concern and would adhere to a reasonable timetable. Congress correctly insisted on specific language in the reorganization act to prohibit more than three plans from being before Congress at one time.[6] When in doubt, the legislative policy belongs in the law.

This is a policy of prudence, not paranoia. We need to dis-

---

[4]Charles M. Hardin, *Presidential Power & Accountability* 63 (1974).

[5]*Congressional Review of International Agreements,* hearings before the House Committee on International Relations, 94th Cong., 2d Sess. 150 (1976).

[6]P.L. 95-17, 91 Stat. 30, Sec. 903 (b). *Providing Reorganization Authority to the President,* hearings before the House Committee on Government Operations, 95th Cong., 1st Sess. 43–44 (1977).

tinguish between objectives and the means used to attain them. Justice Jackson reminded us of our tendencies to ignore fundamentals of government:

> The opinions of judges, no less than executives and publicists, often suffer the infirmity of confusing the issue of a power's validity with the cause it is invoked to promote, of confounding the permanent executive office with its temporary occupant. The tendency is strong to emphasize transient results upon policies—such as wages and stabilization—and lose sight of enduring consequences upon the balanced power structure of our Republic.[7]

Theodore Sorensen, reflecting on his views of presidential power during and after his service with the Kennedy administration, warns against shortsighted reactions to immediate events and the failure to take into account the longer view: "I understand this error, having committed it myself a decade ago."[8]

The literature on the presidency, after emphasizing for many years such vague qualities as "vigor," "energy," and "persuasion," is now more cautious about the ends to which power may be put and the legal boundaries for presidential action. Commentators are taking into account not merely the exercise of power, directed for whatever purpose the president chooses, but the source of authority, rights secured under the Constitution, and the larger system of checks and balances.[9] Too often in the past the legal basis for action has been ignored in the eagerness for results.

Constitutional precepts are important goals even when they cannot be entirely satisfied. There is no need for dismay because we aim high and fall short. Machiavelli, incorrectly remembered as the father of political expediency, encouraged us to establish high standards:

> . . . a prudent man will always choose to take paths beaten by great men and to imitate those who have been especially ad-

[7]Youngstown Co. v. Sawyer, 343 U.S. 579, 634 (1942).
[8]Theodore C. Sorensen, *Watchmen in the Night* xvi (1975).
[9]John Hart, "Presidential Power Revisited," 25 *Pol. Stud.* 48 (1977). Compare with Richard E. Neustadt, *Presidential Power* (1960). Neustadt's original text was not changed in the later editions of 1968 and 1976.

mirable, in order that if his ability does not reach theirs, at least it may offer some suggestion of it; and he will act like prudent archers, who, seeing that the mark they plan to hit is too far away and knowing what space can be covered by the power of their bows, take an aim much higher than their mark, not in order to reach with their arrows so great a height, but to be able, with the aid of so high an aim, to attain their purpose.[10]

The framers of the Constitution settled on a single executive in order to foster unity, responsibility, dispatch, expertise, and a national perspective. To an impressive extent the office of the presidency has alleviated many of the defects experienced by the Continental Congress. Yet the qualities originally anticipated of the executive have undergone profound transformations. It is absurd today to think that a president can be a skilled diplomat, military strategist, macroeconomist, energy expert, and domestic innovator, along with all the other heady roles we expect him to play.

Surely it is arbitrary to highlight the unifying quality of the president. Just as easily we can look at the fragmentation of the executive branch and the many groups within it competing for control. Special interests seek representation within the administration just as they do within Congress. In ways similar to a legislature, these groups barter with one another and conduct their own form of logrolling. Alfred de Grazia put this well when he called the president "a Congress with a skin thrown over him."[11] We need to pierce the skin and comprehend the forces underneath.

The president remains responsible for the operation of the executive branch, but often only in a technical and formal sense. Vast areas are subdelegated to remote sectors of the executive branch. Even presidents and staff assistants with unusual diligence and energy find themselves overwhelmed by the task. Joseph Califano, after serving as an assistant to President Johnson in the area of

[10]Allan Gilbert, trans., Machiavelli: The Chief Works and Others, I, 24–25 (1965), from The Prince, Ch. 6.
[11]Alfred de Grazia, Republic in Crisis 72 (1965). A pioneer in debunking the "superman" image of the president is Thomas E. Cronin; for a recent work see his The State of the Presidency 23–51 (1975).

domestic affairs, recalled that he doubted he ever met, "much less consulted or helped guide, more than one-third of these noncabinet agency and commission heads. Hyperactive as he was, President Johnson met even fewer of them."[12] Congress is frequently advised to confine its activities to "broad policy" questions and leave "day to day" matters to the executive branch. A similar division of labor takes place within the administration. The president is advised to concentrate on broad policy while delegating details to departments and agencies.[13]

Executive officials are often so absorbed by operations, tactics, and short-run goals that they lose sight of national objectives, other than the raising of campaign contributions and the president's reelection. The 1972 campaign was conspicuous for its bartering of the public interest. The Internal Revenue Service, the Federal Bureau of Investigation, the Central Intelligence Agency, and other agencies were used by the White House to violate the constitutional rights of citizens. Raised to high visibility were the administration's relationships with such special interests as International Telephone and Telegraph, milk producers' cooperatives, and grain exporters.[14] Congress is not innocent in such matters, but we are disposed to expect the worst of legislators and at the same time believe in high virtues of the president and his entourage.

Agency officials, even when they have their facts correct, find it difficult to place them in perspective and part company with long-held assumptions and predilections. White House officials, by necessity generalists, may ignore agency expertise when it fails to dovetail with the political needs of the president. Congressional staffers, upon reaching their counterparts in the agencies, sometimes run into this kind of question: "Do you want the official position or the facts?"

The importance of Congress is its capacity for diversity and openness (relative to the executive branch)—the opportunity it

[12]Joseph A. Califano, Jr., *A Presidential Nation* 23 (1975).

[13]*Id.* at 49. See also Stephen Hess, *Organizing the Presidency* (1976).

[14]*The Final Report of the Select Committee on Presidential Campaign Activities,* United States Senate, S. Rept. No. 981, 93d Cong., 2d Sess. (June 1974).

gives to express different sentiments, opinions, and values. It is a disorderly operation and disappointing to those who want firm direction and quick action. But this free play of ideas, as well as the freedom not to move until the time is right, is essential to democratic government. What is needed from Congress is the daily grind of overseeing administration policies, passing judgment on them, and behaving with confidence as a coequal branch. This takes courage and an understanding of constitutional responsibilities.

Congress may stand against the president, or stand behind him, but it should not stand aside as it did year after year during the Vietnam War, looking the other way and occasionally complaining about executive usurpation. There the crucial ingredient was will power, not constitutional power. The source of congressional influence depends on more than access to information, additional staff, or a revamping of procedure and organization. Congress must be willing to participate actively in questions of national policy, challenging the president and contesting his actions. It cannot be viewed as quarrelsome behavior for Congress to independently assess presidential action. Issues need the thorough exploration and ventilation that only Congress can assure.

This does not mean that a congressional product will necessarily be better than a presidential proposal. It is not a question of preferring one branch over another, but of remaining faithful to the form of government embodied in the Constitution. We must learn, especially when the temptation is great, to resist legal short-cuts because "the cause is good." The door is then left open for capricious acts we may deplore. Robert H. Jackson, whose entire career with the federal government lay outside the legislative branch, serving first as attorney general and later as associate justice of the Supreme Court, urged us to hold fast to essentials: "With all its defects, delays and inconveniences, men have discovered no technique for long preserving free government except that the Executive be under the law, and that the law be made by parliamentary deliberations."[15]

---

[15]Youngstown Co. v. Sawyer, 343 U.S. 579, 655 (1952).

Further Readings

In addition to the works cited in chapter footnotes, the following are recommended for supplemental reading.

CHAPTER 1

BENNETT, WILLIAM J. "The Constitution and the Moral Order," 3 *Hastings Const. L. Q.* 899 (1976).

BONDY, WILLIAM. "The Separation of Governmental Powers in History, in Theory, and in the Constitution," *Studies in History, Economics, and Public Law*, Vol. V., No. 2 (Columbia University, 1896).

CARPENTER, WILLIAM S. "The Separation of Powers in the Eighteenth Century," 22 *Am. Pol. Sci. Rev.* 32 (1928).

DRY, MURRAY. "The Separation of Powers and Representative Government," 3 *Pol. Sci. Rev.* 43 (1973).

FAIRLIE, JOHN A. "The Separation of Powers," 21 *Mich. L. Rev.* 393 (1923).

GWYN, W. B. "The Meaning of the Separation of Powers," *Tulane Series in Political Science*, Vol. IX (1965).

RADIN, MAX. "The Doctrine of the Separation of Powers in Seventeenth Century Controversies," 86 *U. Pa. L. Rev. & Am. L. Reg.* 842 (1938).

SHARP, MALCOLM P. "The Classical Doctrine of the 'Separation of Powers,'" 2 *U. Chi. L. Rev.* 385 (1935).

WHEELER, HARVEY. "Constitutionalism," in Fred I. Greenstein and Nelson W. Polsby, eds., *Governmental Institutions and Processes* 1–91 (1975).

WORMUTH, FRANCIS D. *The Origins of Modern Constitutionalism* (1949).

WRIGHT, BENJAMIN F., JR. "The Origins of the Separation of Powers in America," *Economica*, Vol. XII, No. 40 (1933).

CHAPTER 2

BARBER, SOTIRIOUS A. *The Constitution and the Delegation of Congressional Power* (1975).

CHEADLE, JOHN B. "The Delegation of Legislative Functions," 27 *Yale L. J.* 892 (1918).

DUFF, PATRICK W. AND HORACE E. WHITESIDE. "Delegata Potestas Non Potest Delegari: A Maxim of American Constitutional Law," 14 *Corn. L. Q.* 168 (1929).

EHMKE, HORST P. "'Delegata Potestas Non Potest Delegari,' A Maxim of American Constitutional Law," 47 *Corn. L. Q.* 50 (1961).

FISHER, LOUIS. "Delegating Power to the President," 19 *J. Pub. L.* 251 (1970).

FOSTER, STEPHEN A. "The Delegation of Legislative Power to Administrative Officers," 7 *Ill. L. Rev.* 397 (1913).

JAFFE, LOUIS. "Delegation of Legislative Power," Ch. 2 of his book, *Judicial Control of Administrative Action* (1965).

MERRILL, MAURICE H. "Standards—A Safeguard for the Exercise of Delegated Power," 47 *Neb. L. Rev.* 469 (1968).

POWELL, T. R. "Separation of Powers," 27 *Pol. Sci. Q.* 215 (1912) and 28 *Pol. Sci. Q.* 34 (1913).

WEEKS, O. DOUGLAS. "Legislative Power Versus Delegated Legislative Power," 25 *Geo. L. J.* 314 (1937).

CHAPTER 3

CIRILLO, RICHARD A. "Abolition of Federal Offices as an Infringement on the President's Power to Remove Federal Officers: A Reassessment of Constitutional Doctrines," 42 *Ford. L. Rev.* 562 (1974).

DONOVAN, WILLIAM J. AND RALSTONE R. IRVINE. "The President's Power to Remove Members of Administrative Agencies," 21 *Corn. L. Q.* 215 (1936).

FRUG, GERALD E. "Does the Constitution Prevent the Discharge of Civil Service Employees?," 124 *U. Pa. L. Rev.* 942 (1976).

HART, JAMES. "The Bearing of Myers v. United States Upon the Independence of Federal Administrative Tribunals," 23 *Am. Pol. Sci. Rev.* 657 (1929).

_____. *The American Presidency in Action* 155-248 (1948).

MCBAIN, HOWARD LEE. "Consequences of the President's Unlimited Power of Removal," 4 *Pol. Sci. Q.* 596 (1926).

MILLER, CHARLES A. *The Supreme Court and the Uses of History* 52-70, 205-210 (1969).

RICHARDSON, IVOR L. M. "Problems in the Removal of Federal Civil Servants," 54 *Mich. L. Rev.* 219 (1955).

THACH, CHARLES C., JR. *The Creation of the Presidency* 140-165 (1969 ed.).

CHAPTER 4

BELLAMY, CALVIN. "The Growing Potential of the Pocket Veto: Another Area of Increasing Presidential Power," 61 *Ill. Bar. J.* 85 (1972).

CLINEBERG, WILLIAM A. "The President's Veto Power," 18 *S.C. L. Rev.* 732 (1966).

CONDO, JOSEPH A. "The Veto of S. 3418: More Congressional Power in the President's Pocket?" 22 *Cath. U. L.* Rev. 385 (1973).

COOPER, JOSEPH. "The Legislative Veto: Its Promise and Its Perils," 7 *Public Policy* 128 (1956).

_____ AND ANN COOPER. "The Legislative Veto and the Constitution," 30 *G.W. L. Rev.* 467 (1962).

COTTER, CORNELIUS P. AND J. MALCOLM SMITH. "Administrative Accountability to Congress: The Concurrent Resolution," 9 *West. Pol. Q.* 955 (1956).

GIBSON, RANKIN M. "Congressional Concurrent Resolution: An Aid to Statutory Interpretation?" 37 *Am. Bar Ass'n J.* 421 (1951).

GINNANE, ROBERT W. "The Control of Federal Administration by Congressional Resolutions and Committees," 66 *Harv. L. Rev.* 569 (1953).

JACKSON, CARLETON. *Presidential Vetoes* (1967).

KENNEDY, EDWARD M. "Congress, the President, and the Pocket Veto," 63 *Va. L. Rev.* 355 (1977).

LEE, JONG R. "Presidential Vetoes from Washington to Nixon," 37 *J. Pol.* 522 (1975).

Note. "The Presidential Veto Power: A Shallow Pocket," 70 *Mich. L. Rev.* 148 (1971).

———. "The Veto Power and Kennedy v. Sampson: Burning a Hole in the President's Pocket," 69 *N.W. U. L. Rev.* 587 (1974).

"Pocket Veto Legislation," 29 *Record of the Association of the Bar of the City of New York* 724 (1974).

U.S. CONGRESS. *Constitutionality of the President's "Pocket Veto" Power,* hearing before the Senate Committee on the Judiciary, 92nd Cong., 1st Sess. (1971).

———. *The Pocket Veto Power,* hearing before the House Committee on the Judiciary, 92d Cong., 1st Sess. (1971).

WHITE, HOWARD. "Executive Responsibility to Congress via Concurrent Resolution," 36 *Am. Pol. Sci. Rev.* 895 (1942).

CHAPTER 5

BLACHLY, FREDERICK F. AND MIRIAM E. OATMAN, *Administrative Legislation and Adjudication* (1934).

BLACK, HENRY CAMPBELL. *The Relation of the Executive Power to Legislation* (1919).

BRUFF, HAROLD H. AND ERNEST GELLHORN. "Congressional Control of Administrative Regulation: A Study of Legislative Vetoes," 90 *Harv. L. Rev.* 1369 (1977).

CASH, ROBERT B. "Presidential Power: Use and Enforcement of Executive Orders," 39 *Notre Dame Lawyer* 44 (1963).

CHAMBERLAIN, LAWRENCE H. *The President, Congress, and Legislation* (1946).

CHASE, HAROLD W. *Federal Judges: The Appointing Process* (1972).

COMER, JOHN PRESTON. *Legislative Functions of National Administrative Authorities* (1927).

FAIRLIE, JOHN A. "Administrative Legislation," 18 *Mich. L. Rev.* 181 (1920).

HARLOW, RALPH VOLNEY. *The History of Legislative Methods in the Period Before 1825* (1917).

HART, JAMES. "The Ordinance Making Powers of the President of the United States," *Johns Hopkins University Studies in Historical and Political Science,* Series XLIII, No. 3 (1925).

HEBE, WILLIAM. "Executive Orders and the Development of Presidential Power," 17 *Vill. L. Rev.* 688 (1972).

KATZENBACH, NICHOLAS DE B. "The Roles of Executive and Legislative Branches in Judicial Appointments," *New York L. J.* (Nov. 3, 1971).

LEVINSON, L. HAROLD. "Presidential Self-Regulation Through Rulemaking: Comparative Comments on Structuring the Chief Executive's Constitutional Powers," 9 *Vand. J. Transnat'l L.* 695 (1976).

NEIGHBORS, WILLIAM D. "Presidential Legislation by Executive Order," 37 *U. Colo. L. Rev.* 105 (1964).

STEWART, RICHARD B. "The Reformation of American Administrative Law," 88 *Harv. L. Rev.* 1667 (1975).

U.S. CONGRESS. *Executive Orders in Times of War and National Emergency,* Senate Special Committee on National Emergencies and Delegated Powers, 93d Cong., 2d Sess. (Comm. Print June 1974).

CHAPTER 6

BERGER, RAOUL. *Executive Privilege* (1974).

BISHOP, JOSEPH W., JR. "The Executive's Right of Privacy: An Unresolved Constitutional Question," 66 *Yale L. J.* 477 (1957).

BRECKINRIDGE, ADAM CARLYLE. *The Executive Privilege* (1974).

DIMOCK, MARSHALL EDWARD. "Congressional Investigating Committees," *Johns Hopkins University Studies in Historical and Political Science,* Series XLVII, No. 1 (1929).

EBERLING, ERNEST J. *Congressional Investigations* (1928).

HAMILTON, JAMES. *The Power to Probe: A Study of Congressional Investigations* (1976).

HENKIN, LOUIS. "The Right to Know and the Duty to Withhold: The Case of the Pentagon Papers," 120 *U. Pa. L. Rev.* 271 (1971).

KRAMER, ROBERT AND HERMAN MARCUSE. "Executive Privilege— A Study of the Period 1953–1960," 29 *G.W. L. Rev.* 623, 827 (April and June 1961).

MCGEARY, M. NELSON. *The Developments of Congressional Investigative Power* (1940).

_____. "Congressional Investigations: Historical Development," 18 *U. Chi. L. Rev.* 425 (1951).

MURPHY, JOHN F. "Knowledge is Power: Foreign Policy and Information Interchange Among Congress, the Executive Branch, and the Public," 49 *Tulane L. Rev.* 505 (1975).

ROURKE, FRANCIS E. *Secrecy and Publicity* (1966).

_____. "Administrative Secrecy: A Congressional Dilemma," 54 *Am. Pol. Sci. Rev.* 884 (1960).

U.S. CONGRESS. *Executive Privilege: The Withholding of Information by the Executive*, hearing before the Senate Committee on the Judiciary, 92d Cong., 1st Sess. (1971).

_____. *Executive Privilege, Secrecy in Government, Freedom of Information* (3 Vols.), hearings before the Senate Committees on Government Operations and the Judiciary, 93d Cong., 1st Sess. (1973).

_____. *Impeachment: Selected Materials*, compiled by the House Committee on the Judiciary, 93d Cong., 1st Sess. (Comm. Print Oct. 1973).

_____. *Impeachment: Miscellaneous Documents*, compiled by the Senate Committee on Rules and Administration, 93d Cong., 2d Sess. (Comm. Print Aug. 7, 1974).

_____. *Leading Cases on Congressional Investigatory Power*, compiled by the Joint Committee on Congressional Operations, 94th Cong., 2d Sess. (Comm. Print Jan. 1976).

YOUNGER, IRVING. "Congressional Investigations and Executive Secrecy: A Study in the Separation of Powers," 20 *U. Pitts. L. Rev.* 755 (1959).

CHAPTER 7

FUTTERMAN, STANLEY N. "Toward Legislative Control of the C.I.A.," 4 *N.Y.U. J. Int'l L. & Pol.* 431 (1971).

HUZAR, ELIAS. *The Purse and the Sword: Control of the Army by Congress Through Military Appropriations, 1933–1950* (1950).

MILLER, ARTHUR S. "Presidential Power to Impound Appropriated

Funds: An Exercise in Constitutional Decision-Making," 43 *N.C. L. Rev.* 502 (1965).

Note. "The CIA's Secret Funding and the Constitution," 84 *Yale L. J.* 608 (1975).

POWELL, FRED WILBUR. *Control of Federal Expenditures: A Documentary History, 1775–1894* (1939).

SCHWARTZMAN, BERMAN. "Fiscal Oversight of the Central Intelligence Agency: Can Accountability and Confidentiality Coexist?," 7 *N.Y.U. J. Int'l L. & Pol.* 493 (1974).

U.S. CONGRESS. *Impoundment of Appropriated Funds by the President,* Joint Hearings before the Senate Committees on Government Operations and the Judiciary, 93d Cong., 1st Sess. (1973).

——. *Analysis of Executive Impoundment Reports,* prepared by the Senate Committee on the Budget, 94th Cong., 1st Sess. (Comm. Print Feb. 1975).

——. *U.S. Intelligence Agencies and Activities: Intelligence Costs and Fiscal Procedures* (Part 1), hearings before the House Select Committee on Intelligence, 94th Cong., 1st Sess. (1975).

——. *Whether Disclosure of Funds Authorized for Intelligence Activities is in the Public Interest,* hearings before the Senate Select Committee on Intelligence, 95th Cong., 1st Sess. (1977).

U.S. GENERAL ACCOUNTING OFFICE. *Review of the Impoundment Control Act of 1974 After 2 Years* (June 3, 1977).

WALDEN, JERROLD L. "The C.I.A.: A Study in the Arrogation of Administrative Powers," 39 *G.W. L. Rev.* 55 (1970).

WILMERDING, LUCIUS, JR. *The Spending Power* (1943).

CHAPTER 8

BESTOR, ARTHUR. "Separation of Powers in the Domain of Foreign Affairs: The Original Intent of the Constitution Historically Examined," 5 *Seton Hall L. Rev.* 529 (1974).

COHEN, RICHARD. "Self-Executing Executive Agreements: A Separation of Powers Problem," 24 *Buff. L. Rev.* 137 (1974).

HENKIN, LOUIS. *Foreign Affairs and the Constitution* (1972).

MCCLURE, WALLACE. *International Executive Agreements* (1941).

McDOUGAL, MYERS S. AND ASHER LANS. "Treaties and Congressional-Executive or Presidential Agreements: Interchangeable Instruments of National Policy," 54 *Yale L. J.* 181, 534 (1945).

MATHEWS, CRAIG. "The Constitutional Power of the President to Conclude International Agreements," 64 *Yale L. J.* 345 (1955).

ROVINE, ARTHUR W. "Separation of Powers and International Executive Agreements," 52 *Ind. L. Rev.* 397 (1977).

SLONIN, SOLOMON. "Congressional-Executive Agreements," 14 *Colum. J. Transnat'l L.* 434 (1975).

STEVENS, CHARLES J. "The Use and Control of Executive Agreements: Recent Congressional Initiatives," 20 *Orbis* 905 (1977).

TOMAIN, JOSEPH P. "Executive Agreements and the Bypassing of Congress," 8 *J. Int'l L. & Econ.* 129 (1973).

U.S. CONGRESS. *International Executive Agreements*, hearing before the House Committee on Foreign Affairs, 92d Cong., 2d Sess. (1972).

————. *International Agreements: An Analysis of Executive Regulations and Practices*, prepared for the Senate Committee on Foreign Relations, 95th Cong., 1st Sess. (Comm. Print March 1977).

CHAPTER 9

FRIED, JOHN H. E. "War-Exclusive or War-Inclusive Style in International Conduct," 11 *Tex. Int'l L. J.* 1 (1976).

FRYE, ALTON. *A Responsible Congress* (1975).

JAVITS, JACOB K. *Who Makes War: The President Versus Congress* (1973).

JENKINS, GERALD. "The War Powers Resolution: Statutory Limitation on the Commander in Chief," 11 *Harv. J. Legis.* 181 (1974).

LOFGREN, CHARLES A. "War-Making Under the Constitution: The Original Understanding," 81 *Yale L. J.* 672 (1972).

MAY ERNEST R., ED. *The Ultimate Decision: The President as Commander in Chief* (1951).

REVELEY, W. TAYLOR, III. "Presidential War-Making: Constitutional Prerogative or Usurpation?," 55 *Va. L. Rev.* 1243 (1969).

ROSSITER, CLINTON. *The Supreme Court and the Commander in*

Chief (1951).

ROSTOW, EUGENE V. "Great Cases Make Bad Law: The War Powers Act," 50 *Texas L. Rev.* 833 (1972).

SMITH, J. MALCOLM AND STEPHEN JURIKA. *The President and National Security* (1972).

U.S. CONGRESS. *The Powers of the President as Commander in Chief of the Army and Navy of the United States*, H. Doc. No. 443, 84th Cong., 2d Sess. (1956).

_____. *Congress, the President, and the War Powers*, hearings before the House Committee on Foreign Affairs, 91st Cong., 2d Sess. (1970).

_____. *Documents Relating to the War Power of Congress, the President's Authority as Commander-in-Chief and the War in Indochina*, Senate Committee on Foreign Relations (Comm. Print 1970).

_____. *War Powers Legislation*, hearings before the Senate Committee on Foreign Relations, 92d Cong., 1st Sess. (1971).

_____. *War Powers Legislation, 1973*, hearings before the Senate Committee on Foreign Relations, 93d Cong., 1st Sess. (1973).

_____. *The War Powers Resolution: Relevant Documents, Correspondence, Reports*, House Committee on International Relations (Comm. Print April 23, 1975).

_____. *War Powers Resolution*, hearings before the Senate Committee on Foreign Relations, 95th Cong., 1st Sess. (1977).

WILCOX, FRANCIS O. *Congress, the Executive, and Foreign Policy* (1971).

Table of Cases

Index